THE ROHR EDITION

SHAPING
ETERNITY

BECAUSE TEACHERS LEAVE A LASTING IMPRINT

HASHKAFAH, HALACHAH, AND INSPIRATION
FOR THOSE WHO INSPIRE OTHERS

Includes a complete section of halachic responses for educators by
Rabbi Moshe Mordechai Lowy

Mr. Avi Shulman–Editorial Consultant
Mrs. Bassie Gugenheim–Founding Editor
Mrs. Shaindy Appelbaum–Editorial Director

CHOFETZ CHAIM HERITAGE FOUNDATION
THE ZICHRON YAAKOV ZVI CENTER FOR THE TEACHINGS OF THE CHOFETZ CHAIM

FIRST EDITION
First Impression...November 2011
Second Impression...April 2012

For bulk orders contact Chofetz Chaim Heritage Foundation

ISBN 978-1-59826-003-8

Distributed by:
FELDHEIM PUBLISHERS
208 Airport Executive Park
Nanuet, NY 10954
www.feldheim.com

Cover and book design:
Sara Jaskiel

Graphics and page layout:
Justine Elliott

Cover photos:
Natural Light Photography by Aviva Rand
Yehuda Boltshauser–Kuvien Images

Printed in the USA by Noble Book Press Corp.
Brooklyn, NY 11218

שמואל קמנצקי
Rabbi S. Kamenetsky

Study: 215-473-1212
Home: 215-473-2798

2018 Upland Way
Philadelphia, Pa 19131

Dear *Mechanchim,*

On behalf of the Chofetz Chaim Heritage Foundation, it
gives me great pleasure to acknowledge the publication of
this beautiful new book written especially for those who are
dedicating themselves to the *chinuch* of *Klal Yisrael's* children.
Each article in this book eloquently speaks of the exalted role you
play and the eternal impact you have on the children you teach
and the generations that will come after them.

Our organization has undertaken this project to help you
maintain the freshness and enthusiasm to do your vital job as
only you—each individual teacher—can do it. With your own
special talents, knowledge and character traits, each of you
imparts something unique and precious to our children. It is our
hope that this book will be a revitalizing wellspring of inspiration
for those whose job it is to inspire others.

There is no expression of gratitude that can adequately convey
the *hakoras hatov* that all of us in *Klal Yisrael* owe to those of
you who devote your life to *chinuch*. May you be blessed with
strength, good health and *parnassah* to enable you to continue in
this *avodas hakodesh*, as well as the patience, wisdom and insight
to bring each precious *talmid* to his or her full potential.

ב"ה

This volume
is lovingly dedicated in the memory of

מרת שרה רוהר ע"ה
בת ר' יקותיאל יהודה קסטנר הי"ד

Mrs. Charlotte Rohr (née Kastner)

———————————— ■ ————————————

Born in Mukachevo, Czechoslovakia, to an
illustrious Chassidic family,
she survived the fires of the Shoah to become
the elegant and gracious matriarch, first in
Colombia and later in the United States, of
generations of a family nurtured by her love
and unstinting devotion.
She found grace in the eyes of all those
whose lives she touched, and merited to see
all her children build lives enriched by
faithful commitment to the spreading of
Torah and *ahavat Yisrael*
for the glory of the Jewish people.

The Rohr Family
Miami and New York, USA

Kislev 5772   November 2011

THE CHOFETZ CHAIM HERITAGE FOUNDATION

*A not-for-profit foundation
dedicated to the teaching of
Jewish ethics & wisdom*

Dear Educator

Without a doubt, every single member of *Klal Yisrael* acknowledges a boundless debt of gratitude to you, our *mechanchim* and *mechanchos*. It is you who, with unending *mesiras nefesh*, do the holy work of ensuring the continuation of our *mesorah* through our children. What you give is endless, and yet the challenges from within and without grow each day.

With this in mind, nearly a decade ago we began to publish "Impressions," a newsletter developed specifically for teachers, with the goal of offering Torah guidance and wisdom on the issues they face in their many varied interactions and roles. We sought to answer teachers' halachic questions regarding *Shmiras Haloshon*; to offer Torah *hashkafah* on *chinuch* and to uplift teachers with stories of colleagues who made a difference in their students' lives. All this was meant to inspire our readers with recognition of the impact they make through the words they speak and the sensitivity they display to those in their care.

After nearly a decade of publishing this highly-acclaimed newsletter, we have collected some of the finest of its articles to create a *sefer* for you, our teachers. Here you will find a beautiful array of stories from your fellow teachers, Torah directives on issues that affect you in your *avodas hakodesh* and halachic analysis of a wide range of questions you may encounter. We hope this *sefer* will serve as a resource, an inspiration, and most of all, a constant reminder to you of the exalted role you have taken upon yourself on behalf of *Klal Yisrael*.

We lovingly offer you this gift with great humility and everlasting gratitude for taking care of our children and shaping eternity.

Shlomo Yehuda Rechnitz
Chairman of the Board
Chofetz Chaim Heritage Foundation

361 Spook Rock Road
Suffern, New York 10901
Tel 845 352-3505
Fax 845 352-3605

Acknowledgements

Our gratitude to *Hashem Yisbarach* is inexpressible for His having permitted us to produce this book and continue to spread the concept of *Shmiras Haloshon* and *Ahavas Yisrael* in all its facets. With the publication of this book, for the first time ever we are offering teachers throughout the world a gift of inspiration and information crafted especially for them. We hope that we will be worthy, through this book, of enhancing the strength and beauty of the teacher-student relationship, engendering goodness and blessings that will overflow and nurture countless generations to come.

If our teachers, students and *Klal Yisrael* benefit from this volume, their inspiration will be to the eternal credit of **Mr. George Rohr** and the Rohr family, whose far-reaching generosity funded this project. May their deep desire to uplift *Klal Yisrael* and their devotion to this effort be an everlasting merit for **Mrs. Charlotte Rohr**, *a"h*.

We also offer our sincere thanks to **Rabbi Moshe Mordechai Lowy**, *shlita*, Rav of Agudas Israel of Toronto, who has consistently taken precious time from his busy schedule to review and answer questions regarding our publishing projects. As halachic advisor and contributor to "Impressions," he patiently and carefully answers the halachic questions regarding *shmiras haloshon* submitted by teachers and clearly illuminates the path, shining the light of Torah wisdom on real-life challenges both inside and outside the classroom. His sage advice has been essential to our ability to present clear, accurate information through the lens of true Torah *hashkafah*. "Shaping Eternity," as so many of our other projects, bears the imprint of his invaluable input.

We would like to thank **Mr. Avi Shulman**, the editorial consultant for "Impressions," for his astute review of each issue's material, and his keen insights and valuable advice which always enhance the newsletter's content and presentation.

The concept of "Impressions" is the brain-child of **Mrs. Bassie Gugenheim**, director of our Mishmeres program. It is her deep understanding of human nature that pointed the way for a newsletter that would inspire and encourage the rebbeim and teachers who so deeply

influence the next generation. We thank Mrs. Gugenheim for planting the seed that has blossomed into this book, and for placing her prodigious intelligence and talent at the service of our organization, and through it, all of *Klal Yisrael*.

Traveling from idea to reality is often a long, difficult journey, but with **Mrs. Shaindy Appelbaum** steering the ship, no obstacle is too great. Her keen and discerning eye, her dauntless persistence and seemingly limitless energy–all tendered with warmth and humor– have enabled her to accomplish the impossible. We thank her for her ongoing work as editorial director of "Impressions," for seeing to every detail of this project and bringing it to life, and for being the heart and soul of the Chofetz Chaim Heritage Foundation's editorial department for nearly two decades.

Even the best articles cannot be useful unless they are presented in a coherent, logical format. We thank **Mrs. Tzippy Lichter** for performing the painstaking task of cataloguing the issues of "Impressions" by topic, enabling us to develop cohesive chapters for this volume.

With this project, **Mrs. Tova Finkelman** has once again proven the value of her sharp eye for the printed word. We thank her for her efficient and accurate proof-reading, ensuring a high standard of editorial quality.

The unusual artistic quality of the design and layout are the hallmark of our visionary graphic artist, **Mrs. Sara Jaskiel**, whose passion for beauty and perfection have made the cover and design of this volume as inspiring to view as it is to read. We thank her for another job superbly done. We express our appreciation as well to **Justine Elliott**, whose talent and endless hours of dedicated effort are clearly visible in the layout of every page of this book, and to **Michalle Rothschild** for her valuable assistance on graphics.

Our gratitude is extended to **Noble Book Press** for the superlative print job.

Chofetz Chaim Heritage Foundation reaches over 50,000 people through its many programs.

Yet an organization is only as strong as the people who comprise it, and therefore, we gratefully acknowledge the staff, volunteers and leaders who work tirelessly to create a culture of caring and spread the language of *Ahavas Yisrael* throughout the world.

Our success flows from the Torah leaders who map out our path:

The Manchester Rosh Yeshivah, HaGaon HaRav Yehudah Zev Segal, *zt"l*, the founding Rabbinic Advisor of our organization; HaGaon HaRav Shmuel Kamenetsky, *shlita*, the Chairman of our Rabbinical Board; and HaGaon HaRav Avraham Pam, *zt"l*, and *yblc"t* HaGaon HaRav Yaakov Perlow, *shlita*, members of our Rabbinical Board of Advisors.

Rabbi Eliyahu Brog, Rabbi Eliyahu Lamm, Rabbi Hillel Litwack and Rabbi Mordechai Klein, who volunteer their time to answer questions on our Shaila Hotline, provide invaluable halachic guidance to those seeking to properly fulfill the mitzvah of *Shmiras Haloshon*.

We are deeply grateful to the outstanding people of the Chofetz Chaim Heritage Foundation:

To our Chairman of the Board, Reb Shlomo Yehuda Rechnitz, whose vision, enthusiasm, and generosity of spirit has helped us spread the language of *Ahavas Yisrael* even further.

To our board of directors who have been a tremendous help in forging our path into the future: Raymond Beyda, Abraham Biderman, Aba Claman, Nachman Futterman, David Lobel, Yitzchok Mashitz, Ari Parnes, George Rohr, Kurt Rothschild, David Shweky, Gedaliah Weinberger and Moshe Zakheim.

To the many dynamic speakers who have inspired us with audio-visual and taped presentations over the years, we offer our sincere thanks.

If you have benefited from a *Shmiras Haloshon* program or publication over the past few years, it is thanks to the selfless dedication of our staff: Mr. Dovid Kogel, Rabbi Gavriel Jacknin, Rabbi Shlomo Ornstein, Rabbi Yosef Pruzansky, Mr. Boruch Reiss, Rabbi Elchonon Snyder, Chani Bernstein, Pessy Bernstein, Tehila Danzinger, Machla Eichenstein, Rochel Feingold, Malky Fine, Leah Fischer, Tziri Frank, Blimy Friedman, Ruchie Friedman, Rivky Goldstein, Sarah Leah Gordon, Miriam Grossman, Bassie Gugenheim, Kaila Halpern, Chaya Israel, Gitty Kalikstein, Simi Kepecs, Breindy Kertzner, Gitty Kish, Estie Koot, Sussy Kraus, Shira Lazar, Miriam Leiberman, Esther Leibowitz, Blimi Lesser, Suri Levy, Chava Londinski, Rivka Chaya Mayer, Shoshana Miller, Esther Mohr, Shevy Orbach, Leah Ozeri, Ruchy Perlstein, Tzipporah Esther Rosen, Sarah Rosenberg, Chayie Schachter, Leah Sekula, Rivka Sherwinter, Chavi Twersky, Chedva Weinberg, Chavie Weingot, Yitty Zehnwirth, Faigy Zelcer and Sima Zinnes.

We would also like to thank our staff in Eretz Yisrael: Binyomin and Shoshana Cohen, and Mrs. Rochel Orloweck.

The Chofetz Chaim Heritage Foundation is forever grateful to Rabbi Mendel Kessin, whose penetrating taped *shiurim* on *Shmiras Haloshon* were the catalyst that inspired us to start our organization.

Our organization's success is due to friends around the world who have brought our programs to their shul, school or community. To our 450 local coordinators—the *rabbanim*, principals and lay people who have lifted the banner of *Shmiras Haloshon*—thank you so much.

Our building, the Zichron Yaakov Zvi Center for the Teachings of the Chofetz Chaim, is at the heart of all of CCHF activities. We are forever indebted to the anonymous family that graciously dedicated this center, which has been the catalyst for bringing so much of the Chofetz Chaim's wisdom to the world. May the merit of all that is accomplished here stand as an everlasting *z'chus* for the family and for Yaakov Zvi ben R' Menachem, *z"l*, in his place in *Gan Eden*.

To all of the above as well as those who have supported us financially, may the great *z'chus* of *Shmiras Haloshon* stand by you, your families and all of *Klal Yisrael*.

THE CHOFETZ CHAIM HERITAGE FOUNDATION
Cheshvan 5772

In Appreciation

The articles you will read within these pages were written originally for "Impressions," a unique newsletter published by the Chofetz Chaim Heritage Foundation and distributed to teachers and *rebbeim* in Jewish schools throughout the nation. Paying tribute to a teacher's powerful role in influencing the hearts and minds of the next generation, "Impressions" seeks to offer tools and fuel for thought to help our educators make the most of their august role.

A teacher's words and deeds make a lasting impression, and through the articles published in "Impressions," this powerful impact comes to light. We thank the many authors who have contributed their stories and *divrei Torah* to "Impressions" over the years, so that others may be inspired:

Libby Engel is a *mechaneches* in the Los Angeles community who has been teaching for over two decades.

Chany Feldbrand of Lakewood, NJ, is a teacher, writer, lecturer and founder of the Ateres Tznius Movement. She thanks all her friends and colleagues for sharing the heartwarming stories of great teachers, which she shares with our readers here.

Malkie Gendelman, an editor at Israel Bookshop, lives in Lakewood, NJ, with her family.

Rachel Grossberg is a pseudonym for the student—now a grandmother—in the article *Lost Opportunity.*

Bassie Gugenheim of Lakewood, NJ, is the Program Director of Mishmeres, Chofetz Chaim Heritage Foundation's benchmark program for high school girls. She is also the founding editor of "Impressions"; it was her initiative and vision that created the biweekly teacher's newsletter upon which this book is based.

Rabbi Pinchos Jung in the *menahel ruchani* of Bais Rochel High School in Monsey, NY, a noted lecturer who conducts seminars for students, staff and the general public world-wide, and the New York representative of the Ani Maamin Foundation.

Rabbi Mendy Karmel, Assistant Principal and a rebbi at Yeshiva Elementary School, lives in Miami Beach with his family. He has given *chinuch* workshops and has written for educators' publications, including *Rayonos, Hamechanech*, and of course, *Impressions*.

Chana Nestlebaum has played an integral role in the writing of numerous Chofetz Chaim Heritage Foundation projects, including "Positive Word Power," "Loving Kindness," "A Lesson a Day" and "Chosen Words." She is a freelance writer, attorney and mediator living in Lakewood, NJ.

Yaffa Penina is a pseudonym of a free-lance writer and editor who lives with her family in Brooklyn, NY.

Riva Pomerantz lives in Ramat Beit Shemesh with her family and works as a multi-genre freelance writer whose work is featured frequently by The Chofetz Chaim Heritage Foundation, Mishpacha Jewish Family Weekly, and aish.com. Her newest novel, *Charades*, has just been released.

Lauren Roth, MSW, LSW, is a marriage and parenting therapist in private practice in Lakewood, NJ. She also delivers inspirational talks and conducts workshops throughout the United States.

Ben Shalom is a pseudonym for a writer and researcher living on the eastern seaboard of the United States.

Tehila Silverman is a pseudonym for a writer living in the greater New York area.

We also thank the authors of several articles that were reprinted from other publications with their gracious permission. Please see credits at the end of each of those articles.

Your Students, Your Legacy

Like clay on a potter's wheel, our students take shape before our eyes. When the teacher—the potter—applies just the right pressure, a beautiful vessel takes on its form, and knowledge, wisdom and holiness make a home within. With too little guidance, the vessel is misshapen. With too much push and pull, it breaks.

Moreover, a potter intuits that not every mound of clay is the same. Some are meant to become a sturdy jug or jar and some a graceful vase. Shaping and molding is an art, not an industry; each piece demands its own individual approach, its own identity and its own time on the wheel. Only then will it possess the quality of a unique, hand-made work of art.

Likewise, teaching is an art—the highest form of art, for the product is the highest form of Creation, a Jew filled with devotion to Torah, mitzvos and the Jewish people. This is a creation that cannot be mass-produced. A teacher who takes the time to notice the inherent qualities in his or her student, who makes an effort to get a feeling for what the child can become, succeeds in bringing out the student's optimum beauty and productivity.

That is what you, as a teacher, take upon yourself every day. When you meet a former student and see before you a wholesome, happy, Jewish man or woman, you are beholding a vessel of holiness that you helped shape. A little pressure on one side — "Take the test again. I know you can do better!" A supporting hand shoring up the foundation — "That's a great question! Rashi asked exactly the same one!" An expert eye to appraise when the form needs further shaping, and when it is best left alone. A teacher leaves a life-long impact on a student's future. And collectively, teachers shape the next generation. Will they be zealous or lax? Kind-hearted or self-centered? Confident or insecure? Accepting or narrow-minded? The shape of our world a decade or two from now sits on the potter's wheel today.

This volume is dedicated to sharing and enhancing the potter's wisdom. It recounts great moments that teachers like you have experienced in their day-to-day life, throwing a sharp spotlight on the difference a few words, a sensitive act or a moment of wise restraint can have. It relates true stories of modern-day *mechanchim* facing the same challenges you face; it traces their search for answers and the outcomes of their decisions. The eminent wisdom of Mr. Avi Shulman draws powerful lessons and ideas from these stories, adding to the inspiration and guidance they provide.

Yet, as great as inspiration and stories can be, they are not enough to equip a teacher for the vital job at hand. The Torah provides concrete guidance and halachic parameters to prevent stumbling in an endeavor in which a wrong move is too costly to chance. In these pages, you will encounter the hard questions teachers face every day: What can one teacher tell another about a student? How does one weigh the needs of an individual, troubled student against the needs of the class? How does a school get children to report bullying without encouraging loshon hora? How should a teacher handle an antagonistic parent? The expert halachic perspective of Rabbi Moshe Mordechai Lowy takes these questions out of the gray area and answers them with definitive Torah principles.

In the final analysis, it is not only the student but the teacher, too, who is a unique creation. Each brings his or her own gifts into the classroom. Each relates to the students from the depths of his or her own heart. One teacher's magnificent moment may never occur to another teacher. Stories can inspire, but they cannot often be replicated. *Halachos* can be learned, but the exact circumstances of a similar situation may bear further inquiry. What purpose, then, does this volume serve?

It is given to you, *Klal Yisrael's* teachers, to reflect and reinvigorate your passion for your great task. It is here to pierce the veil of routine that clouds any job, and illuminate a clear vision of the everlasting legacy you are creating. With that vision set firmly before you, so many more of your own great moments, great strategies and great achievements will emerge. The potter's clay will remain safe in your hands, as you carefully, lovingly shape it into a vessel whose beauty will endure forever.

TABLE OF CONTENTS

IN THE CRAFTSMAN'S HANDS
REACHING A CHILD'S HEART

SMOOTHING THE VESSEL
THE HOW, WHEN AND WHY OF REBUKE

HASHKAFAH

MASTERING THE ART
HOW TO GO FROM GOOD TO GREAT

STAR CRAFTSMEN
U'MATZDIKEI HARABIM K'KOCHAVIM

"IN THE HANDS OF THE TONGUE"
WHEN AND HOW TO SHARE INFORMATION

THE ART OF RESHAPING
DEALING WITH MISBEHAVIOR

HALACHAH

JUST THE RIGHT TOUCH
HOW TO GUIDE OTHERS

TRIAL, ERROR AND TRIUMPH
OVERCOMING TEACHING CHALLENGES

THE MASTER SCULPTOR
GREAT TEACHERS AND THEIR GREAT MOMENTS

FORMING A CONNECTION
THE POWER OF SHOWING YOU CARE

INSPIRATION

WHEN THE STUDENT DOESN'T CONFORM
STORIES OF WISE INTERVENTION

MOLDING A NESHAMAH
A TEACHER'S IMPACT ON A CHILD'S SOUL

LASTING IMPRESSIONS
SHAPING OUR STUDENTS' FUTURES

Hashkafah:
The Heart & Soul of Chinuch

The *chinuch* of a Jewish child is far more
than education. The wisdom of the Torah
provides a deeper insight into the lofty mission
of *mechanchim*, and the priceless value of the
neshamos entrusted to them, bringing into
focus the immeasurable importance of the
task each rebbi and teacher performs in every
classroom, every day.

The Royal Smile

Y
AAKOV AVINU GAVE HIS SON YEHUDAH the blessing that he should be "red-eyed from wine and white-toothed from milk." Rabbi Avigdor Miller, *zt"l*, explains that these words can also mean that the gift of white teeth—a smile—brings more important sustenance to the body than milk does. And this life-sustaining gift benefits the one who smiles as much as the one who receives the smile.

Why is this gift given specifically to Yehudah?

The question arises, then: why this gift is given specifically to Yehudah. To this question, Rabbi Mund of Montreal answers that, because Yehudah was destined to produce Israel's kings, his smile held special power and importance. What could serve a king better than a smile that delights the hearts of his subjects and makes them feel loved and valued by their leader?

Each of us is the "leader" to someone. As educators we are leaders of the classes we teach and our students look to us for approval and warmth—the feelings conveyed in one powerful flash through a sincere smile. We need not go to great lengths to imagine the feeling of a student when the principal greets him with a smile, when his rebbi shows a friendly face. Everyone has a piece of Yehudah's blessing, and the power to use it within our own individual "realms," each and every day. ⊞

Shaping with Smiles

Think of the people in your life who look up to you. Make a conscious effort to smile in your interactions with them.

Reprinted from "Chosen Words," a publication of the Chofetz Chaim Heritage Foundation.

HASHKAFAH, HALACHAH, AND INSPIRATIO

Full Flavor

A DEDICATED TEACHER, VIEWING his students as they sit facing him, is filled with the desire to help each one become a better Jew and grow close to Hashem. But how?

In *Vaykira*, the Torah offers a paradigm for the proper way to come close to Hashem. In a discussion of the requirements for bringing the meal-offerings, the Torah specifies that they could not contain any yeast or honey; however, they were required to be salted.

Why were the first two ingredients considered an adulteration of the offering, while the third was considered a necessity? Rav Mordechai Gifter, *zt"l*, explained that both yeast and honey create a change in the actual offering—yeast changes the dough, and honey changes its natural flavor. Salt, however, brings out the natural flavor.

In helping *talmidim* learn to serve Hashem, success comes not from trying to alter the characteristics Hashem has given each one of them, nor from trying to cover up those traits with foreign ingredients. It comes simply from helping them find their inborn strengths and bringing out their full flavor. One creative rebbi, on the first day of school, had each student write a list of his strengths, interests and perceived weaknesses. He then dedicated time to discussing with each student how he thought he could use his unique personality in

> **Why were honey and yeast considered an adulteration of the offering, while salt was considered a necessity?**

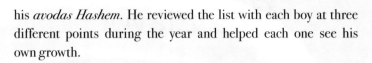

his *avodas Hashem*. He reviewed the list with each boy at three different points during the year and helped each one see his own growth.

When we help our students take stock of what they have to offer, and help them channel their unique abilities and attributes in Heaven's direction, we allow them to experience the joy of knowing that all of them—just by being who they are—possess the ability to fulfill their unique purpose in this world.

Class discussion: If one is not supposed to change or cover his true nature, what can one do with negative personality traits?

Shaping with Salt

▶ A serious student who is exacting with himself and others could be encouraged to become the editor of the class newspaper.

▶ A child who is naturally very bossy can channel his energies more positively when given a leadership role in which he will learn to lead while getting along with others.

▶ The class clown who is distracting and disturbing at times may use his captivating personality to become a great Pirchei leader or camp counselor. He may also use his entertaining style to create skits that explain difficult concepts that the class is studying. ▣

Adapted from "Chosen Words," a bi-weekly publication of the Chofetz Chaim Heritage Foundation

HASHKAFAH, HALACHAH, AND INSPIRATIO

Potential

Potential in Every Child

IN SHEMOS (2:7) we see that Basya told Miriam to find a Jewish woman to nurse the baby that she had rescued from the water. Rashi explains that Basya had arranged for Egyptian women to nurse Moshe, but he would not nurse—because he was destined to speak with the *Shechinah*.

The *Shluchan Aruch* in *Yoreh Deah* teaches that although halachah permits a Jewish child to nurse from a non-Jew, it is forbidden to do so because of this Rashi. HaRav Yaakov Kamenetsky, *zt"l*, was asked, "How is it that we decide halachah based on what was appropriate for Moshe Rabbeinu?" Rav Kamenetsky's answer offers us a profound insight: "We learn from here," he replied, "that every Jewish child has the potential to talk to the *Shechinah* one day—*and that is the way every child should be raised and taught.*"

> **How is it that we decide halachah based on what was appropriate for Moshe Rabbeinu?**

The Power To Soar

THE TALMUD [BAVA METZIA 84A] speaks about the first encounter between Rabbi Yochanan and Reish Lakish. At that

"Potential"
continued

time Rabbi Yochanan was one of the great Sages of the Talmud while Resih Lakish was the leader of a band of thieves. Reish Lakish observed Rabbi Yochanan swimming in the Jordan River and dived into the water and energetically swam to him. Immediately Rabbi Yochanan said to Reish Lakish, "Your strength should be used for Torah." Rabbi Yochanan did not focus on the obvious fact that Reish Lakish was the head of a band of robbers and was very far from living a Torah life. Instead, he focused only on the fact that Reish Lakish had intense energy and undiscovered potential to become a great *talmid chacham*.

> **Motivating someone requires understanding what is important to him.**

The only problem was how to motivate this person to give up his present profession and lifestyle, how to get him to tap into his inner strength. Motivating someone requires understanding what is important to him/her. Listen carefully and people will tell you what is most important to them.

Reish Lakish said to Rabbi Yochanan, "Your beauty is fitting for a woman."

Now Rabbi Yochanan knew how to influence Reish Lakish. "Immerse yourself in Torah study and you can marry my sister who is even more beautiful." Reish Lakish agreed, and this led to his becoming the great Talmudic Sage whose debates with Rabbi Yochanan are quoted throughout the Talmud.

When an artist sees an empty canvas he immediately imagines the beautiful picture that he can paint. This can be our model regarding viewing our students and their inevitable faults. See

HASHKAFAH, HALACHAH, AND INSPIRATIO

their potential, where they can be and what they can become if they use their unique strengths in positive ways. Then focus on motivating them in a way that addresses their specific interests and desires.

Don't give up before you begin. When you believe in someone you give him the power to soar.

A Staff of Distinction

WHEN HASHEM SPOKE TO MOSHE for the first time and told him to go to Mitzrayim, Moshe hesitated and was not certain that the Jews would believe him. Hashem then gave him signs to show *Klal Yisrael* with which to prove himself. The first sign was as follows: Hashem asked Moshe, "What is this in your hand?" It was a stick. He was told to throw it down to the ground, whereupon it became a snake. Then Hashem told him: "Stretch out your hand and take hold of it," and it once more became a stick.

Rabbi Zeidel Semiatitzky, *zt"l*, a *Mirrer talmid* who became a beloved Rosh Yeshivah and inspired countless *talmidim*, saw a profound message in these verses. Moshe Rabbeinu was becoming the leader of *Klal Yisrael*. He knew that the Jews were despondent and at a very low spiritual level. There seemed to be no chance of improvement. Therefore, he asked Hashem, "In their present state, how am I meant to bring them out of Mitzrayim?"

Hashem said to him: "You are mistaken. This people may appear to be beyond redemption, like the *nachash*, the snake. But, *just grab hold of them*, even by the lower end (symbolizing the worst elements), and they will turn into a *shevet*, a staff of distinction.

Every leader, every teacher, must know with certainty, that by reaching out and by believing in their students they give them the ability to achieve.

Caught in the Act

ONE OF A TEACHER'S MOST POWERFUL means of nurturing a child's growth is a word of acknowledgement when the child does something right.

You can almost see the child's spirit rise when he hears you start a comment with "I like how you..." "I respect what you did when..." "I really admire..." These well-placed words build a positive relationship and motivation to keep striving.

> There is no individual who cannot be educated. There is never an individual who is beyond redemption.

It's especially important to catch someone improving in a weak area. The student who seems self-centered offers to help another student in some way. The habitually late student shows up early. The forgetful student brings his homework. Let them know you notice. You'll find that your acknowledgement encourages their newly formed good habit, until it

becomes not only what you expect of them, but what they expect of themselves.

Shaping with Recognition

Realize that to the habitual latecomer coming on time is a victory.

To the self-centered student, helping another student represents a struggle that s/he has won.

Recognize it, appreciate it and celebrate it. ⊞

A Master of Motivation

R'NOSSON ZVI FINKEL, the Alter of Slobodka, was a master at understanding each of his many *talmidim* and motivating each according to his own nature and abilities.

> If a penny can do it,
> so can praise,
> a compliment, or
> even a smile

R' Nosson Zvi would explain, "Nowadays (and that was during his time!) people are not drawn to Torah study or to good deeds by spiritual motives. They must be shown other benefits as well. The chief motivating force in the world is self-benefit; for this people are willing to do anything—even restrain their emotions."

To illustrate this point, he told the following story. "In my youth in Vilna, I saw a woman vendor in the marketplace selling beans. For some reason she got angry at her competitor and began to abuse her loudly. Her anger rose until she actually foamed at the mouth and became drenched in sweat. At the peak of her rage, a customer approached her table and asked for a penny's worth of beans.

"In an instant, the vendor underwent an amazing transformation. He face beamed, her lips curled into a smile, and she graciously turned to wait on her customer.

"This teaches us a great secret of the human personality. A mere penny has the power to change a person from one extreme to

another and make him control his stormiest emotions! This is something no amount of wisdom can accomplish. But if a penny can do it, so can praise, a compliment, or even a smile or a polite word. All of these can win people's hearts and dispel their wickedness.

"This is not yet the end of the story. After the customer paid the penny for the beans, the vendor started to thank him for his kindness and to heap blessings on him, his wife, children and grandchildren.

"From here we see that not only can a penny cause a person to control his bad *middos*, it can even transform him into a fountain of love and kindness."

With this perspective, R'Nosson Tzvi never gave up on a talmid. No one was hopeless. He knew that with the right motivation even a difficult student can be positively tranformed.

Adapted from" Sparks of Mussar," by Rabbi Chaim Ephraim Zaitchik, Pisgah
Foundation, Jerusalem

The Donut

As told to Ben Shalom

IT WAS 1:40 PM ON SUNDAY AFTERNOON *when Yosef* walked into his seventh-grade classroom. The rebbi looked up to see Yosef, a frown on his face, shuffle slowly to his seat after putting a note on Rabbi Fine's desk. It didn't take 10 seconds for Rebbi to understand the situation. Yosef, who never particularly loved school, had left*

Friday morning for an out-of-town simchah and had returned a short while earlier that day. It wasn't difficult to see that Yosef would rather be elsewhere and that his parents had probably prevailed upon him to go to yeshivah. They must have felt that if he came for the last hour, picked up the worksheets and found out what he had missed, he would not be completely lost when Monday came along. But from the looks of it Yosef was already lost today, and tomorrow didn't look too hopeful.

Imagine how happy his mother was when Yosef came running through the front door two hours later smiling from ear to ear, the good cheer in his voice matching the bounce in his step. "Mommy, Rebbi called me over and told me that he was so glad to see me in class even for a short while. He said that it must have been very hard for me to come after the trip and he knew that I really would have preferred to stay home. He gave me a donut for making the effort to come!"

You can be sure that Monday morning found Yosef a lot happier about going to yeshivah than he otherwise might have been. ⊞

* Names have been changed

HASHKAFAH, HALACHAH, AND INSPIRATIO

V'shinantam L'vanecha

AN ELEVENTH-GRADE MESIVTA BOCHUR approached his former fourth-grade *rebbi's* wife at a *simchah*. "It's because of your husband that I am in a top yeshivah today and *shteiging, baruch Hashem*" he told her. To her questioning look, he responded: "When I was in eighth grade I wanted to go to a different, less serious yeshivah. I didn't think I could do it and didn't really want to exert myself. But Rebbi changed that. I used to pass by his classroom on my way to lunch when his class was having recess. Sometimes I got to speak to him. Rebbi always asked me how things were going and he had just the right words of encouragement. It was only a few moments from time to time but it really made a difference. When I mentioned that I really wasn't doing so well and wasn't going to get into a great mesivta Rebbi reminded me of the great questions I asked in his class and what a great mind I had. He encouraged me to aim high spiritually and academically—without even saying so. He believed in me and really cared about the decision I'd make for mesivta. I still remember how happy he was for me when I got accepted into a top mesivta. I went on to learn in my current yeshivah and it has changed my life!"

The oft-quoted interpretation of the words *"V'shinantam l'vanecha"* inspires educators to view their students as their very own children, elevating the task of teacher to the lofty responsibility and privilege of parent.

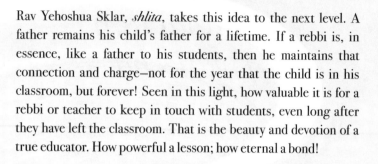

Rav Yehoshua Sklar, *shlita*, takes this idea to the next level. A father remains his child's father for a lifetime. If a rebbi is, in essence, like a father to his students, then he maintains that connection and charge—not for the year that the child is in his classroom, but forever! Seen in this light, how valuable it is for a rebbi or teacher to keep in touch with students, even long after they have left the classroom. That is the beauty and devotion of a true educator. How powerful a lesson; how eternal a bond!

The Chazon Ish considered himself to be the "father" of all yeshivah students. He regularly responded to their letters, offering warm words of encouragement to face the challenges they encountered. His connection to all *talmidim* made every *talmid* feel like his very own son.

To a student in a downtrodden state, he wrote: "Note that you are still in the midst of your educational years and you have the opportunity to establish yourself among [Torah scholars] of the highest caliber...I implore you, do not see yourself as a failure, or as though the challenge before you is too difficult. Remember that all beginnings are hard, but there is nothing that stands in the way of one's will, and he who comes to purify himself is aided. What's important is that you make a decision in your heart, and not be driven back by hurdles..."

To another student, The Chazon Ish wrote: "I was overjoyed to see that you are deeply immersed in your learning. So should you continue to apply your mind to Torah study. Try each day to raise yourself, level by level, with great energy, to bring the words of Torah into your mind and heart, because this is [the purpose of] all of life."

HASHKAFAH, HALACHAH, AND INSPIRATION

May we be zocheh to succeed in forging a life-long bond with every student such that each one truly feels like our very own child.

Shaping by Connecting

Keep in Touch

▸ A short phone call, a post card, a warm hello at a chance meeting go a long way. ⊞

Adapted with permission from Aleinu L'shabeiach, by Rabbi Yitzchok Zilberstein, shlita, rav of Ramat Elchonon

Individuality

■

And If He Is Poor...

"V'IM DAL HU... V'CHIPER HAKOHEN *al hamitaheir lifnei Hashem* —and if he is poor... and the Kohen shall provide atonement for the one being purified" (*Vayikra* 14:21-32).

In his eye-opening work Aleinu L'Shabeiach, Rav Yitzchok Zilberstein, shlita, cites these verses in Parashas Metzora, where the Torah describes the korban offering brought by the person afflicted with tzora'as. A wealthy person is instructed to bring an animal korban, while the Torah specifically stipulates that one who is "lacking" brings a turtledove and achieves purity through this paltry offering just the same as the rich man who can afford to bring a more expensive korban. The poor man brings a korban that cost five percent of the rich man's. Nevertheless, he achieves 100% purity just as the wealthy man with his expensive korban.

Rav Zilberstein chooses this verse to expound upon the task of educators to ensure that they make every effort to accommodate the needs of their "lacking" students. Whereas the Torah specifies a "lacking" person as one who lacks money, teachers often encounter students who lack other commodities—attention span, understanding, patience, and talents, to name just a few.

It is critical to note that Hashem, in His great wisdom and compassion, tailor-made the *halachah* of the *metzorah* according to his standing and abilities. Instead of requiring him to bring an expensive animal *korban* like everyone else, Hashem made

accommodations for the poor person's unique needs and dictated that he should bring an inexpensive bird offering. It is not a step down or a "cop-out"; instead, it is fulfillment of the letter and spirit of the law for this individual, as dictated by Hashem Himself.

The same must apply to our students. The educator is charged with the task of modifying the requirements where students' needs are different than those of the rest of the class. Those who lack must be accommodated, and tailoring requirements is an exalted service, modeled by *Hakadosh Baruch Hu* Himself.

> Write it with *din*;
> Mark it with *rachamim*.

There was a young boy who *davened* in the *minyan* of the Gaon of Tchebin who, unfortunately, did not see much satisfaction from his Torah learning due to his weak intellectual skills.

During the weekly *bechinah*, when the students were being tested on the *Chumash* and *Rashi of Parashas Vayechi*, it came time to ask this particular boy a question on the material at hand. The Gaon, who had come to the yeshivah to conduct the oral test, was concerned that the boy would not know how to answer if the questions posed to him were too difficult. He asked the boy a simple question from the beginning of the *parashah*: How many years did Yaakov Avinu live?

When the boy answered correctly, the Gaon accorded him bountiful praise, reacting as if the boy had answered an intricate *Gemara* problem. He then proceeded to ask the boy another question, from the last *pasuk* of the *parashah*: How many years did Yosef live?

"Individuality"
continued

Upon receiving the correct answer, the Gaon triumphantly exclaimed to the exultant boy: "You see! You know the entire *parashah*, from beginning to end!"

The boy left the test buoyed by new confidence.

___

Rav Binyomin Posen, *zt"l*, a gifted and renowned educator, was known for his sensitivity to the needs of his students. Before his class underwent an oral *bechinah*, Rav Posen would sit with the examiner and instruct him as to the students who should be asked difficult questions and the students who should be given simple questions to answer. His goal was that each and every student feel the sweetness of success.

___

When the Klausenberger Rebbe, *zt"l*, began the famed organization Mifal HaShas, he gathered together the examiners who would be administering the tests to the hundreds of *talmidei chachamim* and spoke to them in private.

"When you design the monthly test," he told them, "compose it with *midas ha'din*, with strictness and thoroughness. But when you mark the tests, mark them with *midas ha'rachamim*, with compassion."

We learn a valuable lesson from this vignette. Tests are an important and constructive educational tool which, when designed to be demanding and thorough, can truly indicate to the teacher whether the student has grasped the material or not. It is certainly not beneficial to make tests too easy, or their educational value is lost.

However, after the student has done his best and has studied well

HASHKAFAH, HALACHAH, AND INSPIRATIO

for the test, then it is not necessary to be overly strict with him. When it comes time for marking, the teacher should review the student's answers with midas ha'rachamim, with compassion and mercy.

Individual Attention

RABBI NUSSBAUM WAS THE PRINCIPAL of Yeshivah Nefashos Rabbos, a large school struggling with many behavior problems among its students. To Rabbi Nussbaum, the school's overwhelming population of 400 was its problem. "It's a challenge just to keep them all moving in the halls. The logistics alone in a school this size uses up your energy."

> **It's a challenge just to keep them all moving in the halls. The logistics alone in a school this size uses up your energy.**

He thought about his colleague Rabbi Rubin who ran Yeshivah Ahavas Yisrael, a similarly sized school. Rabbi Rubin did not seem to be overwhelmed by the challenge. His students had a light in their eyes and a bounce in their steps. Rabbi Nussbaum gave his friend a call and asked, "How do you do it?" Rabbi Rubin explained, "Although it is difficult, I put in the effort to know every student by name. A lot of them come to show me their report cards, and I try to give them some incentive to go even further. Some even return to visit long after they have graduated."

There's no secret to the magic of being acknowledged as an individual. Moshe taught us this lesson as he

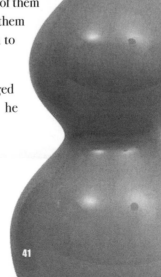

"Individuality"
continued

There's no secret
to the magic of
being acknowledged
as an individual.

guided the Jews through the desert. Hashem commanded him to take a census "according to the numbers of the names." This meant that Moshe had to greet each Jew by name rather than simply taking a count from each family head. Hashem wanted each person to be accorded the respect of individual recognition. The Torah is telling us that no one is just a number; each of us is a name, a face, a person. ⊞

For the Love of Torah

"**D**OES A CHILD NEED TO LOVE HIS REBBI?**" Rabbi Shimshon Pincus, *zt"l*, would often ask an audience of rebbeim.

In his *sefer Ohel Miriam*, Rav Pincus answers this question by defining the primary job of a Torah teacher. The goal is not—as with other studies—just to amass knowledge. Knowledge of Torah itself is not enough; a student must love Torah or the entire purpose of his learning has been missed.

Rav Pincus felt strongly that, practically speaking, it is impossible for a student to love Torah if s/he does not love his or her teacher. A teacher must spend time and effort to create a loving connection with his or her students—not simply because it is a nice thing to do, but because this love is the foundation of the transmission of the *mesorah*, and keeps the flames of Torah study alive.

Unlike all other mitzvos, where the *brachah* for the mitzvah is directly followed by the performance of the mitzvah, the *brachah* on Torah study is followed by a request: "*V'ha'arev na Hashem elokeinu es divrei sorascha b'finu*—Please, Hashem, make the words of Your Torah sweet in our mouths." Rav Pincus states that within these words lies the most pivotal point in teaching Torah. A prerequisite to Torah study is an appreciation for the sweetness and delight of Torah. A child's first introduction to Torah—at age three—demonstrates that sweetness, as he customarily licks the honey off the *alef beis* letters. It is this

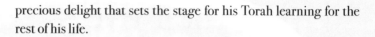

precious delight that sets the stage for his Torah learning for the rest of his life.

The fundamental reason why it is so essential to impart the sweetness of Torah to every child is that loving Torah is synonymous with loving Hashem. This is explained in the Yalkut Shimoni on the words of *Shema*, *"V'hayu hadevarim ha'eileh*– And these words [of Torah] should be..." Chazal comment that these words are an explanation to the first words of the paragraph: *"V'ahavta es Hashem Elokecha*–And you should love Hashem, your G-d." A person may wonder, "How do I follow this command to love Hashem?" This statement teaches us that by immersing oneself in Torah study, which constitutes the "words of Hashem," one will come to recognize Hashem's greatness and thus will come to loving Him.

It is critical for a student to love his teacher, in order that s/he come to love Torah, for that is the touchstone to loving and comprehending the *Ribbono Shel Olam* Himself. A teacher is the conduit between his student and Hashem.

The First Mitzvah

Rav Pincus used to say that the first mitzvah we impress upon our children is not, as many may think, to teach them to say *"Torah tzivah lanu Moshe."* Instead, the first mitzvah that we impress upon a child occurs even before he can talk–when a *sefer* drops on the floor and his mother rushes and says, "Quick! Pick it up and give it a kiss!" That kiss is the child's first introduction to mitzvos. We kiss the *sefer* not only because it is holy, but because we love that which is holy. This love is what we must strive to impart to our

students, so that they will want to continue tasting the sweetness of Torah always.

"Vayikra el Moshe—[And Hashem] called to Moshe" *Lechol dibros u'lechol amiros ulechol tzivuyim kadmah kriah, loshon chibah—*"Calling" preceded every statement, and every saying and every command. It is language of affection."

(*Rashi, Parashas Vayikra* 1:1)

Chinuch Defined

As told to Ben Shalom

TODAY WAS THE DAY. Mrs. Tesser*, the education specialist sent by the Board of Ed, was finally coming to evaluate a struggling student in her first-grade class. Mrs. Fine knew, though, that just telling Sara to go out when the specialist came to the door might leave Sara open to embarrassment and possible scorn. What was the teacher to do?

Several minutes before the evaluator was due to arrive, Mrs. Fine announced, "I'm looking for a well-behaved girl for a special job." She looked around the class and in a voice gushing with enthusiasm that was music to the ears of her first-graders, she pointed out those girls, Sara included, who were sitting nicely. "I need someone who is sitting nicely, and listening well," she continued and then went on with her lesson. A few moments later she added another positive description of the girl she would need for this special task and again announced the names of several girls who "fit the bill," Sara, once again, among them.

All the girls named were obviously pleased, but Sara, a struggling student, without a very long attention span, was absolutely ecstatic. She had done it. She had remained focused (albeit for this short time) and earned the teacher's praise. But the clincher was yet to come. When Mrs. Tesser knocked on the door a short while later,

Mrs. Fine made one final announcement. "Remember that I said I needed a well-behaved, mature girl for a special job. Well, Mrs. Tesser is visiting our school today and she needs someone to help her, someone who knows her way around and knows how to act properly and treat people well. So many of you have been so good, let me see who I can pick today. O.K. Sara Gold, you're just the right one for the job."

> **Does *chinuch* have to be comfortable?**

As Sara left the room she was positively glowing; the admiration of her classmates clearly evident. So much had been accomplished in so short a time by a teacher who knew the true meaning of the word "*chinuch*."

All names have been changed.

All day, every day, the educator is immersed in the noble and valuable mission we call "*chinuch*." In a lecture, Rabbi Zechariah Greenwald, the principal of Meohr Bais Yaakov Seminary, offered insights into the teacher's role and goals by delving into the question of what, exactly, is *chinuch*. *Chinuch* is about preparing our students for their future, helping them become independent and motivated, and instilling in them the desire to grow and develop.

But there is more.

A very interesting *Mishnah* in *Maseches Nazir* discusses an instance of a father who wants to make his child a *nazir* for *chinuch* purposes. In this case, a father genuinely feels it would be best for his child's *chinuch* to

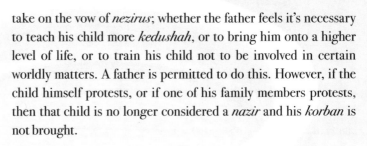

take on the vow of *nezirus*; whether the father feels it's necessary to teach his child more *kedushah*, or to bring him onto a higher level of life, or to train his child not to be involved in certain worldly matters. A father is permitted to do this. However, if the child himself protests, or if one of his family members protests, then that child is no longer considered a *nazir* and his *korban* is not brought.

The *Gemara* (*Nazir* 29a) asks an interesting question: Can someone else affect the parent's *chinuch* of his child? How can a relative protest? It's the parent's responsibility to educate his child! Furthermore, is it appropriate for a child to say to his father, "I know you think this is good for me, but I don't really want to do it!" The *Gemara* offers an answer that cuts to the heart of what *chinuch* truly is.

The *Gemara* says, in the name of Reish Lakish, that any *chinuch* which is not "*chashuv*" is not comfortable. What does the *Gemara* mean? Does *chinuch* have to be comfortable? *Tosfos* gives us a penetrating definition of *chinuch*. At the end of the *nazir* process, all the hair on this child's body will be cut off—he will be left completely bald—and he will be embarrassed and disgraced by this! Therefore, he or others can protest and refuse. Tosfos goes further in his second explanation, "*kol chinuch hu l'hachashivo.*" Long before the advent of modern-day child psychology, Tosfos taught us the very essence of *chinuch*: It is about making a child feel special, feel important. It is about building him up and motivating him to strive higher.

This is "*chinuch*" that will prepare our students for their future. ▣

HASHKAFAH, HALACHAH, AND INSPIRATIO

One Step at a Time

Retold by Riva Pomerantz

CHEZKY KLEIN* WAS A *PROBLEM*. The slightest provocation sent him into fits of rage; his fuse was always either waiting to be lit or already smoldering. The rest of the seventh grade knew that Chezky had to be treated with kid gloves—or else. But no one really knew how to deal with him, how to help him overcome his terrible anger.

> **Rabbi Weinstein was shocked. He had never intended to target Chezky by telling his story!**

"And now, if everyone settles down I'll tell you a beautiful story," Rabbi Weinstein announced. The clamor died down as thirty boys waited expectantly for Rebbi to begin. Today, he told them a story about the Apter Rav who was twice approached by a delegation to address a problem with a member of the community. To their surprise, the Apter Rav refused to take action against the miscreant. Finally, this individual acted in a totally unacceptable way again and this time, when the Rav was told about it, he immediately brought the wrongdoer to justice.

"The *talmidim* were surprised, of course, and they asked the Rav about his strange behavior. The Apter Rav revealed to them an astonishing thing.

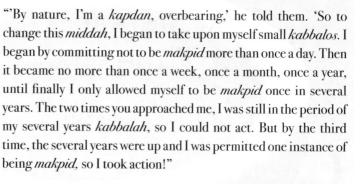

"'By nature, I'm a *kapdan*, overbearing,' he told them. 'So to change this *middah*, I began to take upon myself small *kabbalos*. I began by committing not to be *makpid* more than once a day. Then it became no more than once a week, once a month, once a year, until finally I only allowed myself to be *makpid* once in several years. The two times you approached me, I was still in the period of my several years *kabbalah*, so I could not act. But by the third time, the several years were up and I was permitted one instance of being *makpid*, so I took action!"

Rabbi Weinstein lowered his voice. "Boys, think about what a powerful message this is! A person can change his entire personality, his whole way of life, simply by taking on tiny *kabbalos*, slowly but surely."

In the whirlwind of dismissal, the rebbi felt a shadow fall on his desk. Looking up, he was surprised to see none other than... Chezky Klein, looking somber.

"Rebbi," Chezky said, "I was thinking a lot about that story you told. I think I'm going to try to take on a *kabbalah* not to get angry—all day Friday."

Rabbi Weinstein was shocked. He had never intended to target Chezky by telling his story! But the determined look on his *talmid's* face brought a rush of emotion. "*Hatzlachah rabbah,*" he told Chezky warmly.

No one believed that it could actually work, least of all Chezky, but he held back his temper all Friday. A while later, he extended his *kabbalah* to include Shabbos and Yom Tov, months later he added other days of the week. With incredulous pride, Rabbi Weinstein watched a seventh-grade boy transform himself completely over several years. Gone was the Chezky of old, the explosion waiting

*All names have been changed

HASHKAFAH, HALACHAH, AND INSPIRATION

to happen; this new Chezky was tranquil, even-tempered. It was nothing short of a miracle—and it all happened from one, tiny step.

The *Midrash Rabbah* in *Vayikra* (*Metzorah* 19) highlights the importance of breaking down a big hurdle into smaller, manageable increments.

There is a great pile of dust [which must be moved]. The fool says, "Who could possibly transfer this?" The wise person says, "I will transfer two bucketfuls of it today and tomorrow until I've transferred the entire pile." So it is [with Torah]; the fool says, "Who can possibly learn Torah? Nezikin is thirty chapters, Keilim is thirty chapters..." The wise person says, "Now I will review two halachos today and two halachos tomorrow, until I have reviewed the whole Torah!"

The Midrash contrasts the perspective of a *tipesh*, a fool, and a *pikei'ach*, a wise person. When faced with a challenge, the fool immediately becomes overwhelmed at the thought of accomplishing such an enormous task, while the wise person says, "If I do a little bit each day, over time I will have completed the entire task!"

The *Midrash* is astounding in the treasure it imparts. This is the secret to not giving up when faced with what we feel are major hurdles. Instead of becoming intimidated, the *Midrash* tells us we can take on small increments and build and build...until an entire palace is assembled—one beyond our wildest dreams!

A teacher who can transmit this valuable lesson to his or her students enables them to become like the praiseworthy pikei'ach, giving them a precious tool that will allow them to grow to untold heights! ▣

The Art of Rebuke

◼

A Lesson From Naomi

A PASSAGE IN MEGILLAS RUS eloquently demonstrates the way to correct people without hurting their feelings. Naomi, who models this lesson, was given her name because her actions were pleasing to all. Her method of giving mussar in a gentle manner is the embodiment of who she was, and is an example that we can all learn from.

It says that Boaz told Rus (*Megillas Ruth* 2:8), "Do not go glean in another field...stay close to my maidens." When Rus came home to Naomi she told her how well Boaz had treated her and she repeated her version of Boaz' words, saying, "He even said to me, 'Stay close to my servants'."

Naomi understood that Boaz had said his "maidens" and she wanted Rus to know that she should be staying with the young women, not the young men. But, Naomi did not belittle Rus by correcting her mistake openly. Instead the *pasuk* (2:22) tells us, Naomi told Rus, "It is fine, my daughter, that you go out with his maidens."

In this subtle way, Naomi guided Rus and got the point across that she was to stay with the young women without making Rus lose face.

Shaping with Sensitivity

- ▸ Many times you can make a correction subtly, without calling attention to the mistake made.
- ▸ Even when you're right, you don't have the right to put someone down.

HASHKAFAH, HALACHAH, AND INSPIRATION

Open Lines

IT'S EASY TO BE CALM AND KIND when the class is behaving as we wish. The challenge arises when a student acts in a manner that needs to be addressed and corrected. Teachers face such situations every day. The Torah teaches that reproach should always be given in a way in which it will be accepted, but how does one find that way?

> **The Torah teaches that reproach should always be given in a way in which it will be accepted, but how does one find that way?**

Hashem Himself teaches us the right approach. "Where is Hevel, your brother?" He asks Kayin after he kills his brother. The question, Rashi explains, was meant to keep the lines of communication open with Kayin, to give him a chance to repent. Were he to feel crushed by Hashem's wrath, he'd have no avenue to return.

Kayin in essence killed off one quarter of the world's population. But even for this grave crime, Rashi points out that Hashem came to Kayin with words of calm, with a question, not an accusation. By emulating Hashem's approach, we preserve the dignity and self-respect of those we reprove. Ultimately, this makes the person feel capable of mending his ways and worthy of fulfilling his potential.

Adapted from "Chosen Words," a bi-weekly publication of the Chofetz Chaim Heritage Foundation.

Shaping with Questions

▸ Always ask. An accusation leaves no room for discussion. A question opens the door for communication.

How You Say It

AND HE SAID, *"Look, the day is still long; it is not yet time to bring the livestock in..."* (*Vayeitzei* 29:7).

It's often not what you say but how you say it that determines whether or not your words will find an open ear. The Torah, a few thousand years before modern-day psychologists gave the matter some thought, provided the perfect role model for voicing rebuke of another's actions.

Rabbi Mottel Katz, *zt"l*, the Telshe Rosh Yeshivah, explained that the Torah pays a surprising amount of attention to the conversation Yaakov had with some shepherds as he approached Lavan's house. In all, four consecutive verses record the interchange. The first three verses, in which Yaakov is asking the shepherds for information, begin with, "*Vayomer lahem*—and he (Yaakov) said to them." But the fourth verse, in which he rebukes them for ignoring their duties in middle of the day, begins, "*Vayomer*—and he said."

> There are times when "inference" can be the strongest way to teach a lesson.

Yaakov doesn't address his observation "to them." He merely states what he sees—that there is still much time left in the day, it is not yet time to gather the cattle—and leaves them to infer the rest. Because there is no attack, the shepherds need not mount a self-defense. Instead, they heed his words—the best result for everyone.

HASHKAFAH, HALACHAH, AND INSPIRATION

There are times when "inference" can be the strongest way to teach a lesson.

Adapted from "Chosen Words," a bi-weekly publication of the Chofetz Chaim Heritage Foundation.

Respectful Revision

RABBI SHLOMO HEIMAN, Rosh Yeshivah of Yeshivah Torah Vodaath, treated his students with deep warmth and respect. Whenever a student would suggest a possible explanation, R' Shlomo would begin to repeat the student's words, no matter how ridiculous they initially seemed: "*So* you probably mean to say... yes, yes, that is a deep insight. Perhaps we might want to answer the question we had in the *Gemara* based on your thought as follows..."

> By the time R' Shlomo was done refining the student's garbled thought, a multifaceted piece of insight had emerged.

By the time R' Shlomo was done refining the student's garbled thought, a multifaceted piece of insight had emerged. The *Gemara* was now clear, the student felt confident of his ability, and R' Shlomo had ably fulfilled the dictum of the mishnah (*Avos* 4:15), "*Let the honor of your student be as dear to you as your own.*" ▣

Adapted from, "The Pirkei Avos Treasury," with permission from Mesorah Publications, Ltd.

When and How

I N HIS RENOWNED *SEFER* *Aleinu L'Shabeiach*, Rabbi Yitzchok Zilberstein, *shlita*, brings a beautiful lesson for educators, gleaned from the words *achar hikaso*, "after he had smitten [Sichon...and Og]," (*Devarim* 1:4). This incident highlights the *middos* of the quintessential leader—Moshe Rabbeinu—who addresses *Klal Yisrael* only after he wiped out Sichon and Og.

> How tragic, bemoans Rav Zilberstein, when the bitter-tasting mussar is given alone.

The sequence of events teaches us that Moshe Rabbeinu's first concern was to take care of *Klal Yisrael's* immediate problem—namely that of the persecutors who threatened their safety—and only then did he give them words of *mussar*. How apropos is this lesson for educators! When we find ourselves—as we sometimes do—faced with a situation where discipline or *mussar* is necessary, the most effective technique is the one exemplified by Moshe. First, put all your efforts into helping the student overcome his personal troubles—does the student need food, a break, academic help, a change of seat, a listening ear, etc.—only then impart the lesson that must be taught. How tragic, bemoans Rav Zilberstein, when the bitter-tasting *mussar* is given alone—especially if it is, *chas v'shalom*, transmitted with insensitivity or outright aggression. In such a case is there any hope at all that it will be accepted by the student?

Continuing his discussion on effective rebuke, Rav Zilberstein focuses on another great leader, Nechemiah HaNavi, when he

HASHKAFAH, HALACHAH, AND INSPIRATION

speaks to *Klal Yisrael* on *Rosh Hashanah*, telling them: (Nechemiah 8:10) "*lechu, ichlu mashmanim ushesu mamtakim, v'shilchu manos l'ein nachon lo, ki kadosh hayom laAdoneinu*—Go and eat delicacies and drink sweet delights, and send food portions to those who have nothing prepared, for today is holy to *Hashem*..." The *Aleinu L'Shabeiach* is understandably bothered by a question on this *pasuk*. After all, Nechemiah was addressing the people on Rosh Hashanah. Why, then, was he commanding them to send "*manos*"—food portions—to others, in what seems at first glance to be a displaced Purim-like suggestion?

The *meforshim* explain that on this particular occasion, *Rosh Hashanah* fell on Erev Shabbos*. Thus, *Klal Yisrael* was required to make an *eruv tavshilin* before *Yom Tov* in order to cook on *Yom Tov* for Shabbos. In his message, Nechemiah was commanding the people to send food to those who had forgotten to set aside an *eruv tavshilin* and who were therefore not permitted to cook from one day for the next and would not have cooked food for Shabbos.

Here, another question arises: we know that a person who forgets to make an *eruv tavshilin* may rely on the one designated by his rav. In the times of Nechemiah, therefore, those who forgot to make an *eruv tavshilin* could simply rely on that of the *gadol hador*—Nechemiah HaNavi! It is here that Rav Zilberstein brings an interesting twist by reminding the reader that this dispensation of relying on the rav's *eruv* only applies to the first time one forgets. If one forgets a second time, one may no longer rely on the rav. Harsh words are accorded to a second-time offender in the *Mishnah Berurah*—"He is equivalent to a negligent person, since it is clear that he is not particularly careful with the dictates of this mitzvah."

According to this understanding, Nechemiah was commanding the people to go out of their way to bring

SHAPING ETERNITY

food to those among them who had forgotten—more than once —to make their own *eruvei tavshilin* before *Yom Tov*. Think about this for a moment: the people in question have been cast into the category of "one who is negligent and not careful with a mitzvah"—and they are roundly penalized for their oversight by not being allowed to rely on the *gadol hador's eruv*. Yet despite this, Nechemiah, their true leader, looks out for their best interests regardless. What a pivotal example of "*smol docheh v'yemin mekareves* (rebuke with the left and draw close with the right)!"

> If one forgets a second time, one may no longer rely on the rav.

The teacher-student relationship can be likened to a walk across a tightrope: it requires great skill, patience, and training—and the stakes are very high. When it comes to the delicate issue of imparting mussar and discipline, may we be illuminated by the guiding light of the Torah leaders who have preceded us, and emulate their lofty and effective conduct. ⊞

*This occurred before the standard calendar was established in the year 4118. After the establishment of the calendar it was no longer possible for the first day of Tishrei to be Friday.

HASHKAFAH, HALACHAH, AND INSPIRATIO

58

Rav Wolbe on Punishment

1 THIS IS A TOPIC THAT INTERESTS MANY PEOPLE. To my distress, there is a widespread belief that punishment is the most important educational tool available to both parents and teachers. One school principal published a wonderful book on education, but he entitled it *When to Punish the Child*. I asked him why he called it this, especially since his book dealt with so many other issues, too. Why does our whole perspective have to be: "When should I punish?"

Fascination with punishment stems from a person's desire to control those in his/her care. Many teachers feel that as long as they have the ability to punish, they also have control.

Once, a man filed an application with our school for the position of counselor. He inquired as to the degree of authority he would hold in this position: Would he have license to expel a child from the school? *This was his first question*. It was apparent that this man would never develop into either a good counselor or teacher. If his first concern was whether or not he could expel students— exposing his need to feel complete power over them—then I would never entrust him with students, either in the capacity of counselor or teacher. Such an approach is totally perverse and unworthy of professional educators. The "When should I punish?" perspective is corrupt and undermines all prospects for a healthy education. Punishment must be the last resort.

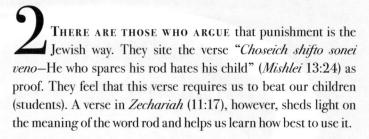

2 THERE ARE THOSE WHO ARGUE that punishment is the Jewish way. They site the verse *"Choseich shifto sonei veno—He who spares his rod hates his child"* (*Mishlei* 13:24) as proof. They feel that this verse requires us to beat our children (students). A verse in *Zechariah* (11:17), however, sheds light on the meaning of the word rod and helps us learn how best to use it.

Zechariah says, "And I took for myself two rods; the one I called pleasantness and the other I called beating, and I herded the sheep." The verse mentions *two* rods: one that we use to beat, and another that we can also use to educate, but through pleasantness— *the rod of pleasantness*. We must recognize that the rod of pleasantness is also a rod, but it causes no pain. When I offer encouragement, this too is a rod. If a child performs well and I give him a piece of chocolate, this is also a rod, but it is a rod of pleasantness.

Bamidbar Rabbah 10 explains that every blade of grass has a malach that hits it and says, "Grow!" Here we see that the force that inspires growth is called a "hit." Of course, this does not mean that on each blade of grass there sits an angel with pink cheeks and white wings, armed with a club (rod). Rather, our Sages are telling us that:

- *There is a force that inspires growth;*
- *Chazal call this force a "hit";*
- *The source of this force is termed a "rod."*

When we read the verse "He who spares his rod hates his child," we must remember that there are two sorts of rods—violent ones and pleasant ones. Why read the verse as a requirement to beat a child, when there are better ways—*using the rod of pleasantness*— to encourage and guide the child's growth? ⊞

Adapted from Planting and Building, by Rabbi Shlomo Wolbe, with permission from Feldheim.

HASHKAFAH, HALACHAH, AND INSPIRATIO

Eye on the Goal

AMONG THE MANY TORAH GIANTS *who strove to bring out the best in their talmidim was Rabbi Meir Chodosh, zt"l, the Mashgiach of Yeshivas Chevron. He perfected the art of censuring with wisdom; encouraging growth and steering students far away from the devastation of despair. Harav Zilberstein, rav of Ramat Elchonon and author of "Aleinu L'Shabeiach," tells a story of one such positive encounter which he heard from the boy—now a grown man—involved.*

The avreich recalled that at one time during his days in yeshivah— for no real reason—he did not show up at the yeshivah's minyan for a month's time. While he was there for the rest of the day, the yeshivah's minyan was just not for him.

One day the Mashgiach called him over, put a hand on his shoulder with genuine concern, and asked, "It seems to me that yesterday you were not at yeshivah for davening; did something happen?"

How much wisdom was hidden in the Mashgiach's words. The Mashgiach certainly knew of the boy's continuous absence from the yeshivah's minyan. He also knew that if he were to ask him why he hadn't come all month, the boy would be overcome with embarrassment, not having anything to answer, and it would be doubtful if the conversation would reach its intended goal. If there was nothing to say and he had truly done wrong for so long, what was the use of trying to improve?

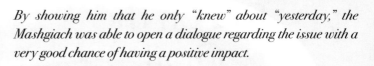

By showing him that he only "knew" about "yesterday," the Mashgiach was able to open a dialogue regarding the issue with a very good chance of having a positive impact.

And judging from the presence of the young *talmid chacham* before him, Rav Zilberstein knew for sure that Rav Meir's words had indeed made their mark.

———————————

As any teacher knows, it is often necessary to censure a student for his misdeeds. But one must ask himself, "Is my goal to 'tell him off,' or is my goal to help him improve his ways? Will he walk away with a determination to do better and the knowledge that he can, indeed, succeed? Or will he be left with the feeling that he is too far gone, that his infraction has sealed his doom forever?"

> **Will he walk away with a determination to do better and the knowledge that he can, indeed, succeed?**

Particularly in our day, when instant gratification is the byword of the generation, and knowing that self-improvement takes hard work, we must find the right way to guide our students without sending them into total despair. We must be careful that our words do not make the student's misbehavior seem—to him—like the most evil deed of the world's greatest villain. If we allow him to view himself as evil, G-d-forbid, from where will he find the motivation to climb out of the rut he finds himself in? What will prevent him from slipping further?

We can learn from Moshe Rabbeinu the delicate art of giving rebuke while keeping a person's self-image intact. When Moshe rebuked the Jewish people at the end of his life, the Torah relates

that Moshe said, "May Hashem, the G-d of your fathers, increase you one thousand times, similar to you" (*Devarim* 1:11).

Why did Moshe need to say that the increase should be *kachem*, "similar to you"?

In his multifaceted *sefer* "Growth Through Torah," Rabbi Zelig Pliskin brings Rabbi Leibel Eger's insightful answer. Moshe was rebuking the people for their errors; he wanted to make certain that they would not feel depressed and discouraged by his criticism. Therefore he assured them that they shouldn't think he considered them to be evil. Rather, he wished there would be a thousand-fold more just like them.

This, then, is the key: to preserve and nurture a person's view of himself as inherently good and worthy while coaching him in the area where improvement is needed. Such an approach will leave the person feeling good about himself and empower him to garner the energy necessary to make positive changes. ▣

Grooming for Greatness

EVERY DEVOTED TEACHER, REBBI, MORAH, and parent invests a tremendous amount of effort into bringing out the best in each child, grooming him for greatness. The true test of how successful they were is only seen when the student is fully grown, when the choices he makes and the refinement of character he achieves stand as testimony to a *chinuch* job well done.

What can we do now to ensure this success?

What was the source of Yosef Hatzaddik's spiritual stamina?

A Rashi in *Parashas Vayeishev*, describing Yosef Hatzaddik, is particularly instructive.

Of the seven pillars of Judaism —Avraham, Yitzchak, Yaakov, Yosef, Moshe, Aharon, and Dovid —only Yosef is known as "*Hatzaddik.*" For even as a lone Jew among gentiles—and a prominent one at that—Yosef resisted every temptation and remained *a tzaddik*. What was the source of this spiritual stamina?

Yosef is called the *ben zekunim* of Yaakov (*Vayeishev* 37:3) and Rashi gives three explanations of the word *zekunim*. Each explanation—as Rabbi Dr. Jacob Mermelstein, a noted psychologist, points out—sheds light on the three ingredients necessary for success in *chinuch*.

HASHKAFAH, HALACHAH, AND INSPIRATIO

A. Yosef was born in Yaakov's old age—*zekunim*.

B. Yosef was a wise son—*zekunim* ("old age") being synonymous with wisdom according to Onkelos—to whom Yaakov taught the wisdom of Shem and Ever.

C. Yosef resembled Yaakov—*zekunim* being an Aramaic contraction of *ziv ikunim,* "facial appearance."

The fact that Rashi brings three explanations shows that he felt that each was not sufficient on its own. So how do these ideas interrelate, and what can we learn from this?

Let's explore each of these points:

A. Yosef was born in Yaakov's old age: Because Yosef was born to Yaakov's beloved wife Rachel, and only after six years of earnest prayer, he loved the boy as though he were his only son born in old age.

B. Yosef was wise: Yaakov viewed him as a wise son. This is reflected in Onkelos' translation of the words "*ben zekunim hu lo—bar chakim hu lei,*" literally, he was a wise child to *him.* Yosef was not just wise, but also, to *him*—to *Yaakov*—he was wise. This recognition of Yosef's G-d-given capabilities underscored all their interactions and compelled Yaakov to groom his son for greatness (as seen by the fact that he taught him all that he had learned from Shem and Ever).

Dr. Mermelstein explains that such a perspective—recognizing the inherent greatness of a child—helps a *mechanech* to focus on the positive, and offer only positive reinforcement, the first step in successful *chinuch*. When dealing with a student whom we perceive as wise and capable, even when he misbehaves we tend to respond in a positive way. Our response might be, "How can a smart boy like you have done such a thing? It must have been a mistake, right?"

C. Yosef resembled Yaakov: Love and positive reinforcement foster a relationship in which the student will want to emulate his rebbi. The student's success, then, will depend on the rebbi being a worthy role model. Yaakov was the ultimate role model and Yosef became a carbon copy of his rebbi, his illustrious father—not only externally, in manner, inflection, and appearance, but internally, in *yiras Shamayim* and *middos*. Seeing himself grow into his father's sterling mold gave Yosef a positive self-concept of who he was and what he was capable of—the ultimate weapon in facing any life challenge.

In this way we can explain the *Midrash* that Yosef resisted Potiphar's wife only when he saw "the image of his father." He saw *himself* in that image, and the moral greatness he had attained; only then did he realize how much he stood to loose. By growing into the "image of his father" he had become someone great in his own right—great enough to want to hold onto that "image," and great enough not to let anything rob him of *himself*, the mirror image of his father.

These three "ingredients"—fierce love, positive reinforcement, and self-example—are vital in producing wonderful children and students. They are the secret of Yosef Hatzaddik's success; a secret we are free to share with each of our students. ▣

Adapted with permission from "There Shall be Light" by Rabbi Yitzchak Meir Goodman, published by Targum Press

HASHKAFAH, HALACHAH, AND INSPIRATIO

The Chazon Ish's Reply

A MENAHEL ONCE ASKED THE CHAZON ISH whether he should expel a very weak student. The Chazon Ish unhesitatingly replied, "Why do you think this boy is a failure? It is relative, only because the others are better than he is. If you expel him on these grounds, then someone else will be the weakest, and in the course of time, you can thus expel all your students!" ⊞

> **Why do you think this boy is a failure?**

Positive Word Power

What Wasn't Said

THE TORAH TELLS US THAT A PERSON suspected of having *tzara'as* was quarantined for one week—kept in isolation, away from family and friends. Because *tzara'as* was a punishment for loshon hora, the ordeal brought shame with it as well. After one week, the person was reexamined, and at that time, if the kohen determined that the suspect discoloration wasn't *tzara'as* at all, the person would go free.

In such a case, it would seem that an innocent person had suffered; he had been shamed and separated from the community for seven days, all for nothing. The Imrei Emes explains that in fact, it was not for nothing. This "false alarm" was a punishment in itself, not for forbidden words that had been spoken, but for positive words that had been left unspoken.

> It would seem that an innocent person had suffered; he had been shamed and separated from the community for seven days, all for nothing.

From this we learn the importance of "loshon tov," of using our power of speech to create good in the world. Sometimes we underestimate the impact of our compliment, our thank you, our quick "moral support" phone call. We think the world can get along fine without it.

HASHKAFAH, HALACHAH, AND INSPIRATIO

But loshon tov is the fiber of *ahavas Yisrael*. Sometimes the context is dramatic—empathy and comfort in troubled times, or *mazal tovs* upon a *simchah*. But, often, the context is commonplace—a hello and a smile in passing, a thank you for a small favor, a compliment on one's new shoes. All of this is just words, yet the words are profound acts of *chessed* as well. . . and we are not allowed to leave them unspoken.

Adapted from "Chosen Words," a bi-weekly publication of the Chofetz Chaim Heritage Foundation.

It's Not Optional!

AS GREAT AS THE PUNISHMENT *will be for a person who speaks a word of loshon hora, that is how great his punishment will be for a good word that came his way to say, and he didn't say it (Zohar, Parashas Tazria).*

We may think that giving a word of praise is doing something extra, but as this *Zohar* clearly explains, a kind or uplifting word is not an extra. On the contrary, if we have the opportunity to say something good and we don't say it, the consequences are as severe as those that result from saying something wrong.

The Softest Piece of Tongue

THERE IS A WELL-KNOWN MIDRASH (*Vayikra Rabbah* 33:1) which relates that Rabbi Yehudah Hanasi served tongue at a feast that he hosted for his *talmidim*. He noted how each student

"Positive Word Power"
continued

carefully selected a tender slice, leaving over the tougher pieces, and utilized this opportunity to teach those present that just as in eating they chose the softer piece of tongue, so too when they speak they must be careful to choose softer words and "leave over" those that are harsh.

In his weekly Motzei Shabbos lectures on the Torah portion of the week, Rabbi Yosef Dov Soloveitchik, Rosh Hayeshivah, of Brisk in Jerusalem, explained: Rabbi Yehudah Hanasi did not have to warn his students not to violate the explicit prohibition of the Torah not to hurt someone with words. Rather, he meant to demonstrate with this vivid illustration the full extent of our obligation in the laws of *ona'as devarim*.

When Rabbi Yehudah Hanasi served tongue at his table all the pieces were certainly edible. Nonetheless, as long as there was a discernible difference in tenderness between two pieces, *talmidim* chose the piece that was only slightly softer. This is the *Midrash's* point. Not only are outright derogatory words and insults prohibited, but as long as there is a noticeable difference between two expressions we are obligated to always select the more pleasant one. People are sensitive and comments that are meant as light banter can cause untold anguish. A person should have the foresight to be aware of the consequence of every statement, concluded Rav Yosef Dov, and be constantly on guard to choose the softest possible approach. ▣

Adapted with permission from "The Power of Words" by Rabbi Zelig Pliskin

HASHKAFAH, HALACHAH, AND INSPIRATIO

A Valid Complaint

AFTER MOSHE AND AHARON APPROACHED Pharaoh and made it known to him that they wished to take *Bnei Yisrael* to the wilderness to serve Hashem, Pharaoh worsened the slavery conditions greatly. He stopped providing straw for the Jews and insisted they keep their former quota while scavenging for straw themselves. The Jewish foremen, as the *pasuk* notes, endured even more beatings from their Egyptian captors after this, and in all, the torment became considerably more unbearable.

Suddenly, Moshe and Aharon were approached by none other than Dasan and Aviram, the heartless evil-doers who epitomized faithlessness and sin, who were responsible for trying to have Moshe killed by reporting on his killing an Egyptian guard. In their despicable arrogance, they turned upon Moshe and Aharon, complaining that the situation has worsened since Hashem had revealed Himself. Furthermore, they scolded the two dedicated leaders unashamedly (*Shemos* 5:20—see Rashi).

What follows this incident is truly astounding. Moshe goes directly to Hashem and brings the complaint of Dasan and Aviram to the fore, questioning why Hashem has caused more agony to befall His People. It is amazing to note that despite the fact that Dasan and Aviram were notorious for their evil ways, Moshe still paid attention and "tuned in" to their—quite legitimate—complaint, and addressed it immediately. We see from here, says Rav Menachem Ben Zion Zaks, as quoted by Rabbi Yitzchok Meir

Goodman, in his book, "And There Was Light," that a true leader always responds to his people, however unsavory they may be.

———————————

Imagine, for a moment, the following scenario:

Akiva is just one of those kids who could only be called a millstone around his teacher's neck, the bane of his teacher's existence. Not a day goes by that he does not capitalize on an opportunity to mock, to disturb, and to disrupt every single lesson in any one of a million creative ways. The rebbi, understandably, is at his wit's end, and it seems that Akiva's days in the class are numbered...

> **Is there a remote chance that dealing with a complaint might plant the seeds of a fresh start?**

And one day, the challenge arises.
Akiva approaches Rebbi's desk, and in a loud voice he declares: "Y'know, Rebbi, we have two tests scheduled for Tuesday. That's not fair!" This sage commentary comes upon the heels of a particularly disruptive day, and in the rebbi's eyes, any word that exits Akiva's mouth is tainted with the bitter taste of his outrageous actions.

There are so many retorts that go through the rebbi's mind, accompanied by a gnashing of teeth at Akiva's gall. But there's no denying it: the kid has a valid complaint! Two tests in one day should be avoided if possible.

What will happen now? How will the rebbi react? Will he disregard Akiva and even dismiss the complaint, or will he take the position modeled by Moshe Rabbeinu and tune in to this complaint

HASHKAFAH, HALACHAH, AND INSPIRATIC

despite the miscreant behavior of the complainer? And is there a remote chance that dealing with Akiva's valid complaint this one time might plant the seeds of a fresh start for the future? Could this possibly be the turning point that is so sorely needed to treat this difficult case?

No matter how far a student has gone, a rebbi or teacher can utilize the valuable lesson taught by Moshe Rabbeinu, who always considered the legitimacy of the complaint, regardless of the character of the one who lodged it.

Shaping with Validation

► Can you imagine what might happen if the rebbi stopped and with a broad smile on his face said, "Akiva, you're right and I thank you for bringing it to my attention." It may be the very first time that Akiva feels that he is being treated fairly. ▣

Whisper Above the Roar

MAKING A LASTING IMPACT is what teaching is all about. But, with the outside world coming at us from all sides, threatening to overtake us with its own negative impact, what is there to do? How do we inculcate the Torah's timeless values, foster solid *middos*, promote proper morals and fortify our students' spiritual growth? Because the evils we face are so pronounced, and the values so contrary to all we hold dear, we clearly need to make full use of every resource at our disposal.

For this reason, there is a prevalent trend to feed our students a steady diet of strong moral messages, employing a great deal of preaching and sermonizing. Everything is spelled out in capital letters and exclamation points. Thus many educators, who use meaningful stories to convey the Torah's morals, reinforce their tales with lengthy sermons that dwell on those morals.

Why do Chazal fill our Seder with mere symbols and vague allusions?

But the clamor of relentless preaching often drowns out the message being taught. When we repeat ourselves over and over again until our point is "coming out of their ears," students begin to associate the values we teach with the suffocation they experience in learning them.

The Torah prescribes a different approach, one which Rabbi Yosef

Leib Bloch, *zt"l*, explains is exemplified by how *Chazal* set up the Pesach Seder. We devote an entire night to reliving the Exodus and a full seven days to its commemoration. Why then, do *Chazal* fill our Seder with mere symbols and vague allusions? Rabbi Bloch's insightful response is vital in our age of ultra-decibels:

Lasting spiritual achievements come through those things that leave only subtle impressions. These, and these alone, can reach the delicate strands of the soul and continue to inspire. We relive Yetzias Mitzrayim, one of the foundations of our faith, with stories, symbols and allusions, for

> **I begin every class with a story, but I never explain its moral. That I leave for the students to figure out.**

that is the way to create impressions that withstand the test of time. The more subtle the approach the deeper it penetrates. Subtle influences make no demands or accusations. They merely plant seeds of awareness—awareness of our obligations and our capabilities—that urge us forward.

We surely need to teach clear moral lessons and define the lines between good and evil in no uncertain terms. But we need to maintain a balance of the overt and the subtle if we want our messages to penetrate.

We *can* get our point across in ways that give our students breathing space. One of today's outstanding *mechanchim* shares his approach. "I begin every class with a story, but I never explain its moral. That I leave for the students to figure out." This is not just intellectually challenging. It enables the student to plug into the story at his level of devotion—and thereby increase that level.

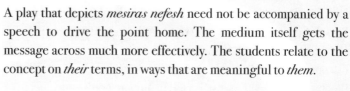

A play that depicts *mesiras nefesh* need not be accompanied by a speech to drive the point home. The medium itself gets the message across much more effectively. The students relate to the concept on *their* terms, in ways that are meaningful to *them*.

> **The ultimate goal was far more valuable than the immediate prize.**

One teacher found a creative, subtle way to accomplish much in enhancing *middos*, morals and values. She brought in a jar of jellybeans and announced that any time a student would do something that was difficult for *him*, he would get a jellybean. Kindness, cleanliness, making a careful *brachah*, keeping the place, waiting patiently, being *mevater*, etc., were all worth jellybeans for those to whom these presented a challenge. When the jellybean jar would be empty the entire class would be rewarded with a special activity, small outing, etc. Additionally, the student would earn the jellybean only if someone else—the teacher or another student—recommended him for one. Since the ultimate goal was far more valuable than the immediate prize, each child would readily recommend others. In an atmosphere of mutual support, "It's not fair" had no place. While rooting for each other they learned to appreciate others' strengths and weaknesses, internalized the awareness that true achievement is measured in terms of personal effort, and discovered that fair treatment must always take that into account. Most important, this was all done naturally, smoothly, without speeches or lectures.

While there are many ways to implement a subtle approach on every grade level, the essential point is the principle itself—one clearly expressed in the Torah: *And behold Hashem passed by, and a great and mighty wind was shattering the mountains and*

HASHKAFAH, HALACHAH, AND INSPIRATIC

breaking rocks before Hashem—Hashem is not in the wind. And after the quaking, fire—Hashem is not in the fire. And after the fire, a still, subtle voice (*Melachim* I 19: 11-12). The *Gemara* (*Chagigah* 16a) concludes: And behold Hashem passed by, i.e. with the still, subtle voice.

Fire and brimstone can proclaim Hashem's presence, but they cannot be its carrier. True spirituality is found—and transmitted—within the still, subtle voice. ⊞

Adapted, with permission, from an article by Rabbi Matis Roberts, Mashgiach Ruchani of Yeshivah Shaar Hatorah of Queens, which appeared in the April 1998 issue of The Jewish Observer.

"*That's* Your Question?"

By Rabbi Pinchos Jung

THIS ARTICLE WAS SUBMITTED TO *Impressions by Rabbi Pinchos Jung, mechanech, author and noted speaker, who felt that Impressions was the perfect forum for this discussion.*

Kids have questions. All types of questions. Sometimes we have ready answers. Sometimes we have partial answers, and sometimes we are caught by surprise, unprepared, maybe even shocked.

Reactions to a challenging question can vary. "Oh, Yanky, that's a fascinating question!' or "Did everyone else hear Yanky's insightful remark?" may be one way that a student's question is acknowledged. Yet, at times, those responding and their responses have been less than inspiring. Some even go so far as to call a child an *apikores* or some other

> **The thoughtlessly worded response continues to reverberate in the student's mind, affecting his entire outlook.**

equally derogatory label in response to his/her sensitive question. There are too many stories of students' innocent—or even not so innocent—questions on *emunah* and *hashkafah* which provoked responses that have left deep, long-term scars. The thoughtlessly worded response continues to reverberate in the student's mind,

HASHKAFAH, HALACHAH, AND INSPIRATIO

affecting his entire outlook. "We don't ask such questions!" or "Who do you think you are questioning that?" may lead him to think, "Well, if that's how they respond, you can be sure that I'll keep my questions to myself in the future!" Countless burning questions remain unasked for just this reason.

Mishandled questions may lead the student to believe, "They don't know" or "They're hiding something" or "There *is* no answer." Worse still—and this *does* happen—is when the student internalizes what he perceives as hostility towards his questions, irrespective of whether this was or was not the teacher's intent. And this thought may play like a broken record in his mind, louder than anything else he hears. "O.K. If that's the way it is, as soon as I'm out of here I'll go my own way..."

This being the case, it behooves us, as teachers, to develop a strategy for welcoming questions and knowing how to deal with them. I'd like to share some thoughts and ideas that have proven helpful.

1. The *Gemara*, whose very *limud* has kept us alive through the ages, is all questions and answers (a small minority are left open). And some of the questions are quite daring.

2. The mitzvah of *Sipur Yetzias Mitzrayim*, relating the story of the Exodus, has as its goal instilling *emunah* in our children. We are instructed to fulfill this mitzvah and conduct the Seder by means of discussion, questions and answers; not through lecturing and narration.

3. There are only a limited number of standard, recurring questions. They have *all been asked* since time began. Compelling answers *are* available. There are very few

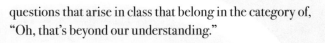

questions that arise in class that belong in the category of, "Oh, that's beyond our understanding."

4. Even if you feel that you personally are not equipped to deal with *emunah* or philosophical issues you can still be a master teacher.

All you need to do is this:

a. React favorably to the student.

b. If applicable, say that this question never bothered you so you haven't looked into it. But:

c. Either promise to research it and return the next day/next week with an answer

d. Or suggest someone you know as an expert in that field.

This approach can be summed up with the useful acronym: **F.O.R.**
  F-First Validate
  O- Offer Your Best for Now
  R- Research or Refer

5. If you feel insecure about a question and your ability to answer it, the most important thing to do is stop for a moment. Never "label" the student or belittle him/her or his/her question. Instead, put yourself in your student's shoes. What do you want your student to be thinking when he hears your answer?

Certainly not: "OK, I wasn't expecting anything better. I'll walk the walk and talk the talk as long as I have to. But when I can do what I want—just you wait!"

Isn't it worth your while to pursue the higher ground, even if it requires much effort on your part, and at times a great deal of

HASHKAFAH, HALACHAH, AND INSPIRATIO

> **Well, if that's how they respond, you can be sure that I'll keep my questions to myself in the future!**

patience, so that your student walks away with a bounce in his/her step, confident that his/her questions are valued?

I still remember the joy a student expressed after one teacher I know took the time to hear him out and help him understand some issues that confused him. This had not been one of the easiest students and his usual demeanor was far from happy. Most often, he walked around with a scowl on his face. Yet, now his face shone as he enthused, "Rebbi made it so clear. He loved my questions!"

You can be sure that this boy's *emunah* was bolstered, his respect for and trust in his rebbi were reinforced, and his desire and love for Torah and mitzvos were raised to a new level. ◪

No Question About It

By Rabbi Pinchos Jung

WHEN IMPRESSIONS FIRST PUBLISHED Rabbi Jung's eye-opening article on dealing with students' questions {See *That's Your Question?*, page 78} the response from teachers was tremendous. Many teachers asked for more guidance and clarification and some expressed reservations as to their ability to step up to the plate. We bring you one such inquiry and Rabbi Jung's enlightening response.

I read with great interest your recent issue,"That's Your Question?," which dealt with responding to your students' haskafic questions. Being a halachah teacher for the past two decades, permit me to explain my problem. I'm basically a technical person and I am comfortable with detail in halachah. Conflicting opinions don't confuse me and I usually manage to get my point across clearly; explaining and discussing hashkafah was never my forte. The student who searches for reasons and wants to explore deep concepts is a challenge to me.

Rabbi Jung responds:
You are obviously a competent teacher, at home in your subject but less secure outside your area of expertise. However, think of it this way: although not everyone is cut out to be a doctor, the tremendous benefit of laymen knowing CPR and the Heimlich maneuver has been proven again and again as countless lives are saved each year by laymen with only the most rudimentary

HASHKAFAH, HALACHAH, AND INSPIRATIO

training in lifesaving techniques. Similarly, although *hashkafah* and answering questions of a philosophical nature are not "what you are cut out for," basic knowledge of *hashkafah* is a must for every teacher—you may yet save a life one day!

Your new-found confidence in this area will allow you to react patiently and properly to those students whose questions may otherwise throw you off course.

Even a small amount of time invested in studying fundamentals of *emunah* yields a great return—for your students, and even more so, for yourself. There are countless *sefarim* in Hebrew, as well as numerous books in English with impeccable *haskamos*, and a great number of CD's by renowned experts which explain these concepts in an enjoyable, engaging way. Permit me to recommend a few: The many books by HaRav Avigdor Miller, *zt"l*, pioneer in explaining haskafic issues to the English-speaking audience. Rabbi Shmuel Waldman, Rabbi Avrohom Katz and Rabbi Leib Keleman have all written excellent books on the subject, and Rabbi Sapirman of Toronto has an incredible series of CDs that clarify all aspects of *emunah*. There is nothing like having a clear understanding and adequate knowledge of relevant, authentic information so that one can provide the correct, compelling answer to satisfy the student when a question arises. Your own *emunah* will grow tremendously from this simple research and your new-found confidence in this area will allow you to react patiently and properly to those students whose questions may otherwise throw you off course.

Knowing, though, that you are more comfortable with a direct approach, as are many teachers, instead of waiting to respond to challenging questions you can inculcate your students with proper *hashkafos* by finding every opportunity to point out the fundamental three principles of *emunah*.

1. There is a creator—Hashem
2. The Torah is from Hashem
3. Hashem is actively involved in every detail of our lives—*hashgachah pratis*

> **There are many students who do not ask the questions that may trouble them.**

Just as you prefer a direct approach over discussion or reacting to challenging questions, there are many students who do not ask the questions that may trouble them and appreciate having this knowledge presented to them. Seeking opportunities to expound on these principles is therefore a great way to respond to your students' needs and have a positive impact on all your students—no matter what their personality, background or temperament.

For more information on how to present principles of emunah to your class and how to answer your students' questions, you may contact the Ani Ma'amin Foundation:

Rabbi Sapirman
(416) 823-9241

Rabbi Jung
(845) 371-0180

Shaping with *Emunah*

Here are just a few examples of how this may be done:

▸ Never miss an opportunity to point out the wonders of Hashem's world and the beauty that is all around us, and stress how impossible it would be for any part of Hashem's world to happen by chance.

▸ There are numerous verses in the Torah that prove its Divine origin. Point out how the promises made in the Torah are impossible for any human being to make and expect to fulfill.

▸ Everyone loves stories. Share personal stories of *hashgachah pratis* with your class and tell stories of *gedolim* and how Hashem rewarded them for their good deeds. One rebbi I know makes a CD each year of *hashgachah pratis* stories that his *talmidim* eagerly record of their own experiences.

Responding to our students' spiritual and emotional needs and strengthening their *emunah*—even if they don't ask us to—is surely one of our greatest mandates as educators. ▣

A Living Example

By Rabbi Mendy Karmel

"He treated me with such respect."
"She never makes people wait."
"He handled that delicate situation with such dignity."

To each one of these comments, the person listening responded, "Of course, s/he's a student of Rabbi _____!"

A S THE JEWISH PEOPLE STOOD at the Yam Suf, watching the Egyptians stampede toward them, Hashem commanded Moshe, "*V'atah hareim es matcha*–and, you lift up your staff" (*Shemos* 14:15). The Ba'al HaTurim points out that there are "*gimmel b'mesorah*," three times that the word "*hareim*," lift up, is mentioned in our *mesorah*, the Torah. The first instance is here, at Kriyas Yam Suf. The second is in *Melachim* II (6:7), "*hareim lach*–lift it up to you," and the third is in *Yeshaya* (58:1), "*kashofar hareim kolecha*–Raise your voice like a shofar."

The Bobover Rebbe, *zt"l*, the *Kedushas Tzion*, writes that the words of the Ba'al HaTurim hint at an insightful and powerful lesson in *chinuch*. "*Gimmel b'mesorah*": there are three ways we can choose to go about relaying our *mesorah*, educating our children and leading the future generations along the proper path. The Rebbe describes these ways as follows: One technique in *chinuch* is mirrored in the first instance of "*hareim*"–"*V'atah*

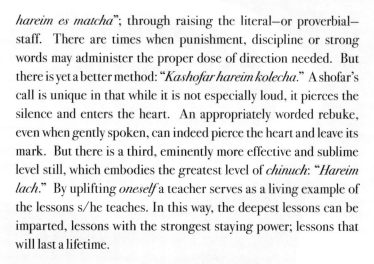

hareim es matcha"; through raising the literal—or proverbial—staff. There are times when punishment, discipline or strong words may administer the proper dose of direction needed. But there is yet a better method: "*Kashofar hareim kolecha*." A shofar's call is unique in that while it is not especially loud, it pierces the silence and enters the heart. An appropriately worded rebuke, even when gently spoken, can indeed pierce the heart and leave its mark. But there is a third, eminently more effective and sublime level still, which embodies the greatest level of *chinuch*: "*Hareim lach*." By uplifting *oneself* a teacher serves as a living example of the lessons s/he teaches. In this way, the deepest lessons can be imparted, lessons with the strongest staying power; lessons that will last a lifetime.

> **It is the unspoken and the unwritten that impact our students the most.**

Rebbis, moros, and teachers invest a tremendous amount of time and effort in preparing lesson plans, making worksheets, and networking with colleagues. But it is the unspoken and the unwritten lessons, conveyed in our every action, that can impact our students the most. As role models who spend a large portion of the day with our students, we serve as the ultimate paradigm for how a Torah-true person should act—and our students absorb every action and word!

When we thank the janitor for cleaning the room or the cook for the lunch each day we help our students learn gratitude. If we pay attention to what is going on during recess and take the time to help a student who is being bullied, we teach the children to be more sensitive and caring. On the other hand, the use of cynicism or negativity to convey our views can breed an attitude of arrogance

HASHKAFAH, HALACHAH, AND INSPIRATIO

and contempt and when directed at people can undo all that has been taught of the importance of ahavas Yisrael. Perhaps the greatest lessons are learned from the ways in which we respond to the unruly student. A response that keeps the student's dignity intact will help students learn that even when someone upsets them, it is not license to respond with hurtful words or humiliation. Not only will this impact their current interactions, but such role modeling is likely to impact the way our students will interact with their future spouses and children. The power we wield with our words and actions is not to be overestimated.

A lesson learned in this way will not remain what they know; it will become who they are.

While there will be times when we may have to resort to the other two methods of *chinuch*—strictness or constructive criticism—let's keep in mind the most effective of all means: raising ourselves to serve as a living example.

A lesson learned in this way will not remain what they *know*; it will become who they *are*. ⊠

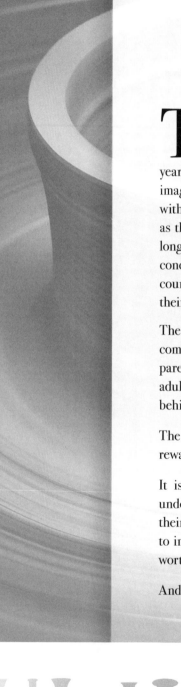

A Worthwhile Sacrifice

THE MITZVAH OF *HAKHEL* requires every Jewish man, woman, and child to come to Yerushalayim every seven years to hear the king read from the *Sefer Torah*. One can only imagine the spiritual heights a person could reach, standing with all of *Klal Yisrael* together in the *Beis Hamikdash*, listening as they had at Sinai to the words of the holy Torah. Yet it was a long procedure that surely must have required maturity and concentration to fully appreciate. Therefore, it seems almost counterproductive to require that children attend alongside their parents.

The *Gemara* asks, what purpose is there in having the children come? The Sfas Emes poses the problem that would cross any parent's mind: the children will just make noise and disturb the adults. Given the spiritual cost to the parents, why not leave them behind?

The *Gemara* explains that the reason the children must come is to reward their parents for bringing them.

It is true that having their small children at their side will undoubtedly disturb the parents' concentration and diminish their spiritual uplift. Yet the Torah maintains that the opportunity to inculcate the children attending with the words of Torah was worth the disturbance and apparent loss.

And so it is with all efforts at *chinuch*.

HASHKAFAH, HALACHAH, AND INSPIRATIO

Sometimes, a *mechanech's* greatest reward is when he sacrifices some of his own personal growth for that of his *talmid*.

Imagine that oft-spoken dream, the long-awaited day of the Mashiach's arrival—the day generations of Jews have prayed for and pined for! How the crowds of ecstatic Yidden will swell, as each person drops whatever he's doing to run to Yerushalayim, to fully experience the *Geulah Sheleimah* and help in the rebuilding of the *Beis Hamikdash*.

And amidst all the hurrying and excitement, the sweet voices of *tinokos shel beis rabban* continue to reverberate, as the rebbi continues to teach Torah to the children in their *cheder*. Surely the rebbi, too, has yearned for this day. He, too, has *davened* each day with fervor, "*V'sechezenah eineinu b'shuvcha l'Tzion.*" Yet *Chazal* teach us that the Torah study of children is dearer to Hashem than the building of the *Beis Hamikdash* and should not cease even for this once-in-history opportunity. So, the rebbi puts aside his own desires, and instead dedicates himself to his *talmidim*. Their learning must not be interrupted. Even at such a momentous occasion, the rebbi sacrifices for his students so that they will know in every fiber of their being how precious their learning truly is. Can there be a bigger *nachas* to Hashem?

It was Rabbi Lipa Zilberman, *zt"l*, who repeated this thought as he encouraged *rebbeim* in their holy task. And it was R' Lipa who lived those words.

The shattering news spread quickly throughout the Torah world. The tragic loss of the leading posek of the generation, the Gadol Hador, R' Shlomo Zalman Auerbach, zt"l, was almost too much to bear. From all corners of Israel and abroad, thousands came to join the levayah. R' Lipa sat in his office lost in thought,

Where was R' Lipa?

overcome with grief. Memories, so many memories, flashed through his mind. He saw himself as a young boy in the Sha'arei Chesed neighborhood of Yerushalayim... the friendly visits between the two. Then as he grew... the divrei Torah they cherished... the chinuch discussions and sage advice... the simchos they had shared... a personal relationship spanning many decades. How clearly he remembered his own mother's levayah, where R' Shlomo Zalman was determinedly present, despite great hardship on his part. And now he was no longer.

Was there even a possibility that R' Lipa would not attend the levayah? And yet, amidst the 300,000 mourners escorting the great Gadol B'Yisroel to his final resting place, R' Lipa was missing.

Where was R' Lipa?

Despite his intense desire to attend, R' Lipa, the devoted principal, remained behind in the cheder with his young talmidim. You see, many of the rebbeim had gone to the levayah, and he, the principal, wouldn't leave his students without a teacher. He, who was so closely connected to the gadol, knew the truth—this was what R' Shlomo Zalman would have wanted. He was certain. Remaining behind and learning with the boys was the only option.

And so it was. His personal feelings were put aside. The chinuch of his precious talmidim was too important. ✠

Translated with permission from "Aleinu L'shabeiach," vol. 4b, by Hagaon Harav Yitzchok Zilberstein, Rav of Ramat Elchonon

HASHKAFAH, HALACHAH, AND INSPIRATIC

Job Qualifications

◆

What Does It Take to Teach?

WHAT DOES IT TAKE TO TEACH? The answer is as complex as the classroom, but we can glean the answer from a lesson that Yaakov Avinu taught in *Parashas Vayechi*.

As Yaakov gathered his children to give them his parting *brachah*, he called Shimon and Levi together and announced, "Shimon and Levi are brothers, their craft of weaponry is stolen (from Esav)."

The *meforshim* explain that Yaakov is referring to the destruction of Shechem, in which the tool of Esav—the sword—was used as opposed to the tool of Yaakov—*tefillah*.

> How is it that those who murdered the entire male population of Shechem, are blessed with the prestigious responsibility of teaching the *tinikos shel beis rabban*?

Yet Yaakov Avinu culminates his admonition with a declaration that seems surprising. He exclaims, "I will spread them throughout Yaakov and disperse them throughout Yisrael. "With this statement Yaakov declared that Shimon would be assigned to travel from town to town with jobs such as *melamdei tinokos* (teachers).

It is truly amazing! How is it that those who murdered the entire

male population of Shechem are blessed with the prestigious responsibility of teaching the *tinokos shel beis rabban*?

HaRav Yaakov Kamenetsky, *zt"l*, explained that only those with great empathy and passion for their brethren will have the strength to withstand the challenges that a *mechanech* faces each and every day in the classroom. The energy of Shimon and Levi when channeled properly makes for the most inspirational *melamdim*.

Adapted with permission from an article by Rabbi Mordechai Spiegel which appeared in Yated Ne'eman.

Preparing to Teach

BEFORE RABBI ISSER ZALMAN MELTZER would deliver his weekly lecture at his yeshivah, he would go for a few minutes into one of the rooms of the yeshivah and close the door. Once, one of the students wanted to know what the Rosh Hayeshivah did during those few minutes before the lecture. Very carefully, the student opened the door just a little bit and peeked inside the room. To his surprise, he saw Rav Isser Zalman walking back and forth repeating to himself over and over again, "Love your fellow man as yourself" (*B'derech Eitz Hachayim* vol 1 p249).

> **Very carefully, the student opened the door just a little bit and peeked inside the room.**

Adapted from "Growth through Torah" by Rabbi Zelig Pliskin, with permission from the author.

HASHKAFAH, HALACHAH, AND INSPIRATIC

Labor of Love

R_AV_ M_ASHINSKY_, _ZT"L_, _OFFERS THE_ following thought in the name of his rebbe, the Klausenberger *Rebbe*: The *Ribono Shel Olom* has created a world where there are manifold needs to be met. Many sorts of craftsmen are required. To meet the myriad needs, Hashem Yisborach endows people with various gifts, each one designed to better the world.

With what special quality, then, are teachers blessed? With a *love of children*. If you are overwhelmed with love for every Jewish child you see, then you can and should be a *mechanech*.

> **With what special quality, then, are teachers blessed?**

Love your *talmidim*. Love them with both your heart and your mind. If your heart yearns to do that which is best for them, then your mind will find the right path to take to help each student succeed.

Adapted from "My Disciple, My Child" by Rabbi Noach Orlowek, with permission from Feldheim Publishers

Qualified for the Job

A TEACHER MUST CONSTANTLY LEARN. Moshe was bidden by the Almighty to show two signs to the Jews letting them know that he was to be their leader (*Shemos* 4: 1-3). His staff turned into a serpent and his hand became leprous when he removed it from his bosom. Rashi explains that the snake indicated that Moshe had slandered the Jews (like the serpent of old) by saying they would not believe him, and that the leprosy was a punishment for having suspected people.

> **What kind of claim
> to leadership was this
> declaration?**

In essence Moshe Rabbeinu was saying, "Look, I've suspected you wrongly and have spoken *loshon hora* against you." Imagine that; a leader admitting to his followers that he was wrong. The question arises, what kind of claim to leadership was this declaration? Rabbi Eliyahu Meir Bloch, Rosh Hayeshivah of the Telshe Yeshivah, explained that Moshe demonstrated he had indeed made mistakes, but he was ready to learn. He was telling the people, "I can teach you, because I myself can learn." ⊞

Reprinted from "Love Your Neighbor," by Rabbi Zelig Pliskin, with permission of the author.

HASHKAFAH, HALACHAH, AND INSPIRATI

Soul to Soul

■

The Color of Their Eyes

THE SACRED TASK OF CHINUCH is a fulfilling yet challenging one. Teachers, by virtue of the intense classroom atmosphere they face, are tested often, and even the best of educators occasionally find themselves reacting to students under stress. It is well known that a teacher's words and expressions make a powerful impression on a student's heart and mind. A well-chosen, encouraging word can uplift a child immeasurably. Conversely, a teacher can do grave, irreversible damage by engaging in *ona'as devarim*. Bitter, angry, abusive words touch the *neshamah* of a person—sometimes forever. It is patently obvious that teachers —who work so hard to help their students grow and flourish— would not want to inflict harm upon their students. Yet given the delicate tightrope that teachers walk almost daily, how can we fortify ourselves?

Rabbi Dr. Yaakov Greenwald emphasizes that the only way to effectively educate a child is to connect with his/her soul. The bond that is forged when a teacher reaches out to the *neshamah* of a student brings the interaction to new ground. The teacher who looks to the *neshamah* of his/her students will never come to hurt them with words.

Rabbi Greenwald often makes a suggestion to *mechanchim* who assure him that they know their students very well.

"I am sure you know your student well," he replies. "But perhaps you can tell me this: What is the color of his eyes?"

The concept that the eyes are windows to the soul is not a secular notion. It is brought down in Midrashic sources, and it is a powerful tool that teachers can use to strengthen their connection with their students. It is not uncommon for teachers to "talk down" to students—both literally and figuratively. But it is difficult to utter hurtful words to a child while gazing directly into his eyes. Indeed, most *ona'as devarim* is shouted across a room, spoken over the phone, uttered as the person turns away or looks down at the victim—all without eye contact.

Perhaps by glimpsing our students through the "windows of their souls" teachers can enrich their efficacy and success. Connecting with a student's *neshamah* not only ensures the most valuable *chinuch* possible; it also offers a powerful guarantee that the roadblock of *ona'as devarim* will never appear. Let us look into their eyes, glimpse their pure souls, and address them with positive, nurturing words!

I Am a Soul

IN A MEETING WITH A GROUP of secular professionals, Rabbi Dr. Greenwald addressed the topic of the soul that lies within every human being. At this foreign concept, a very prominent individual bristled, and stood up during the question-and-answer period.

"Tell me," he said incredulously. "You seem like an intelligent person. Do you really believe that you have a soul?"

"No, I don't believe I have a soul," Rabbi Greenwald replied. The questioner sat down, satisfied.

"Please don't sit down," the rabbi exclaimed. "I'm not finished yet.

I don't believe that I *have* a soul. I believe that I *am* a soul, and I *have* a body."

A teacher who looks into the **eyes** of the student as he/she speaks, and is cognizant of the student's **neshamah**, sees the student as a **fragile** human being who craves proper treatment. The teacher's words will thus emerge more **compassionately**.

Adapted from the Chofetz Chaim Heritage Foundation's Tishah B'Av 2005 Event, "Rebuilding the Bais HaMikdash Word By Word."

Reciprocal Relationship

RABBI ELAZAR BEN SHAMUA says (*Avos* 4:15) "Let the honor of your student be as dear to you as your own; ... and the reverence for your teacher as the reverence for Hashem."

According to the *Lev Simchah*, we may deduce from the *mishnah's* sequence that a reciprocal relationship exists between a *rebbi* (mentor) and his *talmid* (disciple). In an atmosphere in which the *rebbi* respects his *talmid* as much as he esteems himself, the student, in turn, will appreciate the need for *kavod haTorah* and will fear his *rebbi* as much as he venerates Hashem. ⬛

*Adapted from "The Sfas Emes Pirkei Avos" with permission from Mesorah Publications.

Lasting Impression

As told to Riva Pomerantz

IT HAD BEEN A LONG DAY and veteran rebbe Moshe Zions* was exhausted when he walked through the door.

"Hi, Moshe," called his wife, coming out of the kitchen to greet him. "You look bushed! Before you even sit down to eat, you must listen to the message one of your old *talmidim* left on the answering machine! I saved it so you could hear it word for word. I think it'll lift your spirits!"

Curious, Rabbi Zions took the phone.

"Hello, Rabbi Zions, this is David Katz," an enthusiastic voice rang out. "I just wanted to let Rebbi know that I'm getting married out of town tomorrow night!" A pause. "And Rebbi, I just wanted to express my *hakaras hatov* to you. I still remember the song that you taught us at the end of the year, all of fifteen years ago! It went: 'Tick tock, time is passing by.' With that catchy song, you taught us to use our time wisely, and I owe you so much. Anyway, I just wanted to share my *simchah* with you. Thank you, Rebbi! *Simchos* by all and *mazel tov*!"

On that joyful note the message ended and Rabbi Zions was left to contemplate the life-long impact that a teacher can have on his students with even the smallest of gestures. He wasn't this boy's mesivta rebbi, he wasn't his *mashgiach*; he had been his rebbi

HASHKAFAH, HALACHAH, AND INSPIRATIC

in fourth grade! He had taught his students many lessons throughout that year in fourth grade, fifteen years ago. There had been ups and downs, but the simple song he taught at the end of the term held a lesson for life that this student had

> **I still remember the song that you taught us all of fifteen years ago!**

held onto and cherished all through the years. This young man felt connected to his rebbi and was moved to call him right before his wedding. Rabbi Zions was amazed at the magnitude of what his talmid's message taught *him*.

While the message says much about the caliber of the young man who left it, it speaks volumes about the lasting impact of a teacher's parting message to his students.

Names have been changed.

"And this is the brachah..." (Devarim 33:1)

The *parashah* of *V'zos Habrachah* resonates with Moshe's *brachos* to the Jewish Nation, whom he has led faithfully for so many years, through trials, tribulations, and triumphs. Its positive, nurturing, rich essence is in stark contrast to the end of the previous *parashah*, *Ha'azinu*, in which Moshe is told by Hashem that he will soon leave this world. In this solemn dialogue, Moshe grasps the heartbreaking reality that he will never have the privilege of entering Eretz Yisrael.

Rav Yitzchok Zilberstein, in his *sefer Aleinu L'Shabeiach*, draws us into this chapter of Moshe's life and teaches a remarkable lesson to every educator and leader. Imagine

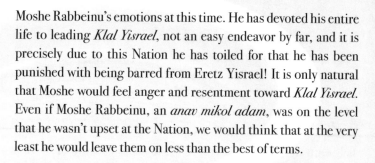

Moshe Rabbeinu's emotions at this time. He has devoted his entire life to leading *Klal Yisrael*, not an easy endeavor by far, and it is precisely due to this Nation he has toiled for that he has been punished with being barred from Eretz Yisrael! It is only natural that Moshe would feel anger and resentment toward *Klal Yisrael*. Even if Moshe Rabbeinu, an *anav mikol adam*, was on the level that he wasn't upset at the Nation, we would think that at the very least he would leave them on less than the best of terms.

But no. Instead, Moshe Rabbeinu launches into a glowing *parashah* of blessings for his people, blessing them with a full, joyous heart. This is the reason for the *vav hachibbur* in the *parashah's* name, *V'zos*—the *vav* connects the "*brachah*" directly to the previous *parashah*, where Moshe is informed of his impending death. This is a true *manhig*, who places the concerns and well-being of his flock above his own to a degree that is truly selfless.

> It's toward the end of a relationship that the connection and the teacher's investment really count.

As *mechanchim*, we, too, experience trials and tribulations with our students, and with Hashem's help, many triumphs in between. But it's toward the end of a relationship that the connection and the teacher's investment really count. Moshe Rabbeinu was about to part with the Jewish People, and he went above and beyond to leave them on a sweet, positive note. The true power of a *mechanech*, writes Rav Zilberstein, is his or her ability to radiate love and caring for each and every student that will stay with them even after the relationship is "officially" over. Just as Moshe Rabbeinu went above and beyond with *Klal Yisrael*, so, too,

HASHKAFAH, HALACHAH, AND INSPIRATIO

every rebbi, every morah, every principal and Rosh Yeshivah, has the power to affect every student simply by ensuring that they leave the year with the sweet taste, the feeling that "My teacher cares about me!"

Every student deserves and benefits from a happy ending. Even if the whole year wasn't as ideal as it might be, a nice send-off can leave a lasting impression—forever. ⊞

Great Lights

IT WAS A REGULAR **S**HABBOS AFTERNOON, *late in the year, and we were leisurely finishing up our seudah when we heard the knock at the door.*

Probably a neighbor's child wanting to play, I thought.

Imagine my surprise when our visitor turned out to be none other than Rebbi T., my son's second-grade rebbi. We invited him in, of course, but we were slightly bewildered as to why he had come. Perhaps he had attended a simchah in the neighborhood and had stopped over for a drink? I finally ventured to ask.

"No, no," Rebbi T. assured me. "I live in the neighborhood." He smiled. "Actually, I came over to see your son, Dovid. I felt like I hadn't really given him enough attention this week so I came by to spend a bit of time with him. If that's okay with you..."

Rebbi T. proceeded to sit down with Dovid and play with him, as my husband, myself, and my other children looked on with amazement. They played a game of Uno, and Dovid proudly showed his rebbi pictures of himself as a small child. They joked and chatted and munched on snacks.

> Any school child today can tell you that there are stars in the galaxies which far exceed the size of the sun.

He left a short while later, with a wave, a smile, and a casual "Good Shabbos." And in his wake, he left behind a deep, palpable feeling of simchah, love, and the unforgettable impact of a rebbi who truly cared.

"I know my rebbi loves me," Dovid told me later that day. "I just know it."

In *Parashas Bereishis*, as *Hakadosh Baruch Hu* reveals the process of the creation of the Universe, we arrive at Day Four, when Hashem places the celestial bodies which He created on the first day in their rightful place in the heavens. The *pasuk* refers here to the sun and the moon as *"hameoros hagedolim,"* "the great luminaries" (*Bereishis* 1:16).

Rabbi Menachem Mark, Rosh Kollel at Torah Academy of Brooklyn, asks an interesting question on this wording. The Torah applies the grand title of "great luminaries" to the sun and the moon, implying that they are *the* biggest lights of the universe. However, any school child today can tell you that there are stars in the galaxies which far exceed the size of the sun and certainly supersede the moon. Why, then, do we crown the sun and the moon with the honor and prestige of the words *"hameoros hagedolim"*?

The answer is profound, one that illuminates the path of the educator in a powerful yet simple way. The reason we accord the sun and the moon the title of "great lights" despite their relatively diminutive size that when it comes to greatness, it's not one's size that makes the difference; it's the impact that counts. While it is true that many stars in the galaxy outshine the sun, there is no question that the sun—and its partner, the moon—have the greatest impact upon the universe.

Every teacher has the potential to be a "great light," casting his or her gentle, formative light on the lives of each and every student in a unique way. A teacher who goes the extra mile to make his or her students shine is truly a "meor hagadol." ✜

With Joy

RAV AVROHOM PAM, ZT"L, *one of the most beloved Torah personalities of our times, took on many leadership positions because of his great sense of responsibility and love for Klal Yisrael. He relished most his primary occupation—that of teaching talmidim. Rabbi Dovid Pam, his son, commented that while his father's 63-year teaching career demonstrated creativity, innovation and dedication, the key to his incredible success in molding talmidim was the joy with which he taught Hashem's Torah.*

I: The Only Way

RAV PAM WOULD CITE A MIDRASH (*Bereishis Rabbah* 22:6) that offers variant approaches to overcoming one's *yetzer hara*:

R' Chaninah bar Papa said: *Push away the yetzer hara with words of Torah*; that is, quell the evil inclination by immersing oneself in the Torah's holy words.

R' Siman said: *Gladden it with words of Torah*. By studying Torah with genuine *simchah*, one can "win over" his inclination and attain a level where his true passion is for Torah and mitzvos.

> **The Torah is acquired through joy.**
> —*Avos 6:6*

Said Rav Pam: In previous generations, rebbeim were successful with the first method, using strict discipline to bring out the best in their *talmidim*. In our generation, however, the only method that succeeds in winning over

HASHKAFAH, HALACHAH, AND INSPIRATIO

a *talmid* is that which R' Siman explains, *samcheihu b'divrei Torah*, to inspire him to experience the joy that can be derived from the study of Torah.

This is the way to teach. The *melamed* needs to be joyful as he teaches, and the student needs to be joyful as he learns. In this way, their spirits cleave to one another in a spiritual bond that is rooted in the joy of Torah study (*Atarah LaMelech*, p. 165).

II: Hashem's Delight

HOW DOES ONE ACHIEVE THE DESIRED state of joy necessary for effective teaching? Rav Pam explained that when a teacher realizes the greatness of teaching Torah and how precious it is to Hashem, he will become infused with joy.

He quoted a Midrash that is homiletically interpreted to describe seven groups of *tzaddikim* who are destined to greet the Shechinah. Which group of them is most beloved? ...These are the scribes, the teachers of Mishnah and those who teach children faithfully. They are destined to stand to the right of Hashem, as it is written, "There is delight at Your right hand for eternity" (*Vayikra Rabbah* 30:2).

Said Rav Pam:
Teaching children Torah places one in the group that is most beloved to *HaKadosh Baruch Hu*. It makes no difference on what level one teaches. The crucial factor is not *what* one is teaching—*Chumash*, *Mishnah* or *Gemara* etc.—but *to whom* one is teaching. One is teaching Jewish children Torah, the mode of behavior expected of a *ben Torah*, and

"With Joy"
continued

the Torah's view of life. A Torah teacher molds people! He takes raw, undeveloped children and transforms them into *zera beirach Hashem* (children that Hashem has blessed).

III: The Best of Both Worlds

EXPOUNDING FURTHER ON THE JOY that one brings into his own life by choosing *chinuch* as his career, Rav Pam cited the *Taz* (*Even HaEzer* 2:3).

...for they [i.e., the ignorant] think that... they will be involved in business and this will bring them goodness in this world. But if they will involve themselves with Torah, then [they erroneously believe that] they will have it good only in the World to Come. The truth, however, is not like this. Torah is "your life" in this world and "the length of your days" in the World to Come.

Rav Pam concluded that the same applies to *chinuch*. There are two divergent attitudes which a Torah educator can adopt when he or she joins the legions of those who will transmit Torah to the next generation. Some view it as *mesiras nefesh* (self-sacrifice). To their minds, they are giving up a lot in this world, but it is worthwhile to sacrifice so that Torah can be transmitted. The other view, the correct one, is that the satisfaction and pleasure of seeing one's students grow in their Torah knowledge and in their appreciation of and commitment to Torah and mitzvos is incomparable. "This pleasure," Rav Pam declared, "has no equal in any other field." He continued:

I can share with you my personal experience. I taught on every level, from first grade to *beis midrash*. I always enjoyed it and the *talmidim* enjoyed it.

~ If you want *olam hazeh*, become a *mechanech*. ▣

Adapted with permission from, "Rav Pam," by Rabbi Shimon Finkelman, Mesorah Publications

HASHKAFAH, HALACHAH, AND INSPIRATIC

Star Attraction

Raising Your Children

THE CHASAM SOFER WRITES in the introduction to his *sefer* that a man who works to strengthen the observance of his fellow Jews will merit to successfully raise his own children in the ways of Hashem. He derives this from the *pasuk* in *Tehillim* (37:26) *"Kol hayom chonein umalveh, v'zaro livrachah*—All day long he is gracious and he lends (of himself), and his children are a blessing."

Along similar lines the Brisker Rav said: "I do not know how to advise people concerning their children's education. However, I have seen that those who work to strengthen the observance of others have good children. This is in accordance with the *pasuk* in *Tehillim* (112:2) *"Gibor baaretz yihiyeh zaro, dor yesharim yevorach*—Mighty in the land will his offspring be, a generation of the upright who shall be blessed."

> I have seen that those who work to strengthen the observance of others have good children.

Holy of Holies

THE PASUK SAYS (SHEMOS 40:10) *"Umashachta es mizbach haolah v'es kol keilav v'kidashta es hamizbeiach v'hayah hamizbeiach kodesh kadashim."*

"You shall anoint the Burnt-offering Altar and all its utensils; you shall sanctify the Altar and the Altar shall be holy of holies."

> Why is the Altar, which was in the courtyard and was used for regular sacrifices, called holy of holies?

The Ramban asks, why is the Altar, which was in the courtyard and was used for regular sacrifices, called holy of holies? His complex explanation concludes with the thought that perhaps this is because through this Altar, others become holy. As the *pasuk* says, "anyone who touches the Altar will be holy."

Rabbi Aharon Schachter, *shlita*, the Rosh Yeshivah of Yeshivas Rabbi Chaim Berlin, explains that from this Ramban we can understand the exalted status of a rebbi or morah. What does a rebbi do? He makes others holy; he is dedicating others to a life of serving Hashem. If he is making others holy, then it is he who is truly a holy of holies.

"True North"

DEAR MORAH W., *You might not remember me. After all, it's been about thirty years since I sat in your classes. At the time, I remember my mother telling me to pay attention to your "pearls of wisdom."*

Fast forward a few years and I got married, baruch Hashem, to a wonderful young man. Some of the lessons learned in your class were starting to make sense as I realized that I wanted to build a Torah home as you so glowingly described.

We eagerly anticipated the arrival of our first child. I imagined

HASHKAFAH, HALACHAH, AND INSPIRATIC

beautiful, pure eyes looking up at me with innocence, and I dreamed about the books we would read together, the songs we would sing together, the first day of preschool.

She was a beautiful, healthy baby, and her first, startled cry brought tears to my eyes. But those tears soon became a torrent when the doctor walked in with a grave look on his face. My precious, perfect baby daughter, he said, was blind. She would never see. My dreams clattered to the ground and turned into dust. I was devastated and in a state of utter despair.

In what way are these teachers comparable to stars?

And then, a dazzling burst of light and hope broke through the dark clouds. It was a memory of you, Morah, from a class you once gave. You told us, unwaveringly, that Hashem never gives a person a nisayon that is impossible. On that day, as I held my baby daughter, your lesson hit me with such force. Its inspiring message gave me the knowledge that everything would be okay.

I became energized. I sprang into action. I was determined not to let my beautiful daughter miss out on life and I knew I could succeed— because of the lesson you taught me so many years ago.

Today, Morah, I stood under her chuppah. Yes, her, my blind daughter who I thought would never attend kindergarten. Not only did she go to kindergarten, she went on to a top seminary in Eretz Yisrael and today she begins building a bayis ne'eman b'Yisrael with a fine ben Torah. And all because of that class you once gave.

OR THOSE WHO INSPIRE OTHERS

"Star
Attraction"
continued

*Now I understand what my mother was saying. Your words are
pearls. Until this very day, thirty years later, I wear them every
moment of every day, strung lovingly around my heart.*

Thank you,
Your talmidah, B.

"*U'Matzdikei harabim k'kochavim l'olam va'ed—eilu
milamdei tinokos.* And those who exert themselves on
behalf of others, they are like stars forever after—these are the
teachers of young children" (*Bava Basra* 8b).

This statement in *Bava Basra* speaks exquisitely about the
singular power of teachers of children, who give their every ounce
of wisdom, patience, and energy on behalf of *Klal Yisrael*,
imparting Torah and *hashkafah* to the next generation. These
teachers, *Chazal* tell us, are like stars that shine forever after, with
a penetrating, infinite light.

In what way are these teachers comparable to stars? Some
commentators explain this parallel by looking at the physical
properties of a star. Today, we all know that it takes many hundreds
of light-years for the light from a star to reach Earth—an arduously
long time. Similarly, there are times in every educator's career
where he or she expends great effort to make an impact on a
student—yet it is only countless years later that the "light finally
dawns." That which the rebbi or morah teaches will sometimes
take effect only years later.

Mr. Avi Shulman brings another facet to *Chazal's* portrayal of
teachers as luminous stars. Imagine a traveler, lost in a desert or in
a great expanse of forest. Imagine a sailor, lost at sea. He has no

HASHKAFAH, HALACHAH, AND INSPIRATIO

sense of direction; he cannot tell his north from south. He is utterly, frighteningly lost. And then he pulls out a special instrument, a sextant, holds it up to the heavens, and calculates the schema of the stars. All at once, he is oriented; he knows which direction to go in! What a relief—salvation!

This is the beauty and innate value of every educator. Just as the stars point a person in the right direction, a teacher guides his or her students in the right direction. As he winds his way through life, the student looks to his rebbi's wisdom. "Where should I go? What should I do? Which way should I turn?" All these questions are immediately answered by his guide—his rebbi—whose leadership is as precise and glowing as a shining star. Instead of floundering in despair, lost, the student looks to his teacher and immediately becomes focused.

Even many years later, a *talmid* can bring to mind a teacher's profound wisdom and utilize it in his life today, as a beacon of light with which to find his way. ▣

Halachah:
The Sure Route to Success

An educator's endeavors often call for consultation with principals, parents, rabbonim, other teachers and sometimes other students for the purpose of enhancing a child's success in school. But when does consultation about a student turn into *loshon hora*? As the questions and answers in this chapter illustrate, only *halachah* can provide a true compass to ensure a route that steers clear of pitfalls and leads ultimately to each child's success.

It is important to point out that *Impressions*, the newsletter on which this book is based, is designed to raise awareness and sensitivity to certain issues that educators may encounter. In-depth details on how to deal with specific scenarios or situations are not provided since every situation is unique and must be dealt with carefully on an individual basis. Educators need never hesitate to consult with rabbonim for any questions that come up in any aspect of their *chinuch* experience.

Toeles for Teachers

1 Information must be accurate and reliable

You must either have witnessed the incident yourself, or investigated the report and found it to be reliable.

2 Judge favorably

Think the matter through and be sure that a wrongdoing was actually committed. Sometimes it appears that a student did something wrong, when in actuality something completely different happened.

With children, especially, we must be careful before jumping to conclusions. It is possible to see part of a chain of events unfold in front of our eyes without seeing the whole story. This can lead one to a very wrong conclusion. It is also important to note that a child can be completely innocent, and have no way to defend himself. The child may simply burst into tears without having the ability to exonerate himself.

3 Try to speak to the student first, before telling others

If it is possible to derive the same beneficial results by speaking to the student in question yourself, you are obligated to do so.

4 Don't exaggerate

Don't add words or embellish. On the other hand, every word that has a bearing, including those details which show the student in a more favorable light, or any detail which will lessen the severity of the wrongdoing (even if it won't exonerate the student), must be mentioned.

HASHKAFAH, **HALACHAH,** AND INSPIRATIO

THE SEVEN RULES OF *TOELES*

Adapted for teachers by Rabbi Moshe Mordechai Lowy, Shlita

5 The teacher's intent must be solely for the constructive purpose of helping the student

When a teacher is wronged, it may be natural to feel hurt or angry. It is, therefore, very important to be honest with yourself and determine that you are not speaking about the incident to alleviate your anger or because of personal prejudice. Your sole intent in disclosing an incident to another party must be positive and constructive, for the benefit of the student.

If you have negative feelings toward a particular student, you should not be the one to relay derogatory information about him. If it is truly important for someone to know, and you are the only one who is aware of the information, it is incumbent upon you to at least temporarily eradicate negative feelings from your heart so that you can transmit the information with the right intention.

6 Consider if there is another way to achieve the same result

If one can bring about the same change without speaking loshon hora, then one must do so. For instance, one could speak about the incident without mentioning names, in a manner that guards the identity of the subject of one's comment.

7 Weigh the harm against the benefit

Consider carefully whether repeating the incident to another teacher, the principal, a parent, or any other individual will cause the student more harm than good. If the student will be punished unduly or if the recipient of the information may be indiscreet and spread the information, which could damage the student's reputation for the future, *chas v'shalom*, then the information may not be disclosed. ▣

The Guiding Light

Your Questions
Answered by Rabbi
Moshe Mordechai
Lowy, Shlita

Q I AM AN EIGHTH-GRADE TEACHER in a girls' elementary school. What do I answer a teacher or principal who asks me for information about my students who are applying to their high school?

A FIRST AND FOREMOST, you must bear in mind that this is *dinei nefashos*. Imagine if the person calling you would begin with the statement, "I'd like to ask you a life-and-death question."

What would your reaction be? Would you stop and think carefully before answering the question? The consequences of giving improper information or withholding necessary information can be severe.

It is extremely important that you, and every teacher, review the Seven Rules of *Toeles* on a regular basis, and that no answer is given without serious deliberation. If the girl is not accepted to the school of her choice, she may wind up in a school where she doesn't feel she belongs. Her resentment or unhappiness can have tremendous negative repercussions. It would not be an exaggeration to say that this decision can be the cause of a girl leaving the *derech* of Torah.

> Imagine if the person calling you would begin with the statement, "I'd like to ask you a life-and-death question."

On the other hand, if a girl would truly be a negative influence on her future classmates, it is of

utmost importance that the high school be made aware of this fact. The lives of these other girls may be hanging on your words. The following seven questions are a great reminder of the Seven Rules of *Toeles*. Keep them in a handy place next to your phone, and ask them to yourself before answering.

Toeles

1. Is it true? Do I know it firsthand?

2. Was I *dan l'kaf zchus*?

3. Am I sticking to facts—no exaggeration, and no opinions?

4. Am I talking with pure motives, only for *toeles*, or do I have a personal vendetta?

5. Is the person I am speaking to the real decision-maker?

6. Can this information be transmitted without giving unnecessary details?

7. Will my disclosure result in the child suffering more than she deserves? Is the person who is receiving the information discreet? Can I trust that he or she will not repeat this information inappropriately or ruin the child's name?

Let's take a look at some true experiences: One Motzei Shabbos, Raizy* walked in to Shloimy's Pizza Shop. As she waited in line for the pie her mother had asked her to get, she eyed the mixed crowd at the nearby table. Just then, she felt a tap on her shoulder. Turning around, Raizy saw the familiar face of Mrs. W., her *Navi* teacher. They exchanged a friendly "*Gut Voch*," and Mrs. W. continued on her way.

The next day the phone rang in Mrs. W.'s house. "Hello, this is Mrs. Lichtenstein from Bnos Brocha. I wanted to ask you about Raizy..." "Well," answered Mrs. W., "I'm not sure, but I think you should know that I saw her in the pizza store last night..." Mrs. W.

Your Questions
Answered by Rabbi
Moshe Mordechai
Lowy, Shlita

had firsthand information—she actually saw Raizy in the pizza store with her own eyes. But, she wasn't *dan l'kaf zchus*.

Mrs. R. called Mrs. L. to ask about Devorah, her student. She wanted to know about her level of *frumkeit*. Mrs. L. answered, "I'm not sure, but she wore her hair down and straightened for graduation pictures."

The significance of the above scenarios is very dependent on the setting, and on the school that is making the inquiries.

Chavi is a poor student scholastically, and her eighth-grade teacher prepares special tests for her. One day the teacher received a call from one of the most academically pressured schools, inquiring if Chavi was among the top students in scholastic ability.

It is not in Chavi's best interest to be in a highly pressured school. If the other requirements of *toeles* are met, it would be appropriate to indicate that this may not be the best school for Chavi. Care should be given to say the very *least* necessary. ▣

*All names have been changed.

Passing It On

Q AS AN ASSISTANT PRINCIPAL, teachers share with me a lot of information about students. I feel I need to pass everything on to the principal since I never know what will become an issue one day. Is this practice okay?

A THE JOB OF AN ASSISTANT PRINCIPAL is to assist the principal. Therefore, anything that the assistant principal feels is pertinent to running the school properly must be told to the principal. However, if there is private information conveyed to the assistant principal that will not necessarily be of benefit in either the short- or long-term, it does not necessarily need to be conveyed.

The role of the assistant principal largely determines his or her responsibility to divulge all information or filter out only that which clearly must be told. If the principal makes it clear that the assistant is acting as the "listening ear" of the principal him/herself, then the assistant principal has the *din* of "*shaliach beis din*" and must repeat every piece of information told, whether it is constructive or not. If, however, the assistant principal is vested with his/her own authority, then s/he should only repeat things that the principal really needs to know in order to make informed decisions. The assistant principal is bound by the Seven Rules of *Toeles*.

If the assistant knows that the principal will react excessively to a piece of information, s/he should not reveal it. In a case where this principal has made it clear that the assistant is a "*shaliach beis din*," the assistant must ask a *shailah* about whether it is permitted to convey the information.

FOR THOSE WHO INSPIRE OTHERS

Your Questions Answered by Rabbi Moshe Mordechai Lowy, Shlita

It is important to point out that even when teachers and principals gather together for important meetings, indiscriminate discussion of students is absolutely forbidden. Only information that meets the laws of *toeles* may be related at these meetings; a "free-for-all" atmosphere is not permissible.

Also along these lines, a secretary who must transcribe information from the principal or other staff members may only do so if utter confidentiality is enforced. The secretary must see her role in the transcription as mechanical, and not pass judgment, nor repeat the information, nor even believe the information that is being handled. In a disastrous incident, a school secretary approached parents and conveyed a piece of information about their child that the principal had decided to deliberately withhold from the parents. The outraged parents stormed the principal's office the next day, and great tragedy resulted from the secretary's actions.

In summation, information that objectively is necessary for the growth of the child or the well-being of the school must be told to the principal. For example, if an assistant principal is told that a child has ADD, this information must be communicated or detrimental ramifications may result.

> A secretary who must transcribe information may only do so if utter confidentiality is enforced.

If, however, the information falls under the category of being merely interesting or biographical, and would serve no clear purpose if it were revealed— such as incidental information about a student's family background, or a mild medical condition that has no bearing on academic performance— then it should not be told. ▣

HASHKAFAH, **HALACHAH**, AND INSPIRATIO

The Boss' Business

Q ONE OF THE TIMES THAT A PERSON MAY SHARE negative information about another person is when there is a *toeles* — constructive purpose, and all the seven conditions of *toeles* have been met. Since one of these conditions is to speak to someone else only if you can't handle the problem on your own, what would the guidelines be for a teacher in discussing a situation with a principal?

A HERE ARE SOME GENERAL RULES TO HELP YOU. It is important for a principal to have a clear, overall picture of each student in the school. This enables a principal to understand a student and guide and help teachers, both current and future ones.

It is therefore justified to speak to the principal:

- In instances where a student's behavior, attitude, etc., are recurring, and the ramifications of it will affect her overall achievement in school—both academically and socially. Often a principal may know some family background or other information about the student which can shed some light and help the teacher deal with the situation.

- In instances where a problem might be a one-time occurrence, but the teacher does not know how to deal with the problem most effectively, it would be justified as well to discuss it with the principal.

OR THOSE WHO INSPIRE OTHERS

Your Questions
Answered by Rabbi
Moshe Mordechai
Lowy, Shlita

It is unjustified:

- If a student does something one time—acts inappropriately or out of character. A one-time action is not something a principal must know in order to understand her students. If, however, a teacher notices the beginning of a serious problem and needs help to nip it in the bud, then advice from the principal may be called for.

> Before you report to the principal, think whether this information is crucial for the overall development of the student.

Advice:

View each student as a person—as a human being. Understand that everyone has some good days and some bad days.

Before you report to the principal, think whether this information is crucial for the overall development of the child. We would not want to cause unnecessary harm to a student's reputation.

Be careful though not to withhold important information when necessary or justified. ▣

HASHKAFAH, **HALACHAH,** AND INSPIRATIO

Teacher Talk

"Since I am known to be a successful mechaneches, the teacher who has taken over my past year's class approached me to ask for a rundown on her new students. She is eager to know as much as possible to enable her to individualize her approach toward each girl."

Q WHICH POINTS AM I ALLOWED TO MENTION, and which should I omit? Can a distinction be made between factual details, e.g. a divorce, behavioral problems, and health matters, e.g. mono? Can I disclose a condition such as mono, which may be very helpful for the teacher, if the parents wish to keep it private?

A IT IS FIRSTLY ESSENTIAL TO ASCERTAIN that the teacher in question will keep the given information to herself. If this is in doubt, then no information may be disclosed, because although it may seem that disclosing the information will be for the child's benefit, it is likely that, in the long run, the child will suffer if this information becomes more widely known.

Having established the integrity of the teacher, the following criteria apply:

- You may only relate information that is considered relevant to her teaching, and fostering the development of the child. Not everything about the student is

When relating permitted information about a student, refrain from any labeling.

Your Questions
Answered by Rabbi
Moshe Mordechai
Lowy, Shlita

allowed to be said. For example, if the student has a cranky nature this should not be revealed unless such information will directly affect the teacher's treatment of the student.

• If it is the parents' desire to conceal information which might be useful to the teacher, you are not at liberty to disclose the information without the parents' consent. If you are personally privy to information which other people do not know, e.g. marital strife at home, you are not permitted to repeat it.

• When relating permitted information about a child, refrain from any labeling, e.g. "lazy," "loud." Refer only to the relevant facts and incidents themselves.

Therefore, after verifying that your recipient is completely trustworthy, you may provide her with information about your former students only to the extent that it will affect her direct dealings with the child—and must omit any labeling of the student. This includes only information which the parents do not object to revealing in these circumstances, and only information which is—or could be—known to other people. ▣

HASHKAFAH, **HALACHAH**, AND INSPIRATIO

Mine Sweeping

Q OUR TEACHERS MEETINGS ARE USUALLY attended by many teachers. When students are discussed by name, there is a strong chance that many of those present don't have a real connection with that student. Also, since I teach in a high school, many teachers will only know the student from a few periods a week. The information given may, therefore, be taken out of context and I worry that it may cause teachers to view the student differently. Practically speaking, how does one know what to say, and to whom, at these meetings?

A A TEACHERS MEETING IS ONE OF THE PLACES where *loshon hora* can be rampant because many things which are said, everyone in the room should not be privy to. For example, a student is singled out for discussion because of her misbehavior. Does everyone in the room need to know about it? Should this be discussed with everybody? If a principal or teacher feels that it would be important for the *issue* to be discussed but there is no purpose in revealing the designated student's identity, s/he should raise the issue without identifying the student in any way. Those staff members who need to know the name for a constructive purpose should be informed of this privately, after the meeting.

> The defining feature of *toeles* is that it enables a teacher to do something constructive with the information.

Your Questions Answered by Rabbi Moshe Mordechai Lowy, Shlita

This, then, is the general rule of thumb: At a large teachers' meeting, where many staff members are present, only information that *all* present will benefit from knowing—for it will ultimately be beneficial for the students and the one being spoken about—should be discussed. Smaller, more individual meetings can be held later to disclose information that would be important for only certain staff members to know. Anyone who is not a direct teacher of the student or will not have a constructive purpose in hearing the information should not be told. Needless to say, any information discussed at a teachers meeting is private and it is forbidden to divulged it to anyone.

The defining feature of *toeles* is that it enables a teacher to do something constructive with the information. For example, if there is bullying going on in school and children are suffering because of it, it would be constructive and essential to warn teachers to be on the lookout for a particular student who has already been proven to be a bully. This *firsthand* information can be conveyed to *all* the teachers in school, including the miscreant student's name, since it will enable teachers to keep a closer watch when they observe this student interacting with others.

Practical examples of *toeles* at a teachers meetings:

1. In a case where a student has been found, through credible, *firsthand* information, to be an extremely negative influence on others, it is important for all the teachers to know and monitor the situation. This will enable them to be on guard against this student having a bad effect on others. In such a case, if the teachers are not told the identity and specific details, they might come back later and say, "If I would have known, I would have protected my students!" Clearly, then, this is a case of absolute *toeles*.

2. If a teacher caught someone cheating and would like to raise the issue at a general staff meeting, she should not identify the student in any way as there is no purpose in doing so—it would be *loshon hora*. After the meeting, the name of the student in question may be privately disclosed to his/her direct teachers so that once they are aware of the problem they can take the necessary steps to help the student improve his/her ways.

3. When a child is caught stealing, there is a question about whether or not it is *l'toeles* to mention this to all staff members. If a child stole one time, the incident should *not* be mentioned in public. However, if there is constant stealing going on, the principal may raise the issue at a staff meeting, alert teachers to the problem, and say, "If you have suspicions about who the culprit may be, please see me privately." In a case where a student is known to steal on a regular basis, the principal may name the student because it is important for teachers to be on the lookout in order to protect the property of the rest of their class. Obviously, the principal would need to be *100% certain*, beyond the shadow of a doubt, that the named child is infact stealing before taking action. ⊞

Your Questions Answered by Rabbi Moshe Mordechai Lowy, Shlita

Meeting of the Minds

Q **I**S IT PERMISSIBLE FOR **L**IMUDEI **K**ODESH staff and English staff—or even two teachers from the same department—to prepare for a parent-teacher conference by discussing their impressions of each student, thereby ensuring that the teachers are "on the same page"?

A **A**NY TIME INFORMATION IS SHARED about another person, it must be done in complete adherence to the laws of *toeles*. This *halachah* applies to teachers with the same gravity as to individuals in any other profession. Disclosing information about students is only permitted when there is a 100% benefit *to the student* in sharing the information. Teachers do not have license to discuss a particular student if they simply want to avoid appearing foolish at a parent-teacher conference by potentially giving completely different reports on the same student!

However, if a teacher is having difficulty with a certain student but discovers that another teacher is successful with the student, s/he may discuss the student with the second teacher as long as the motive is purely to help remedy the relationship with the student. Sometimes personality clashes cause certain students to act out in certain classes whereas they behave angelically in other classes. In these cases, it is often helpful for a teacher who is not experiencing success with the student to get advice from the teacher who is successful. However, the teacher who is having

HASHKAFAH, **HALACHAH**, AND INSPIRATI

difficulty with the student may not share negative stories with the second teacher unless there is a clear purpose in relating the stories. As teachers, we are privy to much personal information but we must safeguard it properly; we have no *heter* to disclose it for improper reasons. It is critical to remember that relating "horror stories" about students is absolutely forbidden, despite the fact that sometimes there is a great *ta'avah* amongst teachers to indulge in this kind of *loshon hora*.

If information-sharing has been deemed *l'toeles*, it is important that teachers refrain from relating unnecessary negative information about a specific student—especially to a teacher who is experiencing success with the student, since this may damage the good relationship.

If a teacher is faced with the uncomfortable task of inform- ing a student's parents of a problematic learning experi- ence, s/he must exercise much tact and sensitivity in the information disclosed and the way it is presented. Par- ents rely heavily on teacher

> **Disclosing information about students is only permitted when there is a 100% benefit *to the student* in sharing the information.**

feedback, and therefore the teacher should divulge only what must be told for the sake of *toeles*. This is also true in the case of a stu- dent who is performing well in other classes but is floundering in one specific teacher's class. In that case, the parents will have been given glowing reports from all the other teachers and will be all the more impacted by a negative report from one teacher if it is not carefully presented. ▣

Your Questions
Answered by Rabbi
Moshe Mordechai
Lowy, Shlita

Should I Say?

Q IN MY POSITION AS DIRECTOR OF THE RESOURCE Room at our school, I get a lot of feedback from teachers about students. Yesterday, a teacher approached me confidentially and told me that a certain student might be experiencing some *shalom bayis* issues at home. My question is, if a teacher knows some specific, confidential information about a student, may that information be disclosed?

A THE MAIN JOB OF A TEACHER IS TO HELP her students reach their full potential. With this goal in mind, there are times that it would be beneficial for a teacher to know certain information about a student because it is in the student's best interest that the teacher is informed. If the teacher of an orphaned student is not made aware of the child's situation, perhaps she might make a comment about the child's deceased parent, causing pain to the student.

There are cases, however, when it would not be in the child's best interest to disclose this kind of information. Before relating information about any student, it is vital to remember that the rules of *toeles* must be met. Careful thought must be given as to whether sharing the private information would be beneficial or detrimental to the student. For example, in the case of a girl who is thriving at school and would be very ashamed if anyone would know about her irreligious sibling, the information must not be conveyed. Teachers most definitely do not have *carte blanche* to reveal any information they are aware of about a student. Instead,

HASHKAFAH, **HALACHAH**, AND INSPIRATIO

they must seek halachic guidance. The same rules apply when the previous year's teacher might feel it necessary to disclose information to the incoming teacher.

Sometimes, the question arises as to what information constitutes *loshon hora*, as opposed to what would simply be considered interesting information. Is it *loshon hora* to disclose that a student is adopted, or that her parent remarried, for example? While every case is different, many factors need to be taken into account in determining whether information is *loshon hora* or not. Particularly, the society, culture, community, and school that the student is part of are important factors. If, for example, divorce is a stigma in the student's community, one must not

The main job of a teacher is to help her students reach their full potential.

disclose that a student's parents are divorced unless all rules of *toeles* have been met. The same rules apply to revealing such matters as *shalom bayis* issues within a family, irreligious siblings, medical histories, and the like. Careful thought must be given before a piece of information is conveyed. Teachers should make it a practice to check with a rav before releasing any private information about a student.

A child privately told her teacher that her father was incarcerated in prison. During her break, the teacher casually mentioned this piece of information to other staff members in the Teachers' Lounge. That night, a shidduch was abruptly called off, only a short time before the chasunah was to take place. Everyone was shocked. The cause for the broken engagement was a mystery—until word got out that a relative of the kallah's family was sitting in prison, as overheard

Your Questions
Answered by Rabbi
Moshe Mordechai
Lowy, Shlita

in the Teachers' Lounge. The teacher who had initially relayed the information was heartbroken. Such is the power of words.

In summary, teachers carry an exceptional responsibility to watch their words, since often they are privy to sensitive information which can have serious consequences if improperly handled.

In accordance with the laws of *shmiras halashon*, a teacher must conceal what must be concealed, and reveal what must be revealed. ⊞

HASHKAFAH, **HALACHAH,** AND INSPIRATIO

Do's and Don'ts

Q AS A TEACHER, I OFTEN WONDER ABOUT how the laws of *toeles* govern Parent-Teacher Conferences. Does a teacher have full license to say whatever s/he wants during this conference? Is the teacher required to take into consideration how the parents might react to the information? May the teacher reveal information about another student as it affects this particular parent's child— for example, if a specific student is having a bad influence on this child?

A IT IS IMPORTANT TO CLARIFY WHAT, EXACTLY, is the purpose of Parent-Teacher Conferences. Is the purpose simply to give out any and all information about the child to the parents? No. The real purpose of "PTA" is to enable the parent and teacher to get together to help the child. It is an opportunity for the two parties involved in the education of the child—the parents and the school—to form a united force to advance the education of the child.

That said, it is clear that a teacher may only give over information that contributes toward this purpose. In the same way, parents should only reveal to the teacher information that pertains to the child's education. When a teacher wants to know what can or can't be told to parents during conferences, s/he must ask this basic question: What will be the *toeles* for this child? To answer this question properly, the teacher must take into account a number of factors. Firstly, what are the parents like? How will they react to the information given? What action will they take if the teacher

Your Questions
Answered by Rabbi
Moshe Mordechai
Lowy, Shlita

shares certain information with them? Will they react in a way that will be detrimental to the child? If the answers to these questions indicate that the parents will not react in a way that will be beneficial to the student then the information *may not be told*.

Parents come to Parent-Teacher Conferences primarily hoping to hear *nachas*. Teachers should try to bring out the best about each child by describing his/her good *middos* and positive scholastic achievements. If a certain child has some faults, the teacher, as stated above, can only mention them if it will be in the child's best interest. If, for example, a student is getting bad marks and the teacher believes that the parents can help by encouraging the child to study better and by staying on top of her homework assignments, then this information must definitely be conveyed. This would be a clear case of how the teacher and the parents can work together to benefit the child, and the *toeles* of giving over this information is obvious. Of course, the parents should be told about the concern without exaggeration or ridicule and fully in keeping with the 7 rules of *toeles*. In short, any concern about a student's emotional, physical, or academic success that could be potentially solved if discussed with the parent should be relayed during PTA—not to tattle on the child, but rather to help.

If a teacher sees that parents are not capable of being partners in this instance, s/he should not share anything negative with them and s/he should try to fix the problem through other means. Any information that, if conveyed, might harm the child may not be shared.

In a case where a teacher feels that for the benefit of a student, s/he must relate information about another student, s/he may do so if there is clear *toeles*. For example, if a teacher sees a student befriending the wrong type of students and is sure that the parents

HASHKAFAH, **HALACHAH,** AND INSPIRATIC

could be helpful in curbing or stopping that friendship, then the teacher may tell the parents about the negative influence of specific classmates—by name. In this case, relating the information is a responsibility incumbent on the teacher who acts as a "pseudo-parent" to his or her students. If the teacher sees that the parents can't or won't do anything about it, then there is no *heter* to share such information. The same rules apply to discussing any other individuals during PTA, including a whole class or even a whole school. Where a teacher is not careful and labels a class as "weak" or "not studious" s/he is speaking *loshon hora* about an entire group, which the Chofetz Chaim says is a far graver sin than speaking about an individual.

> The real purpose of "PTA" is to enable the parent and teacher to get together to help the child.

Discussing other teachers or the principal with parents during PTA, or blaming or speaking about how other faculty members or students interact with the child, is absolutely prohibited unless there is a clear *toeles* and need in doing so. Tragically, PTA often becomes a free market to speak wantonly about students, teachers, classes, and schools, which is an unfortunate and misguided reality. If, for some reason, a teacher does feel that a child should go to a different school or switch to another teacher, s/he may not put down the school or the teacher; instead, s/he can simply say, "I think your child would benefit more from a different school/teacher," without speaking any *loshon hora*. ▣

Better Left Unsaid

Your Questions
Answered by Rabbi
Moshe Mordechai
Lowy, Shlita

Q As a teacher, there are often situations where I am unsure if I should notify a parent of a student's problematic behavior. Can you give me some general guidelines?

A In general, if you feel that the problem can be taken care of without the parents knowing, there is no need to tell them. Here are some points to keep in mind:

People often feel that it is the parent's right to know everything. But, in truth, it is *loshon hora* to tell a parent something negative about his/her child if there is no *toeles*—benefit.

E.g. Rivky W. is usually a good student. One day, she acts up in class, causing some disruption. Later that day Rivky's teacher meets Mrs. W. in the supermarket. It is on the tip of her tongue to let her know what a challenge her daughter was in class that day. Just then, their eyes meet, and Mrs. W. says, "Hello, Morah! How's Rivky doing?"

> **Rivky is much more likely to grow from her mother's compliments and pride in the good report that she received from her teacher.**

Being a competent teacher, her morah knows that she can handle the situation without the help of Rivky's mother. In addition, Rivky's behavior was not serious enough to warrant concern that there may be a situation at home that the school should know about. As these thoughts flash through her

HASHKAFAH, **HALACHAH**, AND INSPIRATIC

mind, the teacher makes a quick decision that there is no toeles in telling Rivky's mother about her daughter's negative behavior. "Rivky's a wonderful girl," she replies. "She's doing very well. Thanks for asking."

Rivky's teacher handled the situation in the correct manner. Who knows what a negative comment to her mother might have caused! Rivky's mother might have gone home and berated her, perhaps she would have been punished severely. At the very least, Rivky's mother would feel disappointed in her daughter. Rivky is much more likely to grow from her mother's compliments and pride in the good report that she received from her teacher.

Nevertheless, there are times when a situation is better off being discussed with parents. Parents are the ones who have the ultimate responsibility to raise the child properly. If the student's behavior warrants the parents' knowledge, and it is believed that they will handle the child in an appropriate manner, it is necessary to let them know.

It is important to note that what is written here is not a *p'sak* that can be applied to every situation. The purpose of these questions and answers is to heighten the awareness of the need to ask a *shailah* when faced with a dilemma. There is no blanket *heter* or *issur*; every situation warrants its own question. The most important understanding to keep with you at all times is that we are dealing with issues that are literally *dinei nefashos*. The future of a child can rest on just one word of a teacher—right or wrong. It is a very serious matter. ▣

Even when you're caught off guard, be careful to evaluate whether there is a toeles in saying what comes to mind.

With Parents

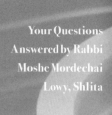

Responsible Disclosure

Q AS A TEACHER, I AM OFTEN UNSURE ABOUT what information to share with parents regarding their children. Some parents press me for information, some don't ask; at times I can't gauge what their reaction will be. Are there guidelines for what I should or shouldn't disclose?

A ALTHOUGH A TEACHER BEARS enormous responsibility for his/her students, ultimately, the responsibility for properly educating a child belongs to the parents. Therefore, it is imperative that, for the child's benefit, parents be active and informed, working out problems that crop up, so that the child succeeds both in school and, eventually, in life.

At the same time, however, it is important to remember that parents are emotionally bound to their children and their responses may not be rational or productive. For this reason, teachers must exercise great sensitivity in relating information, so that the overall goal—of parents working for the child's benefit—is accomplished. Before telling a parent information that may cause an overreaction, or an undesirable effect, a teacher should think carefully about how to present the matter. It is always best to consult one's principal and/or a competent *rav* before speaking to a parent about sensitive issues.

A rebbi received a frantic call from a parent whose eleven-year-old son never came home that day. After a thorough search, the boy

HASHKAFAH, **HALACHAH**, AND INSPIRATIO

was found, hiding in the bushes, crying. "Please don't call my parents," he sobbed. "They said if I got another bad mark, they'd kill me!" The rebbi was at a loss. After careful thought, he informed the parents that he knew

> It is important to differentiate between matters which *must* be told to parents versus issues that are inconsequential.

where their son was, but would only tell them if they promised not to punish him for hiding or for getting a bad mark. Only after obtaining the parents' assurance did the rebbi send the boy home. The next day the boy told his rebbi that this had been the first time he wasn't punished severely for getting a bad grade.

It is important to differentiate between matters which must be told to parents, versus issues that are inconsequential, or will probably go away on their own. A one-time misbehavior which is out of character for the student need not necessarily be reported immediately. In certain situations, perhaps the school guidance counselor should be consulted first. Then, if the problem persists, a teacher should find out how best to inform the parents.

General rules of informing parents are as follows:

A. If the matter doesn't *need* to be shared, do not disclose it. (In case of doubt, ask your principal or rav.)

B. If it is definitely important to inform the parents, there are two options:

   1. If the teacher knows that the parents in question will react in a way that will be beneficial to their child, the information must be disclosed immediately. The teacher should involve the parents both in the problem and the problem-solving.

Your Questions
Answered by Rabbi
Moshe Mordechai
Lowy, Shlita

2. A teacher is in a unique position that allows her to take a more objective view of the issue. If the teacher suspects that the parents will react negatively or overreact, the teacher *must* consult a rav to determine how to present the problem. If at all possible, it would be preferable to try to help the child without the parents' involvement. The rules of *toeles* apply in this situation, so a cost-benefit analysis must be calculated. If it would be more detrimental to the child for the information to be disclosed, then it certainly should not be told. However, if more good would come from disclosing the information, then it should be told.

Example: *A student constantly falls asleep in class. If the teacher knows the parents will respond well to being told, she should certainly involve them in helping the child get more rest. If, however, she feels that they will react inappropriately—punishing their child harshly, imposing unrealistic rules, etc.—she must consult with a principal or rav about whether to bring up the issue. The student's exhaustion during class may be less detrimental to her than her parent's mishandling of the teacher's report.* [This should not stop the teacher from trying to help the student overcome her problem.]

Ideally, teachers and parents should work together to help each child. However, even the best parents can be defensive and sensitive where their children are concerned. Even worse, some parents do not have the skills necessary to intervene properly in their children's *chinuch*. Before speaking, teachers must choose their words carefully to ensure that what they say will help, not hinder. ⊞

HASHKAFAH, **HALACHAH**, AND INSPIRATIC

When Others Are Bothered

Q I TEACH EIGHTH-GRADE GIRLS. At times I have a situation where one or more students are having difficulty with a classmate who sits near them. I want to know the following:

When a mother calls me to complain that a classmate is bothering her daughter, to what extent do I believe it?

If I feel it is necessary to change a student's seat after investigating the matter thoroughly, how should I explain my reason for the seating change to the student who is creating the problem?

There are times when I feel it would be beneficial for the student to know that others are finding her behavior annoying so that I can help her improve. What can I say to the student? Wouldn't it be *rechilus* to let her know that her classmates have complained about her?

A IN RESPONSE TO THE FIRST QUESTION, A TEACHER has a responsibility toward her students that would require her to listen attentively to an allegation that one classmate is disturbing another. Although the teacher *may not accept the report as fact*, she must act upon the information and investigate the matter.

With regard to the second question, it is important to keep in mind the rules of *toeles*, one of which states that if the goal can be accomplished without speaking *loshon hora*, that is the way to

Your Questions
Answered by Rabbi
Moshe Mordechai
Lowy, Shlita

handle the situation. If, for example, you need to change the student's seat and you are concerned that the child will feel that you are just picking on her, formulate a good reason that does not involve revealing the fact that a classmate has complained about her.

> **There are times when I feel it would be beneficial for the student to know that others are finding her behavior annoying.**

If you feel the student needs to know that her behavior is disturbing others, and you feel that this is *rechilus l'toeles*, you must proceed with caution. The rules of *toeles* do not allow one to speak *rechilus* if the words may cause unwarranted harm. In most cases it would be considerably more beneficial to tell a child that you have noticed her doing things that may be causing classmates to dislike her, than to tell her the hurtful fact that a classmate has spoken to you about her.

A student who has low self-esteem will likely be devastated when confronted with such news. If the child is aggressive, s/he may retaliate against the one who complained. It is quite possible that they would discuss it with others in the class, and the situation could erupt into a class-wide *machlokes*.

▶ **INSIDE THE RULES OF *TOELES***

Reviewing the rules of *toeles* and applying them to any situation will illuminate the necessary path of action.

◁ **OUTSIDE THE RULES OF *TOELES***

The potential exists for:
1. Devastating the student.
2. Inciting retaliation.
3. Creating a widening *machlokes*.

HASHKAFAH, **HALACHAH,** AND INSPIRATIO

With Students

When confronted with such dilemmas it is very important for a teacher to be guided by the seven rules of *toeles*. If one reviews these rules and applies them to the situation, they will clarify which path of action to take.

This does not mitigate, in any way, the tremendous need to keep in mind the relationship of the student with the teacher, and the student with his/her classmates. Thought should be given to protect both of these relationships as you decide on the words and actions—within the *halachos* of *shmiras halashon*—that will be the most beneficial to all those involved. ▣

Your Questions
Answered by Rabbi
Moshe Mordechai
Lowy, Shlita

When Someone's Life Is in Your Hands

Q I AM A HIGH SCHOOL TEACHER AND, AS SUCH, I teach a large number of girls from different classes and different grades. Very often I am contacted for *shidduch* information about a girl I have taught. I am always hesitant, however, about giving this information. Firstly, the girl in question may be someone I knew only peripherally, having taught her only one or two periods a week. Secondly, if I taught her in eleventh grade, that may be a good three years ago. In that time, a girl can undergo significant spiritual, emotional, and physical changes. Am I really the right person to give information? Also, if I am not the right person to give *shidduch* information, how do I convey this without making it sound as though like I am trying to hide negative information about the girl in question?

A THE MOST IMPORTANT RULE TO REMEMBER IS THIS: Whenever a person gives information for *shidduch* purposes, s/he must keep in mind that it is absolutely a life-and-death matter. A life can be ruined completely by giving misinformation or, on the other hand, withholding necessary information that should, according to *halachah*, have been revealed. It is critical to realize how severe and vital words are when asked to give *shidduch* information.

HASHKAFAH, **HALACHAH**, AND INSPIRATIC

Shidduchim

That said, a person may only relate information that is known to him, firsthand, to be 100% accurate. Good information can —and should—always be given over, but the information should be stated accurately. If some time has elapsed since the teacher last saw the student in question, s/he can say, "I remember that in tenth grade, he was a very committed learner. I don't know him today." But good information must be genuine, not fabricated. If a teacher teaches

> **Whenever a person gives over information for *shidduch* purposes, they must keep in mind that it is absolutely a life and death matter.**

many students without really getting to know any of them and therefore s/he does not really remember the student in question, s/he can simply say, "I had a hundred girls in the class; I don't really know any of them well." The teacher should not say, "I don't really remember her," as this may imply that the girl was not a memorable or outstanding student.

It is a fact that people change, even in the space of a few years. If a student had a particular character defect or was weak in *frumkeit* during the time the teacher taught him or her, the teacher cannot assume, years later, that the student has remained the same. The student could have done *teshuvah* or overcome the character trait. Even traits that we tend to think cannot be changed, like jealousy, a bad temper, or social awkwardness, can all be remedied. Unless the teacher knows, for a fact, that the student has not changed, s/he may not reveal the defect to the inquiring party. If the teacher *has* been in touch with this particular student and sees, very clearly, that the defect in question is still present, s/he may only reveal it if it is a defect that would definitely and objectively bar the

Your Questions
Answered by Rabbi
Moshe Mordechai
Lowy, Shlita

prospective couple from living a happy life. If the defect in the student is shyness or a difficulty making friends, the best thing for the teacher to say is, "She is a good girl," without mentioning the non-threatening problem.

Another pitfall to be sure to avoid, the Chofetz Chaim strongly cautions, is never to give labels or impressions. If a teacher saw a student get angry one time, s/he may not say, "That student has a temper," based on that single incident. The same would apply if a teacher only has a general impression of a student without actually knowing him or her well. In that case, the teacher can reply, as stated above, "I teach hundreds of students and I don't really know any of them, but so-and-so seems like a nice person." Or, the teacher may state an impression as such: "I don't know her that well, but I have an impression that she always dresses modestly."

A boy and girl were about to get engaged when suddenly the boy began to stall. The surprised parents discreetly tried to find out what the problem was and they discovered that the boy's parents had found out negative—and clearly inaccurate—information from one of the girl's teachers. It was obvious, from the information given, that the teacher could not have been speaking about this girl. The girl's parents called the teacher and confronted her. "Why did you say this about our daughter?" they asked. "Oy!" the teacher replied, distraught. "I mixed things up—I spoke about a different girl!" Despite numerous efforts to set things straight, the damage was already done; the shidduch was ruined.

The moral of this true story is clear: Don't give information if you're not completely sure. If there's any doubt whatsoever, it's far better to say nothing and to ask a *shailah* afterward to verify that you acted correctly. ▣

HASHKAFAH, **HALACHAH,** AND INSPIRATIO

Dangerous Revelations

Q ONE OF MY TENTH-GRADE STUDENTS whom I am close with recently disclosed a secret to me. It is not a life-threatening secret, but it concerns something that this girl did which is against school policy, and she is feeling bad about it. Do I have an obligation to tell the *hanhalah* about this secret, and what are the issues involved in *gilui sod*?

A HALACHICALLY SPEAKING, SOMETHING TOLD IN CONFIDENCE, especially if the speaker specifically asked that it be kept confidential, may not be revealed unless there is great *toeles* in doing so. In a case where a student confides to a teacher, the *toeles* of revealing the secret must be carefully weighed. On the one hand, it may be vitally important that the school know about this problem or confession. On the other hand, will the student be irreparably damaged if the secret is revealed, either because revealing it will cause severe consequences or simply because the student will lose his or her trust in teachers forever after? It is strongly advisable to consult with a competent rav before choosing either to reveal the secret or to remain silent.

Generally speaking, if a student reveals that s/he did something against school rules but promises never to do it again, or if the teacher feels s/he can help the student overcome this infraction, or that it will resolve on its own, then the secret certainly may not be revealed. If, however, the teacher has received a *p'sak* that

Your Questions Answered by Rabbi Moshe Mordechai Lowy, Shlita

the secret is of a nature that demands intervention from the *hanhalah*, the secret must be treated differently. When this determination has been made, it is preferable to begin by trying to avoid revealing the secret outright. Instead, the teacher can try to approach the *hanhalah* and ask that they speak to the student in question, without stating the secret. This way, there is no direct *gilui sod;* the hope is that the student will reveal the secret to the *hanhalah* himself, preventing unnecessary damage. If, however, that is not possible, and the situation is such that the secret must be revealed, then the teacher *must* inform the *hanhalah* directly and completely.

> Like *loshon hora l'toeles, gilui sod* is also governed by the Seven Rules of *Toeles.*

Great care must also be exercised in choosing the right person to reveal the secret to, should the situation warrant it. If a teacher knows that a certain member of the administration is quick to jump to conclusions and punish excessively, delivering a consequence that is disproportionate to the infraction, then that person may not be told. Like *loshon hora l'toeles, gilui sod* is also governed by the Seven Rules of *Toeles*: one of the rules requires that the consequence of revealing the secret not exceed the "crime." Again, a rav can guide the teacher in finding the right person to speak to.

The rule of thumb here is that in cases where a student's secret concerns serious behavior that is clearly damaging to other students, then the student is classified as a *"rodeif"* and we must be concerned about saving the victims, even at the expense of the perpetrator. An example of this would be a case where a student

HASHKAFAH, **HALACHAH,** AND INSPIRATIO

reveals that, tragically, she is regularly *mechalel Shabbos*—and has influenced other classmates to engage in this transgression together with her. In these cases, the school has a responsibility to save the well-being of the larger student population, even if the perpetrator will suffer because of it.

In summation, while secrets and confidentiality are important and paramount, there are times when revealing these secrets and breaching confidentiality are even more vital. With the proper guidance, a teacher can act in the best way possible, averting disaster and bringing immeasurable benefit to individual students and to the entire school. ▣

Revealing a Secret

Your Questions
Answered by Rabbi
Moshe Mordechai
Lowy, Shlita

Who Did It?

Q I TEACH MY STUDENTS *HILCHOS SHMIRAS HALOSHON*, and inevitably the following question arises every year. "What do I do when a teacher or parent says, *'Tell me who did it'?*"

A THERE ARE TWO SIDES TO THIS QUESTION—THE STUDENT'S AND THE TEACHER'S:

The student needs to know that an authority figure does have the right to know information which is needed to enforce rules and order. Just as *beis din* is allowed to send a designated party to make an investigation and report back to them, a parent or teacher has the right to solicit information when someone has committed an offense.

At the same time, an authority figure should be familiar with Rav Moshe Feinstein, *zt"l's* teaching that one should not use the "Tell me who did it" approach, because this encourages the child who enjoys tattling to speak *loshon hora*. Instead, the teacher should make it clear that in this particular situation it is important for the teacher to know who committed the crime, and therefore if someone reports the name of the culprit it would be *l'toeles.*

Even with this understanding, students should be taught that they should not be eager to name the perpetrator. Anyone who is excited at the prospect of belittling his peer is demonstrating a tremendous lack of *ahavas Yisrael.* They can be told that it would be proper to relate the information, only if they are asked about it

HASHKAFAH, **HALACHAH,** AND INSPIRATIO

personally or if the matter pertains to a situation in which there is danger or abuse.

———————◼———————

There is an awe-inspiring story in which both the student and the authority figure illustrate these values beautifully.

It happened many years ago in a yeshivah that had established a firm rule condemning any student who would listen to the World Series during class. The consequence was severe; any *talmid* who was caught was kicked out of the yeshivah.

One day it became known to the Rosh Yeshivah that a student had violated this cardinal rule. The boy had come to class with a radio hidden in his pocket and with a small, well-concealed, ear piece listened to the game the entire afternoon. It was believed that Chaim S.*, a prize pupil, knew which boy was guilty. The Rosh Yeshivah immediately summoned Chaim to his office to question him about the identity of the guilty party.

> The Rosh Yeshivah's poignant appreciation of Chaim's silence is a shining example of a *mechanech* whose love for his students emulates Hashem's love for His children.

Chaim was in a dilemma. It was true. He did know who the Rosh Yeshivah was referring to. He also knew that the culprit was an upright boy who did not cause any other trouble, and if he were to be expelled from yeshivah, he would have a very hard time being accepted elsewhere. Revealing the name of the student would bring this boy untold suffering and might yet cause a tremendous

spiritual loss for the boy. Tormented by this thought, Chaim remained silent.

The Rosh Yeshivah pressed Chaim again, "Tell me the name of the boy." Unable to contain his anguish, Chaim burst into tears. Still, the boy's name did not pass his lips.

For the third time, the Rosh Yeshivah pushed Chaim to give him the information, but Chaim just shook his head in despair.

Witnessing his discomfort and continued silence, the Rosh Yeshivah, who knew Chaim well, understood that this mature, obedient *talmid* surely had a justifiable reason for not revealing the culprit.

At that moment the Rosh Yeshivah got up with a rush of emotion and gave Chaim a kiss. "Thank you, Chaim," he said. "Thank you for not telling me."

Yes, the Rosh Yeshivah had to ask.

And, yes, Chaim had done the right thing, too.

The ripples created by this story in Heaven may never be fully known to us, but one thing we do know. The *neshamah* that was saved is a *neshamah* that brings a lot of *nachas* to Hashem and to *Klal Yisrael* today. ⊞

*Name has been changed.

Forcing the Issue

*Revealing the Culprit:
Teacher*

Q I AM THE PRINCIPAL IN A LARGE GIRLS' SCHOOL. In one of the classes, some students defaced and vandalized the chalkboard to the extent that it became unusable. The teacher responded immediately to the misdemeanor and took action against it. However, as the principal, I feel that I need to take further action. When I approached the teacher to tell me the names of the students, she declined, saying that she felt the matter had been dealt with appropriately already. My questions are: Can I force the teacher to cooperate with me, and is my approach warranted?

A THE PRINCIPAL IS RESPONSIBLE FOR EVERYTHING that goes on in a school—he or she is ultimately answerable if something goes wrong. Therefore, the principal has the right to do what s/he needs to in order to investigate an incident and set things right. Especially in the case cited above, if the principal feels that the students' behavior sets a dangerous precedent, s/he has a right to know the students who are culpable and set an appropriate punishment.

> *U'teshuah b'rov yo'eitz*
> — Salvation comes with plentiful counsel.
> MISHLEI (11:14)

Obviously, the investigation process as well as the setting of consequences must be done within a proper framework, without causing undue shame to the students involved or jumping to conclusions, as discussed in previous cases.

Revealing the Culprit:
Teacher

Your Questions
Answered by Rabbi
Moshe Mordechai
Lowy, Shlita

While the teacher in question may feel that she has done everything correctly and that the matter should rest, she is not the decision-maker; instead, it is the principal who is allowed to override a teacher's judgment. In a case where the teacher is worried that the principal will take drastic action, such as expelling a student from school—which can cause tragic destruction to the student—she must ask a *shailah* about whether she is obligated to forfeit her job by withholding the misbehaving student's name from the principal.

Principals take their responsibilities very seriously and are expected to make good judgments even in difficult situations. In living up to this charge, it is wise to consider the words of Shlomo Hamelech in *Mishlei* (11:14): *"U'teshuah b'rov yo'eitz*—Salvation comes with plentiful counsel." Even in cases where a principal is already convinced of the right action to take, it is possible that s/he may have overlooked something. If a principal sees that a teacher is adamant in a particular situation, it may be prudent to consider the teacher's recommendation since often another perspective proves to be immeasurably helpful. ⊞

Beating the Bully

Toeles: Anti-bullying

Q OUR SCHOOL IS IMPLEMENTING AN ANTI-BULLYING campaign which includes a requirement for children to report incidents and bullying behavior to the administration. How do I reconcile this need with the rules of *toeles*, and what guidelines do I give to the students?

A AN ANTI-BULLYING CAMPAIGN IS A VALUABLE and important project to bring to a school and it is commendable that your school is investing the time and effort to implement this program. Bullying stems from bad *middos* and it is not the *middah* of *Klal Yisrael* to hurt other people and be *miskabed biklon chaveiro* (take pleasure in the degradation of his friend). The bully should be helped to feel that s/he could gain much more by being nice to others so s/he comes to realize that it's better to be the center of attraction for being the one who's nice to everyone, rather than through intimidation and violence.

The delicate balance between *loshon hora* and *toeles* is imperative to understand, especially in the scope of this project. The main rule to remember is that when something is being done for preventive purposes, to protect children from harm, there is no *issur* of *loshon hora* because there's no "bad" speech at play, only constructive speech. The only type of speech that is forbidden is speech whose purpose is to be harmful, to denigrate, or to malign. In the case of your anti-bullying campaign, the purpose is to promote *shalom* and protect children—and these ideas must be properly and deeply communicated to your students at the outset of the campaign. However, in order to invoke the principle of

Your Questions
Answered by Rabbi
Moshe Mordechai
Lowy, Shlita

toeles, seven pertinent rules must be met. It is critical to apprise students of these rules. It's important to stress to children that they may not "tattle" on other students for the purpose of delighting in harming a friend or to take revenge; they may only act in order to protect innocent victims from getting hurt. To put it succinctly, the core of the program must be: Our purpose is not to punish; it's to protect.

Students should be led to understand that the only way the school can eradicate bullying is by children coming forward to name the perpetrators. In fact, participating in this program is not only not an *aveirah*; it's actually a mitzvah, because not only does it help protect people—oneself and others—but it also helps the bullies themselves overcome their negative *middos*, especially when they are young and can be more easily trained. The Seven Rules of *Toeles*, which should be thoroughly explained and demonstrated to all students, are as follows: **1**. Tell only firsthand, eye-witness information; if the information is not firsthand, it must be stated as such. **2**. State in what context the behavior occurred, so it isn't interpreted incorrectly. **3**. Do not exaggerate in any way. **4**. If a positive outcome could be brought about without telling anyone, then it's better to try that avenue instead. **5**. One may not tell on another person for purposes of revenge, only in order to stop the bullying. In the case of this anti-bullying program, a caveat must be stated here: If we tell children they must only act 100% *l'shem shamayim* before naming a bully, they are likely to keep quiet because they won't trust themselves. When this *toeles* condition is stated, it should be framed in a way that shows that as long as they are genuinely trying to act to stop

> **Our purpose is not to punish; it's to protect.**

the bullying, then they may divulge the information. **6**. The information must be conveyed with the least *loshon hora* possible. **7**. The information must not bring more punishment upon the perpetrator than s/he deserves.

Toeles: Anti-bullying

In addition to clarifying the rules of *toeles*, it is also important that the school take appropriate measures to avoid potential pitfalls in this campaign. Before going forward with punishing or rehabilitating a suspected bully, the school must thoroughly investigate the situation even before pointing an accusing finger at a child. There must be a genuine effort to be *dan l'kaf zechus* before taking action and the school must determine whether real bullying occurred or if perhaps something was misinterpreted. Accusing and/or punishing the wrong child is potentially even more damaging than allowing a bully to remain at large! To protect against misinformation being relayed, students must be taught that just as it's a mitzvah to stop bullying, it's a terrible *aveirah* to get an innocent person in trouble. ▣

Your Questions Answered by Rabbi Moshe Mordechai Lowy, ShIita

Teaching *Toeles*

Q I READ YOUR ANSWER *{See page 153, Beating the Bully}* regarding the implementation of a school-wide anti-bullying program, listing the seven rules of *toeles* as they should be explained to students. I am wondering if you could please clarify two of those rules—4 and 7—which seem difficult, especially for young children, to grasp.

A TO BRIEFLY RECOUP, THE SEVEN RULES OF *TOELES* that relate all across the board, and to the anti-bullying campaign in particular, are: **1**. Tell only firsthand, eye-witness information, or state it is not firsthand. **2**. State in what context the behavior occurred, so it is interpreted correctly. **3**. Do not exaggerate in any way. **4**. If a positive outcome could be brought about without telling anyone, then it's better to try that avenue instead. **5**. One may not tell on another person for purposes of revenge. **6**. The information must be conveyed with the least *loshon hora* possible. **7**. The information must not bring more punishment upon the perpetrator than s/he deserves. Now we will clarify rules 4 and 7 with an eye toward explaining these somewhat difficult concepts to students of all ages.

RULE 4: *If a positive outcome could be brought about without telling anyone, then it's better to try that avenue instead.*

The intent behind this essential rule of *toeles* is that one is permitted to speak *loshon hora* only when something constructive will result. However, if the same result could be brought about by

not directly speaking *loshon hora*, then that avenue is far more preferable and must be explored first. In the case of the anti-bullying program, here's an example of this rule at work: Shimon is a child who has been engaging in bullying behavior, but he is really quite unaware of what he's doing. He's not the typical "bully" personality, but rather he's misguided and doesn't realize that his actions are hurting his classmates. In Shimon's case, before a student or a teacher would be required to go to the administration to inform them that Shimon is a bully, a first approach might be to arrange a class or school-wide

> It is incumbent upon the school to ensure that the punishment is not too harsh.

discussion on bullying, explaining exactly what constitutes bullying and how it can be stopped. In this way, perhaps Shimon will suddenly realize that what he is doing is wrong and he will stop. In this case, no *loshon hora* has ever been spoken. However, if Shimon continues to bully, then there's a need to speak *loshon hora l'toeles* and report his behavior to the appropriate party.

The general rule of thumb in *hilchos shmiras halashon* is that before speaking *loshon hora*, the speaker should first try speaking to the perpetrator to encourage him to change his behavior on his own. However, in the case of the anti-bullying campaign, it is potentially dangerous to tell children to first attempt to speak to and reason with the bully himself, as this approach may very well backfire, with the bully heaping even more abuse upon the poor victim. Therefore, we cannot advocate that children approach the bully on their own. However, when a student comes to a teacher to report a bully, the teacher could ask the child, "Do you think if you speak to the bully the behavior

Toeles: Teaching Students

Your Questions Answered by Rabbi Moshe Mordechai Lowy, Shlita

will stop?" If the victim feels certain that it will be okay for him or her to speak to the bully, and the teacher is certain that the bullying will not worsen, then this approach may be explored—but with great caution. In this case, the victim can be advised to gently tell the bully something along the lines of, "You're hurting me, even if you don't realize it."

7. The information must not bring more punishment upon the perpetrator than s/he deserves.

This seventh rule actually presents an important caveat for the school administration when they construct their anti-bullying campaign. Simply put, the rule states that if the perpetrator will be subjected to unduly harsh punishment for his or her actions, then the *loshon hora* may not be said. Therefore, if Shoshana knows that as soon as she mentions to the principal that Miriam is bullying, Miriam will be kicked out of the school, then Shoshana is simply forbidden to divulge Miriam's behavior to the administration.

Thus, it is incumbent upon the school to ensure that the punishment for the bullying is not too harsh, that nothing terrible or cruel will happen to the perpetrator, so that students are free to come forward to reveal the bullies in their classes, in accordance with the seventh rule of *toeles*. It is a powerful lesson for students to be told, when the anti-bullying program is explained, that the punishment for confirmed bullies has been specifically designed not to be excessive, in compliance with the rules of *toeles*. In this way, they see *hilchos shmiras halashon* in action and they internalize the value and importance of these vital rules. Knowing that their classmates will not be punished excessively will empower them to come forward and name the bullies, which is imperative for the program's success.

As schools design programs to eliminate such behavior as bullying, the importance of exercising caution and discretion cannot be overstated. In one school, a child was suspected of bullying and was immediately expelled, without a proper investigation. As a result, he left *Yiddishkeit* completely. When a former teacher met this boy one day, he lamented: "After they kicked me out, no other school wanted to take me. I lost everything I had in this world. And the truth was, I didn't even do the bullying!" ⊞

Toeles:
Teaching Students

Your Questions
Answered by Rabbi
Moshe Mordechai
Lowy, Shlita

Undercover Investigations

Q How should a teacher go about finding out who is bothering a child? Sometimes it's hard to figure out who the perpetrator is and it feels strange to ask the victim to tell. On the other hand, we are here to help the students, and isn't it our responsibility to get involved and take care of the children who are bothering, stealing, hurting, etc. while at the same time taking care of the victim who wants the problem to stop?

A Clearly, in a situation where a child is being bullied, teased, stolen from, or hurt in any way, a teacher must step in and intervene. When a child approaches a teacher reporting that s/he is being bothered, the teacher has a responsibility to investigate the story without casting aspersions on either the victim or the would-be perpetrator in the process. First, it is important that the teacher determine that there is, indeed, a perpetrator involved and that the student's claim is true.

> Divulging information for a constructive purpose is *not* loshon hora and is the proper thing to do.

If the student in question is known to fabricate stories or make himself out to be victimized as an attention-garnering tactic, then the teacher should listen to the student and press for further information. If the student's

HASHKAFAH, **HALACHAH**, AND INSPIRATIC

claim seems plausible, then the teacher can tell such a student: "I don't want to listen to *loshon hora*. Only tell me who is bothering you if you think I can help you solve the problem."

It is best for the teacher to obtain the perpetrator's name from the victim himself, thus eliminating the need to make inquiries that might arouse suspicion and *loshon hora*. When the suspected perpetrator's identity is revealed, the teacher may not shame or embarrass that student. It is best for the teacher to approach this student and simply ask him directly: "Is there anything going on between you and so-and-so?"

If the student is uncomfortable about providing the perpetrator's name because *of loshon hora* concerns, the teachers should *vehemently* tell the student that divulging information for a constructive purpose is *not loshon hora* and is the proper thing to do.

If the student still refuses to reveal the perpetrator's name—for example, in an instance where the perpetrator has threatened the victim with revenge if he snitches, then the teacher must do a proper investigation while trying to prevent any *loshon hora* from being spoken about either the victim or the perpetrator during the course of the investigation. The best solution is for the teacher to make a general announcement to the entire class, in a casual way. The teacher may say: "If anyone knows of any student who is bothering anyone else in the class, it is n*ot loshon hora* and it is a mitzvah to bring it to my attention privately, because you never know how you can help people through this information." This may result in the perpetrator's name being revealed without raising the victim's name in public. If this approach is not successful, the teacher may involve a few other students

Your Questions
Answered by Rabbi
Moshe Mordechai
Lowy, ShIita

whom s/he knows to be trustworthy and honest, and ask them for facts on the matter at hand.

The critical importance of taking a stand against bullying and other hurtful behaviors cannot be overemphasized. A class in which a student was constantly teased by a group of bullies never came forward about this problem to the teacher. Since the victim was too embarrassed to discuss it, she suffered in silence until, at the age of thirteen, she left Yiddishkeit entirely—a direct result of the pain she experienced from her peers. ⊞

HASHKAFAH, **HALACHAH**, AND INSPIRATIC

Negative Report: Positive Response

Q AS A TEACHER, HOW SHOULD I BEST RESPOND when a student comes to report information about another student? What is permitted and what is forbidden in terms of investigating the incident and taking action?

A PART OF A TEACHER'S INTEGRAL DUTY in educating students is to teach them not to engage in the behavior widely known as "tattling" or "snitching." The *Gemara* teaches us that when Yeshoshua asked Hashem to identify the individual who had illicitly partaken of the spoils at Yericho, the *Ribbono Shel Olam* reprimanded him, saying: "Should I be an informant?" This lesson is paramount: we must teach our children to break the rampant habit of "snitching" on other people. Instead, we must emphasize that they should only inform on a fellow student when the laws of *toeles* have clearly been met.

However, in a situation where a student has been harmed by a classmate, he or she should be encouraged to approach the teacher with the problem at hand. As teachers, we bear an enormous responsibility to protect our students—all of our students—and we must make ourselves available to them in every way. It must be remembered, however, that when a student indicates that s/he has been wronged, the teacher does not assume the position of judge and jury; rather, the teacher must be devoted to helping each student—even those who might later be found guilty of misconduct.

Your Questions Answered by Rabbi Moshe Mordechai Lowy, Shlita

> **The teacher must be devoted to helping each student—even those who might later be found guilty of misconduct.**

Before a teacher can listen to a student's report, the student must be reminded of *hilchos toeles* to ensure that the information given over is accurate, firsthand, and completely motivated by *toeles*—an indisputably positive outcome—rather than by a desire for revenge or to cause ill will. If the student presents a problem that potentially incriminates a fellow student, the teacher is forbidden to jump to conclusions without thoroughly and sensitively investigating the allegations. This is consistent with *hilchos loshon hora*, in which the Chofetz Chaim cautions that one is only allowed to *suspect* an individual, based on verified information. Therefore, the teacher should show genuine concern for the student who comes forward with the problem, but s/he may not act hastily to right the wrong.

In the investigation process, teachers must tread carefully and avoid singling out suspect students publicly. Untold pain and emotional scars have resulted from poorly handled teacher investigations where students were either wrongly accused or shamed terribly for their misconduct. When a teacher undertakes to solve a problem, s/he must constantly keep in mind that the task is not to condemn, but rather that the process of the investigation is only to help all those concerned. Even if a consequence must be given to a student who is found to have misbehaved, this must be done gently, wisely, and with the sole intent of helping the student to right the wrong.

With this awareness foremost in a teacher's mind and heart, all actions taken will hopefully reflect this sensitivity and the teacher will not come to *chas v'shalom* hurt a student in any way. ▣

HASHKAFAH, **HALACHAH**, AND INSPIRATIC

Cheating

Q As TEACHERS, WE OCCASIONALLY ARE
CONFRONTED with the uncomfortable occurrence
of cheating on tests. My question is, if a teacher
discovers that a student has cheated, may s/he question
students privately to try to pinpoint the culprit? If this is
permitted, but the culprit is still not caught, can the teacher
collectively punish the class for the cheating incident?

A WHILE CHEATING IS AN UNFORTUNATE and difficult
offense, it must be handled within the confines of
halachah. If a teacher discovers that someone in the class has
cheated, s/he should first announce that the cheater must come
forward and confess (to the teacher privately). The teacher should
offer an incentive to the culprit upon confessing, such as a less
severe consequence—without absolving the culprit entirely. We
learn this from the Torah's teaching of *"Modeh v'ozeiv yerucham,*
The one who confesses and leaves [his sin] will have mercy *shown*
to him"—when a person confesses to his or her wrongdoing, the
sentence is lightened.

If the culprit fails to come forward, the teacher should emphasize
that it is important to discover who has cheated—both for the
cheater's sake, and for the rest of the class. The teacher should
stress, however, that it is not permissible to transgress the laws of
shmiras haloshon in order to uncover the guilty student. Handling
the situation in this way will teach the class a valuable lesson for
life. The teacher should review the Seven Rules of *Toeles* with the
class, carefully explaining each rule. Then the teacher should

Your Questions
Answered by Rabbi
Moshe Mordechai
Lowy, Shlita

announce that if anyone has any information—in keeping with the laws of *toeles*—about the student who cheated, s/he should convey it privately and in a proper way. Most suitable would be to write the information on a note and leave it anonymously for only the teacher to find. The teacher must stress that it is forbidden to fabricate information, misrepresent "hypothetical guesses" as facts, or discuss the situation with others.

If a student does supply information to the teacher, the information must be properly verified and cannot be taken at face value. Only after a careful investigation can a teacher take proper action against a student.

A bachur in a yeshivah broke into the school office and stole the answers to a test. Given the seriousness of the offense, the principal gathered all the bachurim together and warned that if the culprit would not be identified, the entire student body would lose points off the test they just took. One student, Meir H., came forward and disclosed that Shmuel B. was to blame. The principal asked Meir how he knew that Shmuel had stolen the test, and Meir said that Shmuel had confessed his crime. When the principal called Shmuel into the office, though, Shmuel adamantly denied the charges. After several more strong accusations from Meir, the principal decided that Shmuel was, indeed, the culprit, and Shmuel was expelled from the yeshivah.

Only after a careful investigation can a teacher take proper action.

Shmuel's life was ruined by this incident. No other yeshivah would accept him, especially because of the unfavorable cause for his expulsion. He ended up leaving Yiddishkeit entirely. Many years

HASHKAFAH, **HALACHAH,** AND INSPIRATIO

later, Shmuel met the principal of his former yeshivah. "I want you to know that I was not the one who stole the test," Shmuel insisted. The principal decided to track down Meir, who was by now married and living in a different city. Meir remembered the incident only vaguely, but the principal pressed him about whether the information he had supplied so many years ago had been completely accurate.

"Whether Shmuel did it or not, he deserved to be kicked out of yeshivah anyway!" Meir finally asserted. "He was a kid with a lot of problems and I was pretty sure that he had done the cheating—it was a good thing he was expelled."

Pressured by the threat of a loss of grade points, Meir had framed a fellow bachur—and forever altered the course of Shmuel's life. But the ultimate responsibility rests upon the principal, who acted without properly investigating the incident.

Generally speaking, it is not advisable for teachers to threaten or carry out collective punishment. It is forbidden to punish a person for something he did not do. Therefore, it would not be permissible to punish an entire class for the actions of one individual, provided that the rest of the class did not influence or aid the culprit in his/ her misdeed. The only time collective punishment can be carried out is if it would result in an appreciable benefit to the whole class. In the situation described above, the class would not benefit from being punished, since the incident is isolated. However, in a case where rampant cheating is occurring, collective punishment might be necessary. ⊞

Your Questions Answered by Rabbi Moshe Mordechai Lowy, Shlita

Public Admonishment

Q I AM A SUBSTITUTE TEACHER AT A LARGE GIRLS' SCHOOL. At times I find that when a student acts up it should be reported to the principal. I feel it is important for the principal to publicly reprimand the student so that the behavior will not be repeated. Is this permitted?

A THE SCENARIO YOU DESCRIBE RAISES TWO ISSUES: *loshon hora* and *halbanas panim b'rabim*, public embarrassment. From a *shmiras haloshon* standpoint, it is important to bear in mind that only behavior that is *objectively wrong* and needs intervention by the hanhalah may be related by a teacher/substitute to the principal. If students merely "act up," don't listen attentively, or do things that bother the substitute and she wishes to "tell on them," that is *obviously* not permissible. However, when the misbehavior clearly is wrong and needs to be dealt with, a substitute is obligated to inform the principal whose responsibility it is to run the school properly.

> **Does the punishment fit the crime; is this what Hashem wants us to do?**

The next issue involved is a weighty and critical one. Embarrassing a person—whether young or old—is akin to murder, as we know from various Torah sources. Rabbeinu Yonah says on the *pasuk*

Hochei'ach tochi'ach es amisecha v'lo sisa alav cheit (*Vayikra* 19:17) that embarrassing a person is an extremely serious last resort and must be done only after careful consideration. It is important to bear in mind that "embarrassing a student" in this context is defined as making a student feel embarrassed in front of another person. This encompasses a wide variety of actions, including: sending a student out of the room, calling a student a derogatory name, yelling at a student in front of peers, visibly detaining a student during recess, sending a student to a lower grade, and suspending or expelling students.

Given the extreme caution which *halbanas panim* demands, it is imperative that teachers, substitutes, and principals do not take it lightly. Deciding to embarrass a student should be a last resort. Instead, the following is suggested as a means of dealing with student misbehavior.

1. The teacher should try to talk privately with the student about the misbehavior, giving a warning about what will happen if it occurs again.

2. If the student misbehaves again, the teacher can carry out the stipulated punishment, even if it is embarrassing, since the child has already been warned.

3. If the teacher's punishment still doesn't prevent the child from misbehaving, the teacher should go to the principal. It is preferable not to send students to the principal's office, as it often causes them a great amount of shame to be seen sitting in the hallway, questioned by secretaries, etc.

4. The principal should speak to the student, warning about further consequences. In a case where parental

Your Questions Answered by Rabbi Moshe Mordechai Lowy, Shlita

involvement will be helpful, the principal can warn the student that his/her parents will be called, or that further action will be taken.

The question that must be asked before shaming any student is: Does the punishment fit the crime; is this what Hashem wants us to do? Also, the nature of the student must be taken into account— is this a child who will be crushed and destroyed if publicly shamed? Certainly, when a student's misbehavior is influencing other students, the necessity for more forceful intervention increases. However, a student must first be warned that the consequence of continued misbehavior will involve *halbanas panim*.

Perhaps the most critical form of shaming a student is expulsion from school. There are no words that can properly convey the gravity of expelling a child, and it must be weighed with utmost care befitting the halachic question it truly is. The Chazon Ish is quoted as having told a Rosh Yeshivah that expelling a child from school is akin to killing him. On the other hand, a situation where other students are being affected by detrimental behavior of a specific student presents an extremely urgent dilemma. Obviously, there are cases when a child must be expelled, but it should be a last resort and the decision must be made with great clarity and consideration, and certainly with halachic input.

May we merit Divine guidance in all our decisions and actions. ⊞

HASHKAFAH, **HALACHAH**, AND INSPIRATIC

Constructive Criticism

Pointing Out Errors

Q AS A MATH TEACHER, I FEEL THAT IT IS very helpful for students to learn from their own mistakes as well as those of fellow students. I often stress—in a positive way—the need to learn from errors. I encourage students to come up to the board to do equations, and point out their errors so that the whole class can learn. However, I am concerned that this may embarrass some of my students. Despite this, am I justified in this approach?

A IT IS COMMENDABLE THAT YOU RECOGNIZED the need to clarify your approach, especially given the serious nature of embarrassing people—whether students or anyone else. We know that it is forbidden to shame another person—a *halachah* that has been discussed at length in previous articles. Teachers have no license to violate this *halachah*.

As such, it would be preferable if you could point out students' mistakes anonymously, taking them from test papers and homework without naming their names. Thus, you could still give the class the benefit of

> **It is important to stress to students that everyone makes mistakes.**

seeing errors, but individual students would not be shamed. Many teachers utilize the blackboard as a teaching tool that livens up the classroom, and they encourage student interaction to generate enthusiasm. Especially in a subject like Math, where material is often cut-and-dried, calling up students to do problems on the

Your Questions Answered by Rabbi Moshe Mordechai Lowy, Shlita

blackboard can offer some much-needed break in the routine. If you feel that the students' learning will be optimized when students are called to the board and their errors are pinpointed, it is important that you pay special attention to the students you call up. Students who are exceptionally bright or exceptionally weak are more likely to feel ashamed if their mistakes are highlighted. It is best to stress the importance of learning from mistakes and then ask for volunteers to come up to the blackboard. It is important to stress to students that everyone makes mistakes—thereby minimizing any embarrassment that could result. ⊞

HASHKAFAH, **HALACHAH,** AND INSPIRATIC

No Notes

Q I FIND NOTE-PASSING EXTREMELY DISRUPTIVE **during class time. If I confiscate a note, am I permitted to read it? Does the *halachah* change if I clearly warn my students at the beginning of the year that they will forfeit their right to privacy if I catch them with a note?**

A A TEACHER HAS A RESPONSIBILITY TO ENSURE that his/her classroom is a place where the maximum amount of learning will occur. Thus, activities such as note-writing and passing are discouraged. However, another important reason why note-passing must be eschewed is to teach children the importance of not sharing private information improperly. Most often, notes passed during class contain either inappropriate comments that should never have been written, or private information that should not be circulated. Students must be taught about the value of confidentiality and privacy.

Teachers, too, must abide by the *halachos* of privacy and confidentiality. A teacher has no right to see private information, even if that information was passed around during class. A teacher does not have the power to forfeit students' privacy unnecessarily, even if his/her rule has been broken.

When a teacher sees a student involved with what appears to be a note, the teacher can quietly confiscate it. The teacher must take care not to shame the student unnecessarily until the matter is clarified, but s/he should ask to meet with the student after class.

Your Questions
Answered by Rabbi
Moshe Mordechai
Lowy, Shlita

The procedure described would pertain whether or not the teacher made a rule banning note-passing.

In private, the teacher should emphasize that his sole objective is to prevent the student from disturbing class—not to be nosy or interfere in the student's private matters. The teacher should then ask the student whether the confiscated note contains relevant information to the class lesson. If the student responds that the note did, in fact, pertain to class material, then the teacher can ask to read it. If the student responds that the note is not, in fact, private, but that s/he would prefer that the teacher not read it, the teacher can remind the student that it is a teacher's right to read a note that is not confidential. Once the student has specified that the note is not private, the teacher may peruse the note.

> **The teacher should emphasize that his sole objective is to prevent the student from disturbing class.**

It is important to remember that the purpose of a teacher in questioning a student about the content of the note is not to "catch" the student in a lie, or to force him into an uncomfortable position. Rather, the purpose is to educate the student in three areas—on the importance of preserving privacy, on the importance of telling the truth, and to clarify whether the student has or has not broken a class rule.

If the student replies that the note did not pertain to the lesson, and says that it is confidential, then the teacher should not look at the note, but should admonish the student for passing a note during class. However, if based on prior evidence the teacher

HASHKAFAH, **HALACHAH**, AND INSPIRATIC

suspects that the note may contain material of an inappropriate nature—such as chutzpah—then s/he is permitted to scan the note *l'toeles*. If, while scanning, the teacher finds that the note contains confidential information—and not chutzpah—the teacher should stop reading immediately.

Above all else, teachers must bear in mind that the benefit of the doubt applies in every situation, and even a simple matter such as note-passing demands proper clarification.

The rebbi had reached his wits' end with the note-writing epidemic that was disrupting his class daily. Finally, he threatened that the next student to write a note would be suspended from school for a week. Shortly after the warning, he spotted Moshe writing a note at his desk! Incensed, the rebbi seized the note, threw it in the garbage, and announced that Moshe was suspended for a full week. Moshe protested and insisted that he was innocent, but the rebbi refused to listen. Moshe begged his parents to listen to his story until finally they consented.

"The note I wrote said these words: 'V'ahavta es Hashem—es l'rabos talmidei chachamim' (And you should love Hashem—the word es *comes to include Torah scholars), because I wanted to reinforce Rebbi's message."*

Moshe was determined to find the note in the garbage can. Unfortunately the garbage had already been taken out to the dumpster but Moshe resolutely sorted through the garbage dumpster until he actually found the note and brought it to his rebbi—with the exact words that Moshe had quoted! The rebbi asked mechilah from Moshe. The incident made a powerful impression on both of them, as well as on the entire class. ▦

A Teacher's Duty

Your Questions Answered by Rabbi Moshe Mordechai Lowy, Shlita

Q AS A TEACHER, I OFTEN OBSERVE students studying together who are not compatible with one another. Along the same lines, I also see students forming friendships which will have negative results. Am I allowed to interfere and tell the student and/or parent about my hesitations, and try to make a change that will improve the partnering or the friendships?

A A TEACHER IS NOT ONLY *ALLOWED* to interfere in a negative partnership or friendship, she is *required* to intervene. By ignoring a negative relationship, a teacher disregards *"Lifnei iver lo sitein michshol,* do not place a stumbling block before the blind," *"Lo sa'amod al dam rei'acha,* do not stand aside while your fellow's blood is shed," and her responsibilities according to the *Choshen Mishpat.* A teacher must be proactive and look out for every student's well-being. That said, it is important to remember that the Seven Rules of *Toeles* apply in every case. Before stepping in, a teacher must determine whether the information she is acting upon is definitely true, and whether the benefits of interfering outweigh the damage that will be done.

Every situation must be evaluated separately.

Every situation must be evaluated separately. In the case of a bright student studying with a weaker student, the teacher needs to determine if the relationship is, indeed, a deleterious one. Perhaps

HASHKAFAH, **HALACHAH,** AND INSPIRATIO

the brighter student is helping the weaker student, without her own grades being affected? In the case of a girl who will be deeply distressed if a teacher suggests that she terminate a friendship, much care should be taken to determine if the friendship truly will be harmful, or if it's simply not "the best."

The importance of following the Seven Rules of *Toeles* cannot be stressed enough.

A teacher was informed by one of her students that Chaya and Rochel, long-term study-partners, were causing trouble under the pretext of studying. Disturbed, the teacher immediately told Chaya and Rochel that they could no longer study together. The girls maintained that they had always studied well together, and indeed, their grades reflected as much, but the teacher insisted. That night, she called both girls' parents and stressed that their daughters should find other study partners. Over the next few weeks of new study arrangements, the teacher noticed that the girls' marks were dropping drastically. She spoke to Chaya and Rochel again, and they tearfully repeated how well they had studied with each other. After careful analysis, the teacher realized that the original report she had been given had been false. She deeply regretted having acted based on second-hand information, without verifying that it was true.

When a teacher does decide, after careful thought and investigation, that a relationship must be changed, she must do everything to minimize the damage that will be done. In the case of a study partnership, it is best to state that the partners are "not compatible," rather than reveal any negative information. Similarly, a student who is developing a harmful friendship can be guided to choose different friends with statements like, "I think

Your Questions
Answered by Rabbi
Moshe Mordechai
Lowy, Shlita

you and Tamar will do well together." This does not overtly incriminate the unwanted friend, thereby minimizing the amount of damage that will be done.

▼

WHEN SHOULD FRIENDSHIP BE ENCOURAGED...

AND WHEN SHOULD IT BE DISCOURAGED.

△

The responsibility of a teacher to intervene in unsavory relationships is illustrated by this true story: *An excellent student in an out-of-town yeshivah became involved with a bad crowd which influenced him negatively. The parents were unaware of these developments, and were shocked when they were informed that the yeshivah would be expelling him. The agitated parents considered bringing the school to a din Torah since it was negligent of their son's rebbi not to have intervened when the boy began developing harmful relationships!*

Relationships play a vital role in a child's life and future. And who better to observe the effects of those relationships than the astute teacher! With this responsibility in mind, a teacher must use her wisdom and insight to keep a finger on the pulse of her students' relationships, and step in wherever necessary. ⊞

HASHKAFAH, **HALACHAH,** AND INSPIRATIO

Music for the Soul

Q I WOULD LIKE TO MAKE MY STUDENTS **more**
sensitive to the types of music they should and
should not listen to. Am I permitted to mention
specific Jewish singers by name and point out that their
music is not appropriate? If so, in which manner may I state
this? Can I outright "knock" a Jewish singer if I have good
reason to do so?

A WHEN WE WISH TO USE SOMEONE AS AN EXAMPLE
of behavior that should not be emulated, we must carefully follow the Seven Rules of *Toeles,* as explained previously.
Most importantly, what should be remembered is that the
information presented must be absolutely true and accurate—
i.e. no exaggeration—and clearly helpful in achieving a positive
end-result.

However, there is no permission to "knock" a person; only his or
her actions may be pointed out to teach a lesson. A teacher who
"knocks" a person in an effort to convey a lesson instead teaches
students to be cynical and to mock and knock others. Just as it is
forbidden to speak *loshon hora*, it is also forbidden to mock or cut
down other people. It would not be permitted to say, "That singer
is a low-life and not so *frum*!" Instead, a teacher may say, "The
music of this singer is not conducive to *yir'as Shamayim*." If there
is a way of making the point clearly without naming actual singers,
then that would be preferred. As in all instances where the rules of
toeles are invoked, the teacher should convey only the minimum
that can be said to get the point across effectively.

Your Questions
Answered by Rabbi
Moshe Mordechai
Lowy, Shlita

Especially in a case where the person behaving improperly is somebody that a student looks up to as a role model, it is critical to highlight the improper behavior and make it clear that it is incorrect. For this reason, giving guidance on inappropriate Jewish singers—whom students often view as role models and seek to imitate—is paramount.

This question extends to many other areas of *chinuch* as well. Sometimes, for example, teachers may find themselves needing to caution individual students against imitating the mode of dress of fellow classmates. In these cases, too, the immodest student should not be criticized; rather the teacher should focus on the lesson that needs to be brought out: "I don't want you to wear the styles that Leah wears; they are not befitting a *bas melech*."

Can I outright "knock" a Jewish singer if I have good reason to do so?

It is important to point out that there are students who might become cynical and may be "turned off" when a teacher disparages the music of a specific singer. The teacher must be attuned to the attitudes and learning styles of his or her students and educate them accordingly. Often, the best approach is a gentle, heartfelt message that leaves students feeling "This is not conducive to our growth" rather than "The administration is against it." On the other hand, if the teacher knows that the students are honestly seeking strong guidance and fiery tones, then he or she is certainly permitted to express a clear stance against the inappropriate behavior, without disparaging the singer himself.

The importance of listening to the right music cannot be stressed enough.

HASHKAFAH, **HALACHAH,** AND INSPIRATIO

A man once visited the Skverer Rebbe to ask for a brachah.

"My son has always been an excellent masmid, extremely diligent in his Torah study," he said. "But lately, for some mysterious reason, he seems to have lost his desire, his cheishek."

After careful questioning, the Rebbe summoned the son.

"What is different in your life?" he asked. "Have you eaten something questionable? Are you looking at things that might be damaging you spiritually?"

"No," the boy insisted. "Everything is exactly the same. I can't understand what happened."

"Do you listen to music?" the Rebbe asked.

The boy admitted that he listened to the music of a certain frum singer. At this point, the Skverer Rebbe told him that the music of this particular singer came from an impure source. The Rebbe suggested that the boy cease listening to the music for four weeks. By the end of the month, the problem had completely gone away and the bachur's original cheishek was fully restored.

The Mishnah Berurah cites the Shelah Hakadosh who explains the intense power of music. The Shelah writes that many children who end up going off the derech were affected by the impure lullabies sung to them by their non-Jewish babysitters.

May we succeed at keeping our students pure and guide them in making the right choices in every area of their lives. ▣

Your Questions
Answered by Rabbi
Moshe Mordechai
Lowy, Shlita

Forbidden Friendships

Q IF I FEEL THAT A CERTAIN STUDENT in the class is not a good influence on a particular classmate, how and what can I tell the student whom I am trying to warn?

A A TEACHER FACING THE SCENARIO DESCRIBED above is presented with an intricate challenge: s/he is responsible both for protecting Student A from being impacted negatively by Student B, while at the same time ensuring that Student B is not harmed by being negatively spoken about. It is extremely important that the Seven Rules of *Toeles* be applied properly. These include: attempting to use alternate means to solve the problem instead of speaking negatively; knowing with complete certainty that the facts of the case are accurate and are firsthand information rather than hearsay; and ascertaining that relaying the negative information will not result in more harm than benefit.

Before a teacher can take action to prevent a friendship from forming, s/he must be 100% certain that there really is a cause for alarm—in other words, that Student B will definitely exert a negative influence upon Student A. In determining this, the teacher must also ensure that s/he is making an impartial judgment and that no trace of self-interest exists, such as animosity towards Student B. It is best for the teacher to consult with the principal first in order to verify that action must, indeed, be taken.

HASHKAFAH, **HALACHAH,** AND INSPIRATIO

As in accordance with the laws of *toeles*, if there is an alternative method of dealing with the situation other than speaking *loshon hora* about Student B, it must be used. For example, if Student A wants to become Student B's study partner, the teacher may simply say that a different student would be a better match. Or, when appropriate, the teacher could approach Student B and instruct him/her not to befriend Student A, with the understanding that if the request is not honored the teacher will be forced to take further action.

Preventing Negative Influence: Friends

> **Reviewing the rules of *toeles* and applying them to a situation will illuminate the correct path of action.**

Before the teacher makes the decision to speak to Student A about Student B, it is imperative that s/he be sure that Student A will react appropriately. In general, older students are better able to deal with the teacher relaying negative information about a friend of theirs. If there is a chance that Student A will misuse the information—perhaps by going to Student B to repeat what the teacher has said about him or her or will spread the information to others—then the teacher must not take this course of action.

Where there is a concern that Student A will rebel against the teacher's instructions and "*b'davka*" make a more concerted effort to form a friendship with Student B, then the teacher must not speak to Student A. Instead, the teacher can try speaking to Student A's parents, explaining the situation to them and asking them to unobtrusively prevent the damaging friendship from forming. The teacher may only speak to the parents if s/he knows them well enough to be absolutely certain that they will properly deal with the issue and not mishandle the negative information related to them about Student B. ▣

Your Questions
Answered by Rabbi
Moshe Mordechai
Lowy, Shlita

Sound Advice

Q IF PARENTS REQUEST THAT THEIR CHILD be placed in a certain rebbi or teacher's class, but the principal feels that it will not be the right thing for the student, what may be said to the parents? Similarly, if parents want to send their child to a certain school that the principal feels would be a bad fit for the student, what is the principal permitted to tell the parent?

A THE PROHIBITION AGAINST SPEAKING LOSHON HORA does not prevent us from giving correct advice. On the contrary, a person is obligated to advise others properly, with their best interests at heart.

As in all cases of speaking *l'toeles*, it is imperative that the principal has firsthand, 100% accurate information about the teacher or the institution in question and is utterly certain that a harmful outcome will result if the parents are not dissuaded. Also necessary is for the principal to truly know and understand the student in question—a peripheral relationship with the student is not enough to constitute speaking *l'toeles*. When these two requirements are met, and the principal is convinced that the parents are making a big mistake, s/he must try to stop them.

> The prohibition against speaking *loshon hora* does not prevent us from giving correct advice.

The first approach should always be one that doesn't involve any *loshon hora* at all. Instead, the principal can simply tell the

parents, "I know the school/teacher and I don't think it's right for your child. I will advise you on what I really know is best for him." Thus, no negative information is being conveyed while trying to guide the parents toward making the right decision.

If the parents are still intent on their original plan even after this first approach, the principal should try to convey the negative information in as minimal a way as possible. If, for example, the parents are trying to place their child of average academic ability in a school with very high academic standards, the principal can say, "Your child is wonderful, but this school is so challenging that your son's skills will set him back." If the parents of a very well-behaved child want to send him to a class which the principal knows is made up of problematic students who will have a negative impact, the principal can say, "Your child is on a higher *madreigah* (level) and he needs a different class than this one."

If the school or the teacher in question is a rival or competitor of the principal, or there is any animosity between them, the principal is forbidden from relaying any negative information or giving advice against the teacher or school. This is one of the rules of *toeles* and it safeguards against subjective information being relayed, since someone with ill feelings towards another party cannot be impartial. In these cases, the principal should advise the parents to seek a neutral third party for proper guidance in making the right decision.

It is important to note that if the principal knows with certainty that the parents have already made up their minds to send their child to a particular rebbi or school and nothing will change their decision, it is forbidden to say anything. The Chofetz Chaim teaches that it is prohibited to relay negative information "just to have one's opinion known" if it will not bring about a positive result.

Perfect Placement

Your Questions
Answered by Rabbi
Moshe Mordechai
Lowy, Shlita

Q THERE ARE PARALLEL CLASSES IN MY SCHOOL. Every few years they change the makeup of the classes. At these times, parents are allowed some input, if they have a strong preference for one class over the other.

If I feel that a certain student would do better in a particular teacher's class, am I allowed to give this information to the parents so that they can ask the principal to place their child accordingly?

A IF THERE IS TRULY AN OPPORTUNITY for the parent to effect the change by speaking to the principal, then you are *obligated* to relay this information. However, only pertinent information should be given while making sure to follow the seven rules of *toeles*.

If, however, you are faced with a different scenario, where the parents will not be able to act on the information given and change the class that their child is in, it would be prohibited to tell them that their child would be better off with the parallel class' teacher. ◨

> **Am I allowed to give this information to the parent?**

I'm Sorry

Q A COLLEAGUE AND I HAVE BEEN DEBATING about whether and under what circumstances it is appropriate for a teacher to apologize to a student. Can Rabbi Lowy please give us some guidelines?

A WHEN A TEACHER WRONGLY ACCUSES, pains, or embarrasses a student, it is a mitzvah for the teacher to make restitution. In Torah *hashkafah*, admitting to making mistakes is praiseworthy. Therefore, if a student was hurt in public by a teacher's mistake, the teacher must publicly ask the student's forgiveness to undo the damage of the shame the student suffered. This *halachah* applies to students of all ages.

▶ The term "apology," in these cases, does not simply mean saying "I'm sorry." Rather, the teacher must humble him/herself before the student and request forgiveness for the error. While some teachers may worry that such a show of humility might make them look weak in the eyes of their students, the opposite is true. A student will learn a great lesson from seeing a teacher apologize— such an act can lead students to feel even greater respect for the teacher. The vocation of *chinuch* certainly does not give license to harm or embarrass others—no matter how old they are.

▶ If a teacher wrongs a student in private, the apology should only be made privately to the student, but with the same degree of sincerity.

▶ There are varying degrees of mistakes that teachers may make. If a teacher makes an "honest mistake" by misreading a

Your Questions
Answered by Rabbi
Moshe Mordechai
Lowy, Shlita

student's messy handwriting and taking off points for a correct answer, aside from changing the mark, the teacher need not apologize. However, if the mistake was due to the teacher's own carelessness and the child has been hurt, the teacher should apologize for it.

When a teacher needs to discipline students, s/he should not apologize afterwards for punishing them. Similarly, if an entire class is given a consequence, despite the fact that a few students are innocent; the teacher is not obligated to make restitution to them, since s/he is doing what is necessary for *chinuch*. To clarify: if a teacher does something that it is her responsibility to do as a teacher, she need not apologize.

> In Torah *hashkafah*, admitting to making mistakes is praiseworthy.

A powerful and beautiful story is told about the Chasam Sofer:

In the Chasam Sofer's yeshivah, there was a five-year learning cycle which would begin anew every five years. One bachur who had come to the yeshivah at a very young age was blessed with a phenomenal memory. After the five-year cycle was over, he told his fellow students the exact words the Chasam Sofer would use to begin the cycle again. Sure enough, at the next day's shiur, the Chasam Sofer repeated the same words which the boy had quoted. This resulted in some boys smiling and smirking in amusement.

When the Chasam Sofer noticed the disturbance, he was perturbed.

"What is going on here?" he asked, but nobody dared answer.

At this point, the Chasam Sofer announced that he would not continue his shiur until he was informed of what was happening. The boy who had unintentionally caused the ruckus trembled.

HASHKAFAH, **HALACHAH**, AND INSPIRATIO

Apologizing

What would happen to him?

After a few more moments, the Chasam Sofer made a stern declaration:

"Whoever is responsible for this, I do not forgive him because he is disrupting the shiur." With those words, he closed his Gemara and left the room. Eventually, someone told the Rosh Yeshivah what had actually happened. The next morning, the Chasam Sofer announced that every single talmid in the yeshivah was required to come to the beis midrash. The guilty boy was too embarrassed to come, dreading what lay in store for him, so he stayed in his room. To his chagrin, the Chasam Sofer sent a messenger to summon him.

When everyone was assembled, the Chasam Sofer began.

"I really was thinking that I am not worthy to give this shiur," he said. "I cannot begin the shiur because I feel that I made a terrible mistake yesterday. I cannot begin until the boy who I embarrassed is mochel me." He paused. "I want him to come up and be mochel me. I feel that it was because of my own ga'avah that I got angry. I should have been proud of him for remembering everything from five years ago! Instead, I focused on my own hurt pride, and I'm asking for mechilah."

With all eyes on him, the boy said uncomfortably: "There is nothing to be mochel the Rosh Yeshivah for."

But the Chasam Sofer insisted, until the boy finally relented and said he was mochel.

Years later, this boy became a rav in Hungary. He said that this was the biggest lesson he learned from the Chasam Sofer—even more than the Torah he had learned. This was the greatness of the Chasam Sofer, who subdued his own pride to apologize to a talmid. ▣

Airing Out

Your Questions
Answered by Rabbi
Moshe Mordechai
Lowy, Shlita

Q THE TEACHERS ROOM, BY ITS VERY NATURE, is filled with teachers who may return from class feeling frustrated, agitated, and "needing to vent." What are the *halachos* about teachers airing their feelings in a Teachers Room setting, as far as *toeles* is concerned? Where does *toeles* begin and where does it end?

A WE ARE ALWAYS GUIDED BY THE RULES OF TOELES, even where a teacher airing her feelings is concerned. The first question that a teacher must ask is: Is this the right time and place for me to air my problems? The Chofetz Chaim gives a famous, golden rule that any time a person is "steaming," he should not act on it until he pauses, either by going to a different room for a few moments, or counting to himself. This is to give himself a chance to get a better handle on the situation and get clarity about how best to proceed.

There are two reasons for a teacher needing to let off steam. If the teacher is so angry that s/he wants to air the problem in order to get even with the culprit or as an attempt to let others know what the student(s) has done, "venting" is absolutely forbidden since it will inevitably be done in a way that will reveal the student's identity. If, however, a teacher wants to vent in order to enable him or her to go to the next class with more equanimity, s/he may share what has happened, with an individual teacher or a principal, in private, without identifying the student in any way.

In the case where a teacher is not only frustrated about an incident or a student, but also feels a genuine need to hear other teachers'

Venting: Teachers Room

opinions on the subject so as to help in rectifying the situation, the teacher is permitted to speak to a group of teachers in the Teachers' Room. This should be done without identifying the student. The teacher must also be careful not to exaggerate or embellish, and must give completely accurate information.

If a teacher, after careful thought, believes that a student is behaving in a way that is so agitating or disturbing that something must be done about it, s/he should speak to someone—privately—who is in a position to help fix the problem and effect change with the particular student—usually a principal or other administrator.

It is generally forbidden to "air" one's feelings in the public setting of the Teachers' Room, since there is no *toeles* in doing so. Nevertheless, in a school where the Teachers' Room is known to be a place where teachers are careful not to violate the *halachos*

Is this the right time and place for me to air my problems?

of *shmiras halashon*, if a teacher has a one-time, very trying incident and is extremely worked up over it, s/he may vent provided that no identifying details are given. This is only permitted where such behavior will not lead to a widespread habit of teachers speaking about their frustrations amongst each other. ⊞

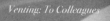

Venting: To Colleagues

Your Questions
Answered by Rabbi
Moshe Mordechai
Lowy, Shlita

Letting Off Steam

Q I HAD A VERY UPSETTING INCIDENT WITH A STUDENT, **and entered the Teachers Room ready to let off steam. Some of the teachers present teach this student, and may be able to offer helpful insights and ideas. I need understanding and advice. Can I tell them what has happened?**

A "LETTING OFF STEAM" IS NOT THE CORRECT APPROACH. Firstly, you must ascertain whether all those present in the Teachers Room have a connection with the student concerned. If not, you must call a separate meeting of relevant teachers.

> Simply "letting off steam" is not the correct approach.

Secondly, you must ensure that all information disclosed and discussed about the student is necessary and constructive, and does not contravene the prohibitions against *loshon hora* or the Seven Rules of *Toeles*.

If the sole need is the opportunity to vent and have a sympathetic ear, it may be a good idea to speak to a qualified and discreet person, such as a rav or *mechanech*, who is not involved in your school. In this scenario, one should not mention the name of the student. ⊞

HASHKAFAH, **HALACHAH**, AND INSPIRATIC

Where to Unload

Q I AM WONDERING IF A TEACHER IS PERMITTED to talk to close family members—either to unburden her/himself, or to get advice. Along similar lines, can a teacher speak to a student's relatives or friends to obtain information that might help the teacher better service the student?

A FIRSTLY, IT IS IMPORTANT TO CLARIFY that the *halachos* of *loshon hora* pertain to family members the same way that they pertain to non-relatives. Therefore, a teacher is only permitted to disclose confidential and/or negative information about students when the rules of *toeles* are met.

Within the laws of *shmiras halashon*, it is permitted for a person to "vent" when certain conditions are met. The criteria for disclosing *loshon hora* for the purpose of unburdening oneself can be seen by answering the following questions:

1. Is this the right person for me to unburden myself to?

2. Will s/he tell others this information?

3. Will s/he think badly about the people whom I am discussing? Will s/he act upon this information (i.e. when asked for information for a *shidduch*, will s/he disclose what I am about to tell her/him)?

4. Will the benefit of my telling about my stressful experience outweigh the risk of what will result from my disclosing the information?

Your Questions Answered by Rabbi Moshe Mordechai Lowy, Shlita

If the criteria are met, a teacher may speak with one person about the troubling matter. However, it is preferable to withhold the names and identifying details of the people being spoken about. If a teacher can "vent" to a family member without the listener ever guessing who the subject is, then this would not be considered *loshon hora*. However, it is often difficult to conceal identifying details carefully enough that the listener will not realize who is being spoken about; then the conversation would be *loshon hora*.

> **While the criteria for unburdening oneself pertain to the speaker him/herself, the laws of *toeles* pertain to the person being spoken about.**

The other aspect of the question deals with a different matter—speaking to others about a particular student. In a case where a teacher wants to get advice or information, s/he must act within the parameters of the *halachos* of *toeles*. While the criteria for unburdening oneself pertain to the speaker him/herself, the laws of *toeles* pertain to the person being spoken about. It must be clear that an unmistakable benefit to the student will result from the discussions. Since it is difficult to determine what is true *toeles*, before a teacher considers taking action, it is helpful to ask him/herself this question: If I would be in the same situation as this student, would I want this information divulged and/or discussed?

If, after extensive thought, a teacher decides that it is in the student's best interests for him/her to discuss the student with others, it must be done according to *halachah*. When the seven conditions of *toeles* are met, the teacher can initiate a conversation by saying, "I'm trying to help this student, and it would be beneficial for me to know x and y about him/her."

The importance of teachers maintaining student anonymity and a

high level of discretion cannot be stressed enough. Consider the following true story:

An elementary school rebbi casually mentioned to his wife that a certain boy cheated constantly and the rebbi and the hanhalah were working with the student to help him overcome this problem. Some time later, the rebbi's wife, Mrs. Dibur, met the mother of the boy in question, and the two began to chat.

"I hope you took care of the problem," Mrs. Dibur said off-handedly.

"What problem?" asked Mrs. Kapton.

"You mean you don't know that your son has a terrible problem with cheating?" Mrs. Dibur exclaimed.

The next morning the principal summoned Rabbi Dibur and told him that the Kaptons had asked that he fire Rabbi Dibur immediately due to his indiscretion in speaking to his wife about his talmidim. In addition, the principal told Rabbi Dibur that the boy's parents—who were extremely strict and overbearing—had severely punished their son when they heard he had cheated, by taking away his privilege of going to camp that summer!

The rebbi didn't mean any harm by schmoozing with his wife, nevertheless look what their conversation caused: he nearly lost his job, and a child received a devastating punishment because of the information that inadvertently escaped—information that had been deliberately withheld from the parents due to the known severity of their disciplinary techniques.

Teachers hold the key to their students' minds, hearts, and *neshamos*. It is an enormous privilege and a tremendous responsibility—one that cannot be taken lightly. Even in the heat of the moment, a teacher must consider the serious ramifications of any breach of confidentiality, which can result in unimaginable tragedy and pain. ▣

Venting: To Family

Your Questions
Answered by Rabbi
Moshe Mordechai
Lowy, Shlita

Last Year's Student

Q I AM A FIFTH-GRADE REBBI IN A LOCAL YESHIVAH. The mother of a *talmid* from last year—an excellent student—called last night to discuss with me some difficulties her son is facing with this year's rebbi. What can I do in this situation? If I approach the rebbi to speak about the boy and just ask how he's doing I will be soliciting *loshon hora*. If I tell the rebbi that the boy's mother called me about the situation, I will be guilty of *rechilus*. What should I do?

A A REBBI'S MAIN PRIORITY AND OBLIGATION is to help his *talmid*, and this must always be carried out within the framework of the Seven Rules of *Toeles*. The first and most important point that cannot be stressed enough is that when a parent calls a previous rebbi to discuss a current rebbi, it is absolutely forbidden for the rebbi to speak disparagingly to the parent about his successor, saying, "I know that rebbi and he's not really the best teacher." Even if the previous rebbi knows some negative information about the current rebbi, communicating it to the parent is not only unhelpful, it is completely forbidden and constitutes pure *loshon hora*. In cases where teachers have told parents negative things about other teachers, the result has been terrible harm and even serious consequences.

The rebbi is correct in that he is not permitted to tell the sixth-grade rebbi that the mother called with a complaint, because this is *rechilus* and does not meet the criteria for *toeles*.

Even after a rebbi is no longer the official teacher of a student, he

HASHKAFAH, **HALACHAH**, AND INSPIRATIO

Rechilus vs. Toeles

still has an obligation to help out when needed. In a case where a rebbi is tipped off by a parent that a former *talmid* is having a hard time, he should make an effort to speak directly with the current rebbi to try to remedy the situation. He can casually approach the current rebbi and say, "I'm very close with so-and-so from last year and I notice he seems unhappy. I'd really like to talk about how we can help him succeed."

The current rebbi may be reluctant to discuss his student, worrying that doing so constitutes *loshon hora*. However, in a case like the one described here, there is a great *toeles* for the conversation to take place because the previous rebbi really has a

> **A rebbi's main priority and obligation are to help his talmid.**

good handle on the student and knows how to help him. The previous rebbi can reassure the current rebbi of this when he initially approaches him.

Last year's rebbi can work directly with the current rebbi to help iron out any difficulties, or, if he thinks it is advisable, he can suggest to the parents to be in touch one-on-one with their son's current rebbi. ▣

Your Questions Answered by Rabbi Moshe Mordechai Lowy, Shlita

Walking a Tightrope

Q SOMETIMES, WHEN I AM TEACHING HALACHAH, a student will raise her hand and insist that her parents do it another way–a way that is clearly against the *halachah*. I am not talking about cases where the student is describing a different custom or a lack of a *chumrah* (stringency). How do I address this in a way that would not be *loshon hora* against the student's parents, and at the same time in a way that will not cause the student to lose respect for the parents or to speak *rechilus* (by going home and telling the parents: "My teacher said that you are wrong!") It is not always possible to just tell the student that I will discuss it with her privately, as the comments are made in class and other students start questioning.

A TEACHING HALACHAH TO A CLASS OF DIVERSE students can often result in the scenario described above. When a child announces that his/her parents do something different than what the teacher states as the correct *halachah*, it is important to preserve both respect for the parents in question and the child's respect for his/her parents while clearly communicating the proper *halachah*.

The teacher must be careful not to say anything negative about the parent. But the teacher should first try to be *melamed zechus* and tell the student that it is possible s/he misunderstood his/her parents' behavior. The teacher can also then question if perhaps the parents learned the *halachah* differently or if they received a *p'sak* from a rav to act as they do in the area discussed. Lastly, the teacher can tell the student that maybe what s/he saw in this case

was an exception. At the same time that the teacher is trying to exonerate the parents from being cast in a bad light, the teacher must emphasize the correct *halachah*. By stating: "The *halachah* is such-and-such," and not addressing individuals, the teacher avoids speaking *loshon hora* since s/he is not maligning the parents in any way.

> It is important to preserve both respect for the parents in question and the child's respect for his/her parents while clearly communicating the proper halachah.

There is no concern about the child speaking *rechilus* if the teacher has not spoken negatively about the parents. If the teacher has simply stated the correct *halachah*, then the child will not come home saying "My teacher said you're wrong"; instead, the child will say "We learned that the *halachah* is this way."

It is important that the teacher know with certainty whether the *halachah* being taught is black-and-white or if there are different opinions about its observance. In the first case, where the *halachah* is absolute, it is advisable for the teacher to disallow questions from students in order to forestall uncomfortable scenarios such as the one described above. However, where various *minhagim* (customs) and *chumros* (stringencies) exist, it is very beneficial for a teacher to encourage students to discuss how their parents observe the *halachah*. This serves as a valuable opportunity to show respect for all halachic opinions and demonstrates the beauty of *"eilu v'eilu divrei Elokim chayim."* If a student insists that s/he has been given a *p'sak* from a rav to observe the *halachah* in a certain way, it is imperative that the teacher

Your Questions
Answered by Rabbi
Moshe Mordechai
Lowy, Shlita

show respect for this ruling even if it differs from the way in which the teacher originally presented the *halachah*.

In some cases, a student may insist that his/her parents act in a way contrary to *halachah* when really the student is attempting to adhere to a level of stringency over and beyond the parents' perfectly adequate Torah observance. If this occurs, it is the teacher's responsibility to encourage students to respect their parents and not adopt a "holier than thou" attitude toward them. ▣

A Clean Slate

Q IS A TEACHER ALLOWED TO GO THROUGH STUDENTS' report cards/record cards from the past year(s) before teaching them, as a means of getting to know who they are? Would this change if s/he has already begun to teach the class? May s/he look at a specific student's report card whom s/he is having difficulty with?

A PREVIOUS YEARS' REPORT CARDS AND RECORD CARDS inevitably convey a certain impression of a student that is often not an accurate reflection of who the student is today—or even who s/he was then. Therefore, before a teacher looks at students' report cards or school records, it is best to meet the students, to avoid forming a false impression. If, after forming her own opinions during the first few weeks of school, a teacher finds herself having difficulties with a specific student and she wants to know whether the problem is a new one or it also occurred during the previous school year, then she may look at the records after seeking the principal's input in the matter.

Handling negative information is only permissible if a definite, specific purpose will result. Therefore, a teacher is certainly permitted to look at specific students' report card if she is thoroughly convinced that it will help her help the student. If a teacher is having widespread difficulty with the entire class, however, it would be better for her to speak directly to the previous year's teacher instead of looking through report cards because she would probably obtain more accurate information that way. Often, report cards do not reflect anything more than grades,

FOR THOSE WHO INSPIRE OTHERS

Your Questions
Answered by Rabbi
Moshe Mordechai
Lowy, Shlita

which is not the information a teacher needs to know in order to address a discipline or behavior problem.

An additional problem presents itself if a teacher teaches only one subject or even one department, such as *limudei kodesh*. In this case, she does not need to know how well or poorly her students do in other, unrelated subjects. Thus, seeing additional, non-*l'toeles* negative information about students would be prohibited. As a safeguard against receiving negative information that is not *l'toeles*, a teacher of a certain subject could ask the school secretary to print out the student's marks from the previous year only in that specific subject or department. This way, she will not be privy to any unnecessary information about the student.

> **Often, report cards do not reflect anything more than grades.**

It is important to clarify that teachers should only be privy to information that directly affects their teaching of the class. A teacher does not need to know everything that goes on in her students' lives. Only that which is relevant to her role as teacher can be clarified or revealed. As is the case in any other inquiry about relevant information, such as *shidduchim*, job interviews, etc., a teacher is only permitted to inquire about information that will directly help her teach the student.

Any time a teacher receives negative information about a student's past, s/he must handle it with care, as the following true story illustrates.

A fourth-grade rebbi "helpfully" told the incoming fifth-grade rebbi some extremely uncomplimentary things about a certain student in the class. This negative information severely affected the current

HASHKAFAH, **HALACHAH**, AND INSPIRATIC

rebbi's impression of the student in question and he exhibited, from the very start, a bad outlook toward this student, penalizing him for even slight offenses and becoming extremely irritated with his behavior. The student, in turn, complained to his parents about his teacher's negative behavior. "He's always picking on me! I never did anything wrong and I want to be good!"

After a while, his parents became concerned about their son's constant complaints and they came to speak to the rebbi about what was going on.

"We already know from last year that your child is a problem," the rebbi remarked, off-handedly, revealing the source of his animosity for the student.

Understandably, the parents became very upset at the previous year's rebbi and also chastised the current rebbi for his attitude. "Did you even try to succeed with our child?" they asked him. "It could be that he simply didn't 'click' with last year's rebbi and things will be dramatically different this year!"

The rebbi took these parents' words to heart and actively worked to erase his former impression of the student. And wonder of wonders—the boy became the best student in the class!

First impressions are priceless. We must be exceedingly careful to form them properly. ⊞

Inspiration:
Golden Moments,
Lasting Impact

These are the moments every educator hopes for—the moments when it suddenly becomes clear that he or she has reached a child's heart, uplifted his spirit or penetrated his mind. Sharing these moments helps to keep teachers inspired to continue the search for the best ways to connect to their students and shine a light into their lives.

For Shabbos and Forever

Retold by Yaffa Penina

I T WAS FRIDAY. THE BOYS had all been dismissed and everyone was heading home to get ready for Shabbos. But not Rabbi Fried*. He had to make sure that those boys who had been absent would get their Shabbos sheets. Rebbi had sent home Yehuda's sheets with his neighbor and Shloimy's booklet with his brother. Shimmy Weiner, though, did not live close to anyone in the class and had no siblings in yeshivah. So Rebbi got ready to do what he often did, drive over to his *talmid's* house and hand-deliver the Shabbos sheets along with a treat and best wishes for a *refuah sheleimah*.

> **What could possibly be so important about Shabbos sheets that Rabbi Fried just had to make sure Shimmy Weiner got them?**

What could possibly be so important about Shabbos sheets that Rabbi Fried just had to make sure Shimmy Weiner got them? Most people wouldn't understand, but Rebbi put so much into his *talmidim* and the Shabbos sheets extended that bond all through Shabbos. It wasn't the booklet itself as much as the *kesher* it represented and the ability that it afforded each one of his Pre-1A, budding *talmidei chachamim* to take yeshivah home, that drove Rabbi Fried to go the extra mile.

Before he left, Rabbi Fried called the Weiners to inquire about Shimmy and make sure someone was home. Mr. Weiner answered and told Rebbi that Shimmy had strep throat, but was on the mend.

He had started antibiotics the day before and would surely be back in yeshivah on Monday.

"I'm so glad to hear that." Rebbi enthused. "I've got to get you Shimmy's Shabbos sheets," Rabbi Fried said warmly.

Mr. Weiner, almost ready to leave the house with his family to spend Shabbos at his in-laws' in another borough, was a bit distracted. "Well, we're leaving very soon to spend Shabbos at my in-laws'; I guess Shimmy can always make up the work when he comes back to school next week."

"No, no," Rabbi Fried assured him. "This is much more than work—this is...it'll make his Shabbos! I wouldn't want Shimmy to miss out. Let's see now...,"

Rabbi Fried made a quick calculation; even if he left yeshivah that minute he couldn't possibly make it to the Weiners' house in Friday traffic in under twenty minutes, and the Weiners were eager to leave. "How about a fax machine? Do you have access to a fax, by any chance?"

Mr. Weiner was quiet for a moment. He didn't own a fax machine, but the rebbi sounded like it would really make a big difference.

"Oh—I have an idea," Mr. Weiner said suddenly, remembering. "Let me give you a fax number. You can fax it over to this machine."

"Wonderful!" Rabbi Fried exclaimed, blissfully un-aware of the hectic Weiner schedule. "I'll fax it right over."

After a brief exchange with Shimmy in which he wished him well and let him know just how pleased he would be to see him back in yeshivah, Rabbi Fried hung up happily, and got into his car to head home. He soon allowed the incident to slip from his mind.

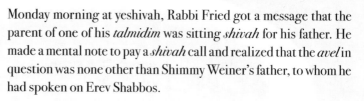

Monday morning at yeshivah, Rabbi Fried got a message that the parent of one of his *talmidim* was sitting *shivah* for his father. He made a mental note to pay a *shivah* call and realized that the *avel* in question was none other than Shimmy Weiner's father, to whom he had spoken on Erev Shabbos.

But he was ill prepared for the welcome he received when he walked into the Weiner *shivah* the next day.

"Rabbi Fried!" Berish Weiner cried. "You have no idea what you did for me!"

"Uh, no," the rebbi replied, taken aback.

"Sit down and let me tell you," the *avel* said quickly. When Rabbi Fried complied, he continued. "Do you remember that you insisted on faxing over the Shabbos booklet to my Shimmy on Friday?"

Rabbi Fried nodded.

"Well, I'll tell you the truth: we have no fax machine in our house, but you were so insistent that I finally gave you my father's fax number. We stopped off at my father's house, on our way to my in-laws, just to pick up the sheets. And...," he paused, and his eyes misted over, "and that was the last time I ever spoke to my father."

Silence reigned in the small living room.

"Rabbi Fried," Berish said tearily, "I had no idea that my father would pass away right after Shabbos. If it wasn't for the five minutes I spent at his house picking up that fax, I would not now have my father's smile and his warm 'good Shabbos' freshly etched in my heart, where it will remain as my cherished, final memory of him."

Here was a devoted rebbi, completely focused on what he could do for a talmid, and he ended up doing so much more than he ever imagined! ⊞

*Names have been changed.

More Than I Could Handle

By Tehila Silverman

I ENTERED MRS. WEISS*, the principal's, office and put down my briefcase with an emphatic thud. A mixture of feelings welled up inside me; frustration, disappointment, defeat, even a good measure of anger and resentment. They were simply impossible. Completely and totally impossible. And I was at the end of my rope.

It was my eighth-graders. Never before in my 20+ years of teaching had I encountered such a difficult class. I couldn't even get my finger on what exactly made them so difficult; was it the level of chutzpah they exhibited, the attitude problem they had, the airs about them? Was it the general lack of interest in learning, a fact they had no problem openly admitting to, that I found so demoralizing? Or was is the combination of so many girls struggling with major personal issues that so bogged down the entire class and affected them negatively?

I didn't know. But I did know that this could not go on. It had become exceedingly difficult for me to teach them and I needed to have a long talk with the principal.

And a long talk we did indeed have. We talked about Rivky, whose situation at home warranted immediate professional intervention, but there was no way her parents would ever hear of it. We

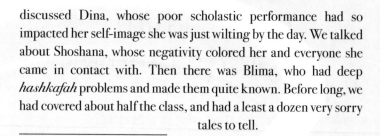

discussed Dina, whose poor scholastic performance had so impacted her self-image she was just wilting by the day. We talked about Shoshana, whose negativity colored her and everyone she came in contact with. Then there was Blima, who had deep *hashkafah* problems and made them quite known. Before long, we had covered about half the class, and had a least a dozen very sorry tales to tell.

> **I feel so bad for anyone who has a daughter in this class...**

I closed the roll book I was holding and sighed heavily. For some reason, images of my own *kinderlach*, my own sweet, precious daughters, popped into my mind. *Each of these girls has a mother, a mother who loves them and cares so deeply about them,* I suddenly found myself thinking. *If this is hard for me as the teacher, imagine how hard it must be for their parents.* "I feel so sorry for their mothers," I said aloud, to myself as much as Mrs. Weiss. "I feel so bad for anyone who has a daughter in this class..."

"Indeed I do," Mrs. Weiss's response came, almost inaudibly. "I do indeed feel so sorry for anyone who has a daughter in this class..." A pause. "And I have so many..."

The problems were indeed real. Mrs. Weiss had just handed me the key to facing the challenge.

How fortunate are the students whose principal views them as her own precious children! And how fortunate am I to have such an exceptional principal as a guide and role model! ⊞

Names and identifying details have been changed to protect privacy.

HASHKAFAH, HALACHAH, AND **INSPIRATIO**

19° and Heartwarming

Retold by Chany Feldbrand

THE NUMERALS ON MY DASHBOARD glowed in the mid-morning frost: 19 degrees Fahrenheit. I shivered in my warm coat and woolen gloves, grateful for the relative warmth my vehicle afforded me; glad I wasn't outside in that biting cold scraping ice off a windshield. "No one should be outside in such weather," I thought to myself as I navigated through the local traffic and made my way to work. My warm breath was creating a rising vapor in the chilled car as I slowed down at the traffic light.

And then I saw them.

> I saw boys jump and dance around in a valiant effort to keep warm.

Boys. Lots of them. In fact, it was a whole elementary school full of boys. Outside. Lining the sidewalks. Without coats, without hats, without gloves or scarves or earmuffs or any of the other things their mothers had thoughtfully and carefully purchased for them. I knew in an instant—this must be a fire drill. But why on earth in such weather? Drills are always fun, a welcome diversion on a monotonous day, perfect for the balmy sunshine of a spring day. A fire drill is certainly not the kind of thing one enjoys in 19°-degree weather.

Then I noticed the fire engines. So it was not a drill after all. This was something real. (As I later found out, it was just a small mishap in the kitchen, but enough to have the fire alarm go off and necessitate evacuating the building for a good 15 minutes.) I watched a whole cheder's worth of boys line the sidewalks in teen-digit temperature. I watched the boys shiver and huddle together to ward off the numbing cold. I saw boys jump and dance around in a valiant effort to keep warm.

And then I saw something truly heartwarming.

There stood a rebbi. He was surrounded by his precious *yingelach* and, oddly enough, he was standing in his shirtsleeves. What had happened to his jacket? I looked a bit closer. He had his boys lined up in pairs. He had his jacket in his hand. And he was spreading it over each pair of boys for two minutes at a time. Two minutes and then it was time for the next pair. Each boy had a precious two minutes to escape the cold, a precious two minutes to restore some warmth to a freezing body, a precious two minutes to wrap himself in rebbi's jacket.

Two minutes to envelope himself in a rebbi's warmth.

And a lifetime to remember the selflessness of a rebbi's love.

In honor of the unknown rebbi who literally gave the "shirt off his back" for his dear talmidim. May Hakadosh Baruch Hu reward your act of selflessness. ▦

French Fries

Retold by Chany Feldbrand

I BELONG TO A SPECIAL GROUP OF MOTHERS. Vigilant mothers. It's not so simple, this caution mothers like me must exercise. Think about it; your son comes home with a note about a *siyum*. Without a second thought, you prepare his white shirt and the $2.50 to cover the cost of the pizza or franks or whatever the rebbi happens to decide to serve.

In our house it just doesn't work that way. When Yossi* comes home with a note about a *siyum*, my antennas shoot up and I get to work. It's one thing managing his issues on a regular day-to-day basis. It's quite another when there is a change in routine.

You see, Yossi suffers from severe food allergies.

Lunches, snacks, parties, *siyumim*; all these pose special challenges for him, and I find I must always be on top of a situation that is potentially life-threatening, *chas v'shalom*.

But by now I have it down to a science; Yossi comes home with a note about a party and I try to arrange for some other, permissible food for him to enjoy so that he doesn't feel

He did what the moment called for.

excluded from the festivities. And this *siyum* on *Parashas Vayeira* was no exception. As soon as I read the note about the upcoming

pizza party, I called the principal, Rabbi Pinter, and reminded him about the problem. We had been through this before. "Don't worry about it," he reassured me. "Just call Pizza Palace and tell them to add two fries to the order and put it on the school's bill." I thanked him for his understanding and immediately called the pizza store. Explaining the situation to the cashier, I asked him to please put a note in a prominent place stating that two packs of fries be delivered to the school along with the pizza order. I even called back several hours later to ensure that this had indeed been done. "Yes, ma'am," came the response. "We have the note right here and we'll be sure to send the fries tomorrow." I hung up the phone, satisfied that my son would be enjoying the *simchah*—and food—together with his classmates.

It was not to be. For some reason, the fries were not delivered together with the pizza. My son was devastated. His rebbi, who knew nothing of my arrangement with the principal, tried to mollify him with an extra half-donut that had remained, but my son was only partially pacified. So when he crossed paths with Rabbi Pinter after the *siyum* was over, he told him, ever so respectfully, that the fries had never arrived.

"Why didn't you tell me right away?" Rabbi Pinter asked, his voice full of surprise and concern. "Okay, Yossi, I want you to wait right outside my office. I'll be back in a few minutes."

With that, Yossi saw Rabbi Pinter grab his jacket and quickly exit the building.

Indeed, not quite ten minutes had passed, and Rabbi Pinter was back. His face was slightly flushed and tiny beads of perspiration glittered on his forehead. In one hand he held his car keys.

And in the other he held two packs of fries.

"*Mazel tov*, Yossi," he said, extending his hand and the fries. "May you always *shteig* in your learning!"

The sparkle in Yossi's eyes as he thanked Rabbi Pinter said it all. An impression for a lifetime had been made in that one moment.

In one moment and two packs of fries. ⊞

*All names have been changed.

OR THOSE WHO INSPIRE OTHERS

"Help!"

Retold by Chany Feldbrand

"**N**INTH GRADE WAS A ROUGH YEAR for Leah*," I thought as I maneuvered my car into the school parking lot. "And tenth isn't turning out much better."

It was PTA night and I could feel the familiar mix of trepidation and dread well up inside me. All teenagers are tough, but some are tougher than others. Something deep inside me, perhaps that small flower of a mother's hope that refuses to wither, reassured me that it was a passing stage, that she'd eventually straighten out, but heaven knew how much strength and emotional stamina I'd need until we got there...

I entered the building and was greeted by a wave of animated chatter. Judging from the lines of women waiting, it would be quite a while before my turn came. I didn't mind; it would give me a chance to sort out my jumbled thoughts, to reign in my turbulent emotions.

Leah was going through a hard time and even I, her mother, couldn't figure out exactly what her issues were. But the way they were manifesting themselves was unacceptable to the school we had chosen. Her mode of dress, while conforming to the "letter" of the school's code, surely didn't reflect the "spirit" of it, and the administration was understandably concerned. After a very tumultuous freshman year, with confrontations and ensuing hard feelings on both sides, we came to the conclusion that perhaps

it was in Leah's best interest to change schools. And so began the application process, the interviews, and by June's end it was all set.

September 2 the bombshell fell. Because of some unfortunate snag, the school was forced to

September 2 the bombshell fell.

change their mind. Leah, who was already removed from the class roster at her former Bais Yaakov, would be back there for her sophomore year.

She didn't like that one bit.

I felt it at home, and I was sure the teachers sensed it in school. I imagined her sitting through the classes with that blank, empty look on her face that had become so familiar to me. She rarely did homework and never once made a positive comment about school. And now, here I was, to meet her teachers.

Mrs. Weissman interrupted my thoughts as she smilingly gestured to the chair opposite her. I quickly glanced at the sheet in my hand. Mrs. Weissman: *Kesuvim*, two periods a week. "Can't be too bad," I thought as I braced myself for what I was sure to come.

Suddenly I heard Mrs. Weissman's voice. "Leah has so many positive attributes, but I was wondering–is she happy in school?" she gently inquired.

I don't know what compelled me but I was brutally honest. "No, not at all, in fact she's pretty miserable" I answered, too upset about the whole situation to worry about PR or anything else.

All names have been changed.

"I thought so." Mrs. Weissman's face radiated concern. "I try to give her a smile and a good word whenever I can, but I wanted to ask you if there's anything else I could do to help the situation?"

Anything else to help the situation? The situation that was robbing me of sleep at night and of my peace of mind during the day? The situation that tore at my heartstrings and hurt my soul to the core? The situation that was spiraling out of control and growing worse each day? Anything to help? The utter helplessness and desperation I felt turned to a mighty storm that clouded my vision and threatened to overwhelm me. I averted her eyes; I certainly didn't want to fall apart in front of this stranger. As the seconds ticked by I sensed the teacher's compassionate gaze upon me and I lifted my head.

It was then that I noticed the moisture in Mrs. Weissman's eyes as she leaned forward and asked, in an almost inaudible whisper, "If there's nothing you feel I can do for Leah at school, do you mind giving me her name for *Tehillim*... I want to daven for her..."

Almost at once, I felt the storm inside me beginning to subside, as if the tide had turned. Suddenly it wasn't a teacher and mother conferring, it was two mothers... hoping and praying for a precious *Yiddishe neshamah*.

Shaping with Prayer

▶ A devoted teacher is concerned with a student's complete well-being, not just the student's success in a particular subject.

▶ "*Kol hamelamed es ben chaveiro Torah k'ilu yoldo*, Whoever teaches his friend's child Torah, it is as if he gave birth to him." **Sanhedrin 19b**

▶ Because this is so, a teacher, like a parent, would certainly pray for each child's success. ▣

HASHKAFAH, HALACHAH, AND **INSPIRATIO**

HALLELUKAH!

Retold by Chany Feldbrand

IT WAS ROSH CHODESH CHESHVAN, a date principals associate with a deep sigh of relief and the feeling of finally settling down to business: Long weeks of uninterrupted learning and growing stretched ahead. On this particular *Rosh Chodesh Cheshvan*, as I walked the hallways of my school, a feeling of satisfaction came over me; the wonderful *Yom Tov* season, with its accompanying flurry of activity, was over. Teachers were back with renewed strength, classes were in full swing, and I was enjoying the sweet sound of childish voices coming in muted tones from behind the various doors I was passing.

And then I passed the first grade. A pang. *Rosh Chodesh Cheshvan* was always a special day for our first graders, for it was the first time in their lives that they would recite *Hallel*. Our first-grade teacher, Morah Stern*, always made this auspicious occasion exceptionally meaningful for her girls. As someone who had an intensely special connection to *tefillah*, she went to great lengths to make the first recitation of *Hallel* a mini-celebration. From the pep talk she would give them beforehand, which caused the stars in her eyes to leap to the mesmerized eyes of her little charges, to the special treat she gave each girl afterwards, the deep impression was made: Reciting *Hallel* was a privilege to be cherished, and not just in first grade, but forever.

So why the pang on this *Rosh Chodesh Cheshvan*? Simple. Morah

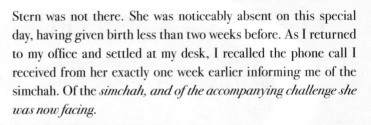

Stern was not there. She was noticeably absent on this special day, having given birth less than two weeks before. As I returned to my office and settled at my desk, I recalled the phone call I received from her exactly one week earlier informing me of the simchah. Of the *simchah, and of the accompanying challenge she was now facing.*

Her newborn daughter was born with a complex cardiac disorder.

My heart skipped a beat.

A stream of thoughts flooded my mind... Images of a tiny baby hooked up to intricate machinery in a NICU, fighting for every breath... Images of a smiling, exuberant Morah imparting the joy and privilege of reciting *Hallel*, ... Images of little, wide-eyed girls in freshly starched uniforms, drinking in every word and then proceeding to enunciate the precious words of *Hallelu Avdei Hashem* for the very first time... Images of a tiny heart pumping valiantly, and a mother's heart being ripped asunder as she bears witness to this moment-to-moment struggle for survival...

Suddenly, I couldn't remain in my seat any longer. Something was drawing me back to that first-grade classroom. I soon found myself peering through the little window on the classroom door.

My heart skipped a beat.

There was Morah Stern, *one week after giving birth*, in her classroom. She was on the way to the hospital, on the way to her baby, but she had to make a short stop first.

She had come to sing *Hallel* with her precious *tinokos shel beis rabban.*

Her baby was in ICU fighting for survival, and she was here in the classroom, to sing Hashem's praises, for His kindness is forever. With her trademark fire and enthusiasm she was once again preparing her little girls for the tremendous merit of reciting *Hallel*, of singing of Hashem's greatness, of Hashem's goodness. The children sat at the edge of their little seats, eyes glued to their beloved teacher as she spoke her words of introduction with awe and love.

And then, shivering with excitement and anticipation, they opened up their *siddurim*.

With the sense that a Presence far greater than anything in the universe was hovering just overhead, I observed from the window. The children were gazing intently into their *siddurim*, carefully pointing to the proper place on the page, haltingly, lovingly, joyously, enunciating each word. And she stood in the front of the room, *siddur* clutched tightly in her hands, eyes deeply closed, brow furrowed in concentration, her melodious voice blending with their childish ones...

Moshivi akeres habayis, eim habanim semeichah, Hallelukah!

And then, before I even had a chance to thank her for the infinitely precious gift she had given her students—and me—that morning, Morah Stern was gone. She had gone on, to be at her baby's side, her lips no doubt still murmuring the hallowed words of *Hallel*...◪

*Name has been changed.

Connections

∎

Global Reflections

They say three fourths of the earth's surface is water.
I can believe it, looking at our globe, looking at all the blue.
The brown-gold of land, continents, sparse spread.
We're water globes, each of us—
One fourth continental, visible;
Three-fourths ocean deep, invisible, unattainable, submerged.

Reprinted from Memo to Self by Ruth Lewis, with permission from Targum Press

∎

A Lovely Trait

What a lovely
trait it is
to say kind words.
How much lovelier to
say them right away
before the moment's
flown, to phone
early in the morning,
to make the whole
day sweet,
to set hearts singing.

Reprinted from Memo to Self, by Ruth Lewis, with permission from Targum Press

HASHKAFAH, HALACHAH, AND **INSPIRATIO**

Never Alone

An elderly man entered the yeshivah of Rav Simcha Wasserman to say *kaddish*. Following the prayers, he introduced himself to the Rosh Yeshivah, explaining that he was the retired chairman of the history department of a large American university.

"Nowadays, I'm pretty much alone," he lamented.

"How could that be?" asked Rav Simcha. "How many students do you think you had in the course of your career?

"Well, let's see. In the 30 years I taught, I probably had about 30,000 students."

"Don't any of them come to speak to you or invite you to their weddings?" Rav Simcha asked.

> **To create a lasting bond, a teacher must teach with love.**

The answer was no. Not one student had established that kind of personal connection with their professor. Yet in the Rosh Yeshivah's life, every week brought weddings, visits, requests for advice and guidance.

Rav Simcha explained the power of connecting through Torah. "Torah is given with love." The bond between people who learn Torah together is saturated with this love. It is deep and lasting.

To create a lasting bond, a teacher must teach with love.

Although no other subject carries within it the love that is integral to Torah, any teacher, through love of her/his student, can create a lasting bond. ▣

Adapted from "Rav Simcha Speaks" by Yaakov Branfman and Akiva Tatz, with permission from Mesorah Publications, Ltd.

The Sweetest Ice Cream

As told to Riva Pomerantz

HE WAS A MASTER REBBI. With talent and eminent wisdom, he worked tirelessly with each of his *talmidim*, always seeking to understand and reach every boy; to maximize his potential. To Rabbi Janowsky, each student was a unique diamond, waiting to be polished under the rebbi's gentle guidance and love.

So it was, as he looked out at the twenty-five eager eighth-graders seated before him, Rabbi Sholom Janowsky felt a surge of joy tinged with a certain sadness. It had been a wonderful, uplifting year for both the students and their rebbi, and now, with one month left, came the annual angst of separation.

"Boys," Rabbi Janowsky declared, "I cannot even tell you how amazed I am by all the efforts each of you has put in this year. Now, as our year together is coming to an end and you will soon be going out on your own to mesivta, I'd like for us to work on strengthening a certain problem area we've been having lately: coming on time to davening in the morning."

The class squirmed uncomfortably. Although the rebbi constantly emphasized a desire for the boys to *daven* together at school, many preferred *davening* in shuls closer to their homes where the pace was quicker and the times more flexible.

"Listen up, boys," continued the rebbi. "I'm offering a super-deluxe barbecue at my house to anyone who attends *davening* on time at school every morning from now until the end of the year. Deli, hot dogs—the works!"

A ripple of excitement spread across the room. Such an offer was hard to refuse.

"Remember, only boys who meet the requirement will get the reward," the rebbi cautioned. "I hope to see all of you at the barbecue!"

Despite frequent reminders and encouragement from Rabbi Janowsky, it was clear that not every boy would be attending the gala barbecue. Especially of concern to the rebbi was Dovi Goldmark's lack of participation. Dovi had worked hard all year and enjoyed a particularly close relationship with Rabbi Janowsky, but he simply was not interested in making the commitment to come to *davening* on time.

The last day of school—highlighted by the long-awaited barbecue—arrived. Despite the fact that he had made a conscious choice not to meet the *davening* goal, Dovi felt especially disappointed about missing the barbecue. The whole year had been a fantastic one, and now it seemed spoiled by the exclusive party at his rebbi's house that he was not permitted to attend.

Chinuch was *Chinuch*, and he simply couldn't back down on his word.

Similar thoughts were running through Rabbi Janowsky's mind, even as he cheerfully hosted the boys who had earned their reward.

Dovi's absence weighed heavily upon him; he worried about ending on a sour note—after all, he had come such a long way. But what could he do? *Chinuch* was *chinuch*, and he simply couldn't back down on his word.

When the telephone rang in the Goldmark's house at 10:40 p.m., Dovi answered it morosely. He had spent the entire night sulking in his room, bemoaning his exclusion from the party even though it was his own doing.

"Dovi!" came the tired but caring voice of none other than Rabbi Janowsky. "I know the hour is late, but I've been thinking about you."

The rebbi's next words made Dovi's breath catch in his throat.

"How about if I come over now and quickly take you out for some ice cream and a little schmooze?"

And schmooze they did. About everything on Dovi's mind and about keeping a *kesher* next year as well. A smiling Dovi felt a huge burden lifted from him. Ice cream had never tasted as sweet as it did that night, when, nearing midnight, a rebbi cemented a relationship with his *talmid* that could truly be called life-changing.

An incredible and true story of an exceptional rebbi. He not only taught the eighth grade; he was truly a rebbi for life.

Shaping with Sweetness

▸ The *sweetness* of the relationship is often as important as the lesson itself.

▸ The answer doesn't always have to be yes or no... Often there are alternatives. ▣

HASHKAFAH, HALACHAH, AND **INSPIRATIO**

Three Minutes and 23 Seconds

Retold by Chany Feldbrand

THE *TZIMMES* WAS BUBBLING GENTLY on the stove, while the round challos stood cooling nearby. The girls were putting the finishing touches on the festive Rosh Hashanah table, while I tended to some last-minute details in the kitchen. Suddenly, the ringing of the phone penetrated the noisy chatter of our earnest preparations. I glanced up at the clock as I searched for the cordless. 5:10 p.m. Yom Tov would commence in just about an hour and a half, I thought, "Who would be calling now?"

"Hello?" I said breathlessly when the elusive cordless had finally been located. A rich baritone voice came clearly across the wires; a voice I immediately identified.

Rabbi Bendet*.

> **What could possibly have compelled him to call.**

I was completely taken aback. Rabbi Bendet was my 12-year-old Yehuda's rebbi. My mind raced. What could possibly have compelled him to call on such a hectic day, *and* at such a late hour? Had my son done something wrong? Something terribly wrong that warranted a call at this most inopportune time?

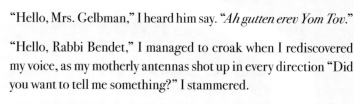

"Hello, Mrs. Gelbman," I heard him say. *"Ah gutten erev Yom Tov."*

"Hello, Rabbi Bendet," I managed to croak when I rediscovered my voice, as my motherly antennas shot up in every direction "Did you want to tell me something?" I stammered.

"Actually, no," came the response. I could practically hear the smile coming through the line. "I called to speak to Yehuda. Is he available?"

I covered the receiver with my palm and motioned for Yehuda to come get the phone. "It's your rebbi," I mouthed. "He asked to speak to you."

Yehuda's face registered surprise and curiosity as he took the phone. "Hello? Rebbi?" he asked tremulously.

I watched Yehuda's face intently. The surprise and hesitation was soon replaced by a small smile, which proceeded to grow as the moments ticked on. Yehuda's brow then furrowed slightly, and his head nodded ever so imperceptibly, as he concentrated intently on what he was hearing. After a few long minutes, I heard him thank his rebbi, answer a fervent and hopeful *"amen,"* after which he handed me the phone. "Rebbi wants to tell you something," he said, the huge smile still threatening to split his face in two.

"I really called expressly to speak to Yehuda," explained Rabbi Bendet. "But I didn't want you to think that I didn't want to talk to you, so I asked him to hand you back the phone. I want to wish you a *kesivah v'chasimah tovah*, and a healthy year filled with *nachas* from Yehuda and all your children. Have a good Yom Tov!"

I pressed "end" on the receiver and glanced at the timer displayed on the small screen of the phone. "Three minutes and 23 seconds" it read. I was astounded. What had propelled a busy man to spend

HASHKAFAH, HALACHAH, AND **INSPIRATIO**

his time, on one of the busiest days of the year no less, calling a student of his?

"Yehuda," I called out, determined to get to the bottom of this. "Why did Rebbi call you?"

"Oh, he wanted to wish me a good year," answered Yehuda simply.

"But didn't he wish all of you boys a *kesivah v'chasimah tovah* in yeshivah yesterday?" I gasped.

"Yeah, he did. But he said he wanted to tell it to me personally and give me a special *brachah*. And he gave me a real good one." Yehuda's eyes were still shining.

Three minutes and 23 seconds. A personal *brachah*. Erev Rosh Hashanah.

I was too awed for words.

But that was not all. After Yom Tov, when the boys gathered in yeshivah to "compare notes," the extent of Rabbi Bendet's devotion became clear. It was not just my son, *but every single talmid in his class of 25*—including Rabbi Bendet's own son, who was called from another line in the house!—received a personal phone call on that erev Rosh Hashanah. A personal phone call, a personalized *brachah* and a few personal minutes with a great person.

My mind tried to do the math. Three minutes and 23 seconds times 25... I hopelessly gave up. But judging from the warmth that spread through my son—and his entire class—that day, there was no need to calculate anything.

It all added up to one rebbi's giant heart filled with love. ▣

*Names have been changed.

Reaching Sarah

Retold by Bassie Gugenheim

ROCHEL BERNTSTEIN,* *Tova Richter, Yael Cohen...* The tension in the air was palpable as I took attendance on the first day of the school year.

Malky Feinstein, Brocha Friedman...

I read a name, then glanced at the girl. Each time I was met with the bright hopeful eyes of another nervous ninth-grader.

Esti Sandler, Sarah Klein...

I could barely detect any response from the back corner seat. Sarah sat staring down at her desk, face blank and expressionless. I felt a tug at my heartstrings. She seemed so alone.

As the days progressed, the anonymous names on the list began to take form and meaning. Each day brought novel discoveries of talents and refreshing personalities. My class was coming to life. Everyone but Sarah. Sarah seemed to be living in a different world. She did not participate in class. Her work was often incomplete. There was no interaction with her classmates. It was as if she didn't exist. I knew that I could not let things continue this way.

With no prior experience in dealing with a challenge of this nature, I gave the matter some serious thought. As a teacher, my obligation was to get this girl to learn. It seemed to me that the first step was to show Sarah that she was capable of producing. I called her over after class and requested that every evening she write down the *psukim* we learned in class, the English interpretation of the

words, and a summary of our learning in her own words. The next morning her first completed assignment was on my desk, and I knew I was headed in the right direction.

Within a short while I was able to involve Sarah in class review. Her homework enabled me to know what questions she could handle with ease. I could call on her, and she could answer.

> The student in this story had been promoted each year without ever being pushed to produce. Her turnabout came when she was finally shown that she could.

At first her classmates were quite surprised. Over the years they had grown accustomed to her silence. It was almost as if a classroom fixture had suddenly come alive.

Soon, the inevitable took place. Students respond to their classmates according to the way their teachers interact with them. "If Morah speaks to Sarah, then we can speak to Sarah." I spotted her talking to a classmate during recess, and she no longer ate lunch alone in the classroom.

A new girl had been added to the class, a girl with a pretty face and a lovely personality that somehow had gone unnoticed until the year I was her teacher.

*Names have been changed.

Shaping, Slowly but Surely

- The teacher's intervention in this story was effective because it was direct and consistent, yet not overly time-consuming.

- Direct, small, consistent steps go a long way toward solving even the most difficult issues.

- The greatest gift a teacher can give her student is to show her that she can succeed. ⊞

The Highest Mark

Retold by Riva Pomerantz

IT WAS A HECTIC THURSDAY NIGHT for Mrs. Springer*, and eight-year-old Boruch's distress had gone unnoticed. Now, as she walked passed his bedroom door, she was surprised to hear him moving around.

"Boruch," she asked gently, "are you still up? Is everything okay?"

Her questions were met with silence. Mrs. S. approached her son's bed and put a loving arm around his shoulder. "What is it, dearest?"

Beneath the quilt, Boruch's shoulders rose in a deep sigh. Then suddenly the dam burst, and a torrent of tears burst forth. Slowly, painfully, the words came out. His teacher had ignored him today... she knew he needed her help yet she deliberately looked away from his raised hand... and now he was going to fail his math test... he was going to be a failure!

Mrs. Springer caressed her son lovingly. "Don't worry, sweetheart," she said soothingly, "I'll study with you, and teach you whatever you don't know. I won't let you fail your math test. And I'm sure that your teacher didn't ignore you on purpose. I'll call her tomorrow and find out what happened. She probably didn't even realize that you were raising your hand. Okay, my boy?"

Mrs. Springer's reassurances calmed her son's distress, and

Boruch's tears gradually subsided. A few moments later, she tiptoed away from the bedside of her sleeping angel.

The next morning when all her children had made their way to school, Mrs. S. called Morah Rosen. After introducing herself, she told Binyomin's teacher all that had transpired the evening before.

Mrs. Rosen felt terrible. She explained to Mrs. Springer that the class had been working on a major review for a math test the following Monday. She had noticed Boruch's hand in the air fleetingly, but her focus was on those students who she knew had trouble with math. Because Boruch generally did very well, and he had not continued to ask for assistance, she did not realize that he was still struggling with his examples.

After expressing her deep regret for the unintentional pain that she had caused Boruch. Mrs. Rosen asked Mrs. Springer to please do the following:

• Be sure to tell Boruch that she is very sorry that he felt hurt.

• Tell Boruch that she commends him for not disrupting the class when he felt that he was being ignored. At the same time, explain to him that in the future, if he still has a question after class, he should come over to her and tell her about it.

• Last but definitely not least—Mrs. Rosen asked Mrs. Springer to please bring Boruch to her house on Sunday afternoon for fifteen minutes, so that she could review with him the points that he was unclear about.

Mrs. Springer was more than happy to take Mrs. Rosen up on her special offer. Sunday afternoon a very joyful Boruch knocked on his teacher's door. Twenty minutes later, he not only knew his math, but he felt like a million dollars. Boruch scored a 103 on his math test the following day, and his self-esteem soared to new heights.

I think we'd all agree that the highest mark of all goes to the teacher who took a negative situation and turned it into a most positive experience in true education for all those involved.

Shaping Together

Parent-teacher communication

▶ For this remarkable experience to take place it required a caring parent who was sensitive to the teacher and a caring teacher who was sensitive to the student.

▶ Even a good student should not be taken for granted and can benefit from encouragement. ▣

All names have been changed.

HASHKAFAH, HALACHAH, AND **INSPIRATIC**

Dear Michal
From a Parent's Diary

Retold by Chany Feldbrand

RUMMAGING IN MY SECOND-GRADER'S briefcase is not one of my favorite pastimes. I never know when my unsuspecting hand will dig into something old and soft (a forgotten peach perhaps?) or something dry and crumbly (a mass of crumpled potato chip crumbs mixed with pencil shavings?). But it's a task that must be done from time to time, and if I don't, I can be sure no one will. So that's how I found myself one day, cleaning out Michal's backpack, praying that no unwelcome surprises come my way.

Well, guess what. A surprise did, but it was most welcome.

It was a dog-eared, coverless, frayed spiral notebook that, six months into the school year, I still hadn't seen. Curiosity overtook me and I opened it up.

It was full of letters. Letters from seven-year-old Michal to her teacher, Mrs. Milstein, and letters from Mrs. Milstein to Michal. Intrigued by this brilliant way of getting the students to hone their writing skills while building a personal relationship with each child, I began to read.

In the childish scrawl so dear to me, I read of my daughter's love and adoration of her teacher, of her hopes and ambitions for the

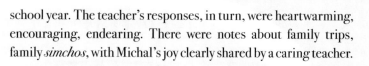

school year. The teacher's responses, in turn, were heartwarming, encouraging, endearing. There were notes about family trips, family *simchos*, with Michal's joy clearly shared by a caring teacher.

> **This short note encapsulated the ultimate in a teacher/ student relationship.**

And then I turned the page. There on the lined page, in large, juvenile print, was a note from Michal expressing her excitement upon her teacher's return from a trip to Eretz Yisrael. Indeed, I now recalled that Mrs. Milstein had been away over Succos and how sorely Miriam had missed her. I read the words, fascinated, and this short little private exchange encapsulated for me the ultimate in a teacher/student relationship:

Dear Mrs. Milstein,
I am so happy that you are back in school.

Love,
Michal

Dear Michal,
I am also so happy to see you.
You know, Michal, when I was at the Kosel, I davened for you. I davened that you should grow up to be a true bas Yisrael and that you should bring a lot of nachas to your Tatty and your Mommy and also to Hashem.

Love,
Mrs. Milstein

HASHKAFAH, HALACHAH, AND **INSPIRATIO**

As I blinked away the moisture in my eyes, I prayed from the depths of my heart that those *tefillos* be answered in the fullest sense.

With appreciation to Mrs. Milstein, who surely wouldn't want her real name in print, and who has done so much for her precious students. May she be blessed with continued siyata d'Shmaya. ▣

Lost Opportunity

By Rachel Grossberg

CHAYA, A LONELY NINTH-GRADER from a troubled home, stood in the still unfamiliar hallway of her new high school. Somewhat overwhelmed by her new surroundings, she wondered how she would manage to adjust ... Chaya's thoughts were interrupted by the kind greeting of the school's guidance counselor. Putting an arm around Chaya's shoulder, the guidance counselor asked her how things were going. Then, pulling her aside, she said, "I know you're going through a hard time. If you ever need someone to speak to, I'm available ... any time."

For one brief moment Chaya felt tremendous comfort and relief. Somebody cared about her; somebody was there for her; she didn't have to deal with it all on her own. But this new surge of hope was dashed only an instant later as Racheli tapped her on the shoulder and said with a grin, "I see the school 'psychologist' got a hold of you ... Better watch out!"

Chaya's stomach tightened; she realized that being caught talking to the guidance counselor would label her a "case." She never did talk to the counselor again.

How many Chayas are in desperate need of help today, but are too afraid of being labeled a "problem" by their classmates? Many of these girls are shortchanging themselves by not having the opportunity to talk through problems or decisions with a mentor.

All teachers occasionally find themselves in a situation similar to that of Chaya's guidance counselor—wanting to extend a hand to a student that needs a little extra. It is important to be careful to do this *chesed* with wisdom, being careful not to be seen with the student in a way that will make her peers talk.

Below are some ideas and advice from schools that we have spoken to.

Shaping with Discretion

► Be careful not to be seen speaking to a student in public when it could be misunderstood.

► If the guidance counselor is involved in other school-wide activities, it is a lot easier for him or her to speak to a student without arousing the unwanted attention of classmates.

► A teacher who is involved with several students who need help should make it a point to be seen in conversation with well-adjusted students, too.

► One school has an envelope in an inconspicuous location for students to leave a confidential message for the guidance counselor. (Keeping the envelope with a secretary may be a good idea.)

► Another school has evening hours during which students can call their guidance counselor.

► The location of the guidance counselor's room is key to the privacy of those who need his or her help. ▣

Someone Knew...

Retold by Chany Feldbrand

IF YOU'D LOOK AT HER, YOU'D NEVER KNOW.

You'd never know that this regular tenth-grader was dealing with anything but what regular tenth-graders deal with.

You'd never know that this tenth-grader's mother was just diagnosed with a dreaded illness and she was petrified beyond words.

You'd never know that as the oldest child, she was running the home, caring for six younger siblings, all at the tender age of 15.

You'd never know that between cooking, cleaning, feeding, homework, organizing and juggling, this regular tenth-grader was being crushed under a burden far too great for her frail shoulders.

You'd never know because that tenth-grader—who was me—came to school each morning with a big smile pasted on her face as if everything was just fine. She sat in her seat, dutifully took notes, socialized at recess time and then went merrily on her way.

But, somewhere deep inside, I was crying out. I wished someone would notice. I wished someone would say *something*, anything, to relieve the constriction in my throat and the ache in my heart. I wished someone would just tell me that she knew and how sorry she was that it was so hard on me. As I'd listen to the frivolous banter of my classmates I'd think to myself in frustration, "How

HASHKAFAH, HALACHAH, AND **INSPIRATIO**

can you be so busy with such pettiness when there are issues of life and death going on?"

I was an emotional paradox. On one hand, I took a sort of pleasure in keeping my "secret" and seeing how well I could cope on my own. Yet, I wanted—*and desperately needed*—the empathy and warmth of another human being to soothe the pain and give me the strength to forge on. So did I want acknowledgement and support or not? I didn't even know myself what I needed.

But someone did. My principal. A wise woman indeed.

"Sarah*," my teacher called on me one day, "I left my plan book in the teacher's lounge. Would you mind getting it for me?"

Dutifully, I made my way there. In response to my knock, who should open the door but Mrs. Heller, the principal, herself. (I later learned that she had told my teacher to leave something in the lounge as a pretext to send me there.)

"Why, Sarah," exclaimed Mrs. Heller. "It's so good to see you! I've actually been meaning to look you up to see how you are and how things are going." Mrs. Heller looked at me meaningfully. My gaze met hers. And what I saw in her eyes can only be described as... as nothing other than undiluted *nesi'as ol*.

That was it. That compassionate gaze and my thin veneer began to crack. Against my will, hot tears began stinging my eyes. I struggled to regain composure, to give Mrs. Heller a semblance of an answer, but it was no use. As I stood there, for an interminable moment, washed against the shore of utter aloneness, I suddenly felt the human touch of caring the frail child inside me had so craved. Mrs. Heller stretched out her hand and reached for mine. Without a word, she put her arm over my shoulder and gave me a

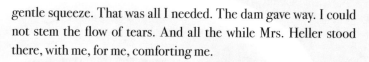

gentle squeeze. That was all I needed. The dam gave way. I could not stem the flow of tears. And all the while Mrs. Heller stood there, with me, for me, comforting me.

Honestly, I do not remember even one word of what she said. I do not recall the whisper of comfort, the soft voice of empathy on that gray morning when my mother lay in her hospital bed and I felt my world collapsing. But it does not matter. Because I recall what really mattered.

What really mattered was what Mrs. Heller's gesture meant to me.

It meant I wasn't alone. It meant that someone realized. That someone cared. It meant that I would once again muster the courage and the fortitude to sail on no matter how stormy the seas would turn.

> **Teaching means reaching.**

Someone knew that there was one girl, one out of hundreds in the school, who needed a show of empathy and support. *Someone knew* that being a teacher did not just mean teaching; the material, the curriculum, the student's mind.

Teaching means reaching; the heart, the core, the *neshamah*.

Mrs. Heller's lifeboat certainly reached mine.

Though years have passed, Mrs. Heller and I have maintained a special relationship. I have benefited greatly from her wise counsel and warm guidance. It all began with a seemingly small gesture, but one that left a lasting impression on my life. For that, I am eternally grateful. ⊞

*All names have been changed.

HASHKAFAH, HALACHAH, AND **INSPIRATIO**

A Teacher's Devotion

Retold by Malkie Gendelman

IT WAS WELL KNOWN AMONG THE STAFF at Bais Miriam* that Reva Feingold had been accepted as a student only through many pulled strings. Having left her old school after seventh grade for personal reasons, Reva was anything but the kind of girl that Bais Miriam wished to attract. She was a difficult girl with a negative attitude towards life in general, and especially towards school. Added to that, she had a rebellious nature that forebode trouble on her teen horizon.

And yet, a dedicated community member to whom the school was indebted had gotten on Reva's case and had begged the administrators to give her a chance and accept her into their school. Left with little choice, the school reluctantly consented.

True to her nature, Reva showed up on the first day of school with a chip the size of a boulder on her shoulder. She spent the entire day with her head down on her desk, refusing to cooperate with anything the teacher said.

Day after day, week after week, and month after month, this behavior continued. Reva did not participate, do her home-

> Reva showed up on the first day of school with a chip the size of a boulder on her shoulder.

work, or fill in any answers on her tests. All of the teacher's efforts to reach out and draw her into the class were soundly rebuffed. It was as if the eighth grade at Bais Miriam had twenty-one students, instead of twenty-two.

And then, one Friday, already towards the end of January, the miracle occurred. Mrs. Brander, the eighth-grade teacher, stopped by the principal's office after school, her face shining like the sun. Wordlessly, she handed the principal a note. It read:

Dear Mrs. Brander,

I want to thank you for everything you do to try to help me out. Even when I pretended to ignore all the efforts you put into teaching me, you still never gave up. It's because of this that I've decided that I want to turn over a new leaf. If you haven't given up on me by now, I won't give up on myself. I want to behave like a regular student. I'm going to go out and buy all the school supplies which I never got, and I'm really going to try to pay attention in class and do well.

A million thanks for keeping the door open for me.

Love,
Reva Feingold

The principal looked up at Mrs. Brander, her eyes wet with tears. Turning back to the note, she noticed, for the first time, a small line scrawled as a P.S. on the bottom:

P.S. Mrs. Brander, thank you for calling me **every single night since the beginning of the year**, to review with me what we learned in class that day. 🔲

*All names have been changed.

A Show of Empathy

Retold by Riva Pomerantz

FOR A MONTH NOW, "Production" had become a household word for every family with girls in Bnos Chaya Academy*, anticipating the day when they would find out what this year's production would be. The Steinbergs were no different.

The door burst open, and Mrs. Steinberg ran out of the kitchen to greet an excited Shevy. After all the wait, the school-wide Production Meeting had taken place today.

"How did it go?" she asked.

Shevy swung herself onto a kitchen chair.

"You're not going to believe the day we had today," she exclaimed.

"When we got to school, they told us to meet in the auditorium after *davening*. We all crowded in, and they showed us a very interesting video on the bombing of Pearl Harbor. Then they announced that buses were waiting outside to take us somewhere.

"It turns out that downtown, there was a huge exhibit on Pearl Harbor, and that's where we visited. It was very well-done. We were each given 'passports' with names of actual soldiers who had been serving on the base at the time of the attack. They took us onto a ship and explained to us all the historic events and showed

us photographs, video clips, and memorabilia from Pearl Harbor.

"At the end of the tour, our teachers gave out snacks and led discussions with us about the frailty of life and how, without warning, the whole world can suddenly change. It really made us think and appreciate the good times.

"Then, before we got on the bus, the principal, Mrs. Freilich, gathered us together to talk about Production."

"What a great break-out!" Sara interrupted. "I'll bet you all weren't expecting it would be so exciting. Nu—what play are you doing this year?"

A strange look crossed Shevy's face.

"Uh, Ma, actually, Mrs. Freilich announced that we're not having a Production at all this year."

Sara Steinberg's heart sank. Could it be? After all the excitement, the discussions, and the anticipation? The girls must be devastated!

"What she said was that she and Mrs. Lehrer, who usually write the play together, were overwhelmed with other jobs and personal obligations and just couldn't pull it off this year. Mrs. Freilich stressed to us that she knew we were probably very disappointed, but that she wanted us to brainstorm about other fun things we could do this semester to make it the best winter ever. After that, the teachers asked us to express our feelings about the Production being

> **We could tell that they were very serious about wanting us to have a great time.**

canceled. Everyone had a chance to really talk about how frustrated and disappointed they were, and the teachers and Mrs. Freilich listened very sympathetically.

"They set a date for next week to have a real brainstorming session to plan activities, and we could tell that they were very serious about wanting us to have a great time."

Sara looked at her daughter. Shevy was composed, even cheerful.

"Wow," she said gently. "I'm sure this news must have caught you by surprise."

"Y'know, Ma," Shevy said thoughtfully. "I think it was the fact that we could really see how much they cared about our feelings that made a difference. Some schools would have just made the announcement and that would be the end. In this case, though, we really felt understood and cared for."

Sara hugged her daughter and went to make supper. Top priority that evening was definitely a gratitude phone call to that sensitive principal, Mrs. Freilich. ▣

*All names have been changed.

The "Forever" Smile

By Lauren Roth

The following story, submitted by a former high school teacher, is a
beautiful illustration of the tremendous impact a teacher can have
on a student. Sometimes it just takes a moment.

I WAS A HIGH SCHOOL TEACHER, and girls would often come
to me privately to discuss personal problems and issues. One
day, a ninth-grader (not one of my students) came to me to discuss
her difficulties acclimating to the new school. Not all of her friends
from elementary school had come to this particular high school.
She missed some of her old friends who had gone to other schools,
and she was finding it difficult to navigate the new constellation of
peers in her class. We discussed strategies for her to build
relationships with her classmates in this new environment.

Three months later, this ninth-grader asked to speak to me
privately again. I was stunned by what she had to say. "Mrs. Roth,
do you remember that time, about four weeks ago, when you
passed me in your car when I was on my way to school and you gave
me that huge smile?" Completely unaware of having done that, I
answered slowly, "N-no. I have no recollection of doing that." I
honestly didn't remember having smiled to her at all; it must have
been just a regular, cheerful smile of greeting, given in passing.
"Mrs. Roth," she continued, "that smile changed my entire life!

You know that I was having difficulties getting along with the people in my class. And I was really down about it. Because I was down, I guess that perpetuated a negative cycle: I was down, so the girls really didn't feel like talking to me. And their not talking to me made me more morose. I felt lonely and unliked. But that morning, I was walking to school, and you gave me this huge smile. It made me feel so good that when I got to school, I was in a really great mood. I was happy, and cheerful, and I went over to some of the girls and started talking to them, and they responded by talking to me, and then they started calling me at night, and I called them, and this amazing, positive cycle of cheerfulness and friendship developed, and now I am so happy. And it's all because of that one smile you gave me. Thank you, thank you, thank you!"

Her story was incredible to me; one smile, that I hadn't even remembered giving, had actually changed someone's life. After that, I have always made sure to smile and interact positively with everyone I meet, even if it is "only" in passing. You never know which smile will linger in somebody's heart—forever. ▣

A smile is a mitzvah that costs nothing
but is **priceless**.
It **enriches** those who see it,
and those who **give** it.

It takes but a moment;
it lasts **forever**.

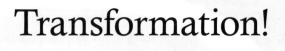
Transformation!

Retold by Chany Feldbrand

I T WAS REPORT CARD TIME. My eye carefully followed the lines on the rating sheets as I meticulously recorded my students' grades. Rochel; she had made marked improvement in test scores, good. Dina; she had shown extra effort which earned her a significantly higher mark. Tzipora, hmm. I chewed my pencil top thoughtfully. She had been out quite a bit during performance practice and had therefore slipped markedly in her grades. After a while, my head began to swim a bit as student after student marched before my mind's eye, up for complete scrutiny, as I weighed and debated how best to convey who she is and what she has accomplished in a curt, impersonal numeral.

And then came Liba's turn.

Liba. Instinctively, my eye traced back a column to her mark for first term. Wow. I would never have dreamed that something so intangible, so imperceptible, could make such a dramatic difference. My mind wandered back to the early months of the year.

Liba. I didn't know *what* to do with her. I mean, this was twelfth grade, so why were we dealing with this? Weren't we supposed to be past the age of mumbled comments, rolled eyes, defiant shrugs of the shoulder and most of all, "*the attitude*"? I did not know what was goading her to act this way, but I firmly decided that *it could not go on*. She somehow managed to spoil the pleasure I had always found in teaching and was negatively affecting the entire class.

And it was quite difficult to discuss this with Liba. Ask any teacher of teenagers: How does one explain negativity, attitude and undercurrents to a child who will assume a virtuous air and vehemently proclaim innocence while insisting, "Tell me exactly what I'm doing wrong."

No, I could not say exactly what she was doing wrong, but *something* was very wrong. It was time to speak to the principal.

It turned out that I had only seen part of the picture. There was something major churning beneath the surface, and once I was enlightened as to what emotional baggage this child lugged to school each day, my whole perception of her changed.

> **The student didn't change, the teacher didn't change, the behavior hadn't yet changed, but something did.**

In my close to two decades in the classroom, never had I had such an experience. The student didn't change, the teacher didn't change, the behavior hadn't yet changed, but something did.

And that something was my heart.

I recall reading an anecdote about Rav Yaakov Yosef Herman, of "All for the Boss" fame. There was a particularly difficult *meshulach* who frequented the Herman home, yet Reb Yaakov Yosef treated him with utmost understanding and respect. "When you have *rachmanus*, you don't need *savlanus*," was his explanation.

After hearing about that one missing link in the picture, my heart filled with overwhelming *rachmanus* and empathy for this child

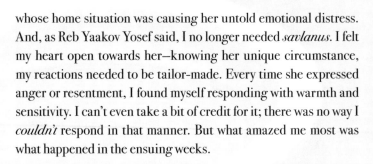

whose home situation was causing her untold emotional distress. And, as Reb Yaakov Yosef said, I no longer needed *savlanus*. I felt my heart open towards her—knowing her unique circumstance, my reactions needed to be tailor-made. Every time she expressed anger or resentment, I found myself responding with warmth and sensitivity. I can't even take a bit of credit for it; there was no way I *couldn't* respond in that manner. But what amazed me most was what happened in the ensuing weeks.

Shlomo Hamelech expressed it best (*Mishlei* 27:19): "*Kamayim hapanim l'panim...*" Liba must've subconsciously sensed that something in my understanding of her had changed, and she responded in kind. Over the next few months, without any overt overtures, Liba and I developed a positive, even close, relationship. She began coming over to me after class, with an endearing smile on the face that had previously sported a perpetual scowl. She'd come and ask me to explain a concept we learned or a *hashkafah* topic we discussed. She'd come ask me for advice on various issues or just for a friendly chat. Never once did she mention anything of a personal nature or give any clue to her difficult situation, but I could tell that she felt secure and comfortable in our relationship. In addition, her marks soared, as she endeavored to live up to the confidence I subtly instilled in her.

And now, with rating sheets in hand, I had to encapsulate all this into a simple, numerical grade? I had to put what I can only call a triumph of the heart, the transformation of a child *and her teacher*, into a measly number? No, there was no way I could do that.

So I sat down and wrote this article. ▣

HASHKAFAH, HALACHAH, AND **INSPIRATIO**

Hearty Appetite

Retold by Yaffa Penina

BREINDY* WAS BUSY PREPARING for her upcoming wedding. The shopping, the fittings, the apartment, *kallah* classes, her job, invitations, her *chasan*... There was so much to do; the days seemed to run away from her. Yet she made time to call Mrs. Gross, even calling several times until she got through; she just had to thank her and personally invite her to the wedding.

Mrs. Gross was pleasantly surprised when she got the call. Breindy Deutsch had graduated from Bnos Brachah elementary school 7 years before, and Mrs. Gross remembered hearing that Breindy was a *kallah*. After exchanging pleasantries and wishing Breindy a hearty *mazel tov*, Mrs Gross wished her well on her upcoming wedding. Breindy thanked her for her good wishes and then said that she had something else to thank her for.

"Mrs. Gross, I doubt that you remember this, but to me it meant so much that I had to call you now to share the memory and ask you personally to attend my wedding." Now Mrs. Gross was all ears. What could she possibly be going on about?

"I must have been in second grade at the time. My teacher caught me eating in class one morning and sent me out to YOU! I was shaking and shivering, terrified of what you, the principal, would do to me. I stood in front of your door and knocked hesitantly. While you said 'come in' softly, to me your voice sounded like a cannon's roar. I tiptoed in as slowly as I could; wanting nothing

> To me you seemed larger than life, and my imagination began to run wild, thinking of what you might do to me.

more than to vanish into thin air. But, alas, there I was face to face with you, THE PRINCIPAL. To me you seemed larger than life, and my imagination began to run wild, thinking of what you might do to me.

"It took me a while to find my voice and answer when you asked why I had been sent to the office. I bit my trembling lip to stop the tears that threatened to cascade down my cheeks at any moment, looked down at the floor, and answered in a hesitant whisper, 'I—w-a-s—e-a-t-i-n-g—i-n —c-l-a-s-s.'

"What you did next warms my heart until this day. You came around to me, touched me gently on my shoulder and quietly asked, 'Are you hungry? Perhaps you didn't finish your breakfast and ran out to the bus?'

"You continued to talk softly even as I stared at the floor. 'Here, come have a seat, I'll get you some cereal and milk.' And that's exactly what you did. By the time I left your office a few minutes later, my stomach was full and my heart was fuller.

"I have cherished that feeling of love and concern that you showed me that day and I always will. Thank you!"

Mrs. Gross hung up the phone with a smile on her lips and a heart overflowing with satisfaction. She could not help but marvel at how a seemingly small, long-ago incident in her busy day as a principal had continued to warm the heart of her student as she grew from a shy second grader into the lovely kallah she was today. ▣

*Names have been changed.

HASHKAFAH, HALACHAH, AND **INSPIRATIO**

The "Sole" of Matter

Retold by Chany Feldbrand

SOME THINGS NEVER CHANGE. As a school secretary for over 20 years, I can attest to that with a fair amount of certainty. And the thing that changes the least is the relationship between high school students and the ubiquitous school rules. Especially rules having to do with uniform and dress code. I am sure this is not unique to our school, a typical in-town Bais Yaakov, nor to our students. What I feel is unique to our school is the exceptional principal we are blessed with.

And the story with Rina* is just one case in point.

It all started as a typical boring day in December, with all the regular things to do; photocopying to take care of, checks to mail out and transcripts to type up. As I busily went about my work, I sensed a stir in the teachers' lounge adjacent to my office. It was not hard to catch on to what was going on.

> We've seen infractions in this area before, but this... This is completely unacceptable!

"We've seen infractions in this area before," Mrs. Golding, the *mechaneches* who was responsible for enforcing the student dress code, was fuming. "But this... This is completely unacceptable!"

"Unacceptable indeed," agreed the teacher who had spotted the offending party. "I've seen borderline colors and borderline tastes. We've even had one or two girls we had to tell not to wear such shoes again. But this?"

"She should be sent home immediately, and told not to return until she gets a pair of normal, acceptable shoes," Mrs. Golding stated emphatically. "I've had enough. It's not the first time she's tried to bend the rules and get around them. We have to teach her a lesson once and for all."

At this declaration, silence reigned in the room. I found myself also holding my breath, wondering what the verdict would be this time. Now that I had gotten a glimpse of Rina standing nervously near the office, I was inclined to agree with the teachers' assessment. The type of footwear she had come to school in was indeed completely unacceptable, never before seen in our school. And the insolence her face purportedly expressed was no simple manner, either. I continued my filing quietly, waiting to hear what the outcome would be.

> **Wasn't this a "cut and dried" case of breaking a school rule, and breaking it in a most unacceptable manner?**

Having said her piece, Mrs. Golding's eyes then turned questioningly towards Mrs. Bergman, our principal, who had been standing quietly by, listening to the exchange. It was clear that she was seriously thinking the matter through, with a calmness and clarity that was so characteristic of her. Then she spoke. "I'd like to go have a word with Rina first," she

stated softly. "I want to hear what she has to say."

Mrs. Golding's eyes expressed surprise. Wasn't this a "cut and dried" case of breaking a school rule, and breaking it in a most unacceptable manner? How could Rina possibly justify herself? But the principal's word is final, and Mrs. Golding knew from experience to accept the wisdom and intuition that is Mrs. Bergman's hallmark.

Mrs. Golding and I watched as Mrs. Bergman approached Rina. Although she was out of earshot, we were able to feel the vibes of Mrs. Bergman's warmth and acceptance as they enveloped Rina and we then observed as Rina slowly shed her façade and responded to Mrs. Bergman's queries. After a few moments, Mrs. Bergman returned to her office.

Without a word, she reached for her pocketbook. She withdrew her personal credit card and, clutching it firmly, approached me. Handing me the card, she said quietly, "If you don't mind, can you please drive Rina to Shoe Empire? I would like her to select a pair of shoes, and please charge it to my credit card. I will cover for you here in the office."

As I would learn later, Mrs. Bergman, with her caring interest and desire to look just a bit deeper and see the whole situation, had won Rina's confidence. It seems her family had come upon hard times financially, and when Rina's shoes tore, she had no heart to ask her parents to get her new ones. Left with no choice, she pulled out an old pair of footwear she normally just wore lounging around the house, and with a heavy heart donned it, promising herself that she would try to land some babysitting jobs in the next few days to earn money to buy herself a decent pair. It was Mrs. Bergman who had the sensitivity and intuition to realize that there

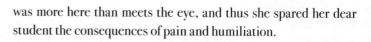

was more here than meets the eye, and thus she spared her dear student the consequences of pain and humiliation.

It took a credit card and a new pair of shoes to accomplish that.

And Mrs. Bergman gets the sole credit.

All names have been changed.

Shaping the Whole Picture

▶ The principal did not just assume guilt even though the student had a negative track record.

▶ Would the teenager have disclosed the private information about her home situation to the teacher as she did to this principal? Why or why not? ⊞

When you try to
influence someone,
it is **important**
that the **message**
he hears is that you
love him and **care**
about his welfare.

—Vilna Gaon

HASHKAFAH, HALACHAH, AND **INSPIRATIO**

Sweet Rebuke

Retold by Bassie Gugenheim

CHAIM KNEW HE HAD PUSHED THINGS TOO FAR.

For a short, suspense-filled moment, the ninth-graders waited, wondering how Rebbi would respond to Chaim's latest offense. But their fear was unwarranted. In a firm, quiet voice, Rabbi G. let Chaim know that his behavior would not be tolerated, and he would have to sit detention the next day.

The dreaded hour arrived, and Chaim watched as his classmates rushed out the door to catch the waiting buses. Slowly, he walked to the classroom assigned for detention. The secretary handed him an assignment prepared by his rebbi, and he sat down resignedly to begin his work. He glanced at the clock. Only ten minutes had gone by. How would he get though the rest of this period? What was the point anyway? Who needed school? Who needed a rebbi? Although he knew he had been wrong, Chaim was beginning to feel very resentful.

A movement by the door caught his eye, and Chaim looked up just in time to see his rebbi walking in the door.

> What was the point anyway? Who needed school? Who needed a rebbi?

"Here Chaim," his rebbi said handing him a paper bag, "I brought something for you."

Curiously, Chaim peered inside. Seeing a chocolate danish and a can of Coke, he looked up questioningly at his rebbi.

"I knew you would be here late, and I thought you might get hungry," his rebbi said simply.

The anger that had been simmering inside melted away. His rebbi cared about him. He was a person who mattered. If someone could treat him like that, maybe it was worth putting in effort after all. Tomorrow, he would behave a whole lot better. He wanted to make his rebbi proud.

The Wise Answer

A TRUE LEADER WILL FIND WAYS *to uplift a student even when rebuking him. The following anecdote is a beautiful example:*

Rav Nosson Tzvi of Slobodka once summoned a student who was chronically late for prayers.

"Rebbi," the student protested, "human beings aren't angels."

"Indeed they are not," said Rav Nosson Tzvi, "they are greater than angels." ▣

Adapted from "A Touch of Wisdom, a Touch of Wit" with permission from Mesorah Publications, Ltd.

HASHKAFAH, HALACHAH, AND **INSPIRATIC**

A Bull in a China Shop

Retold by Riva Pomerantz

HESHY* WAS ONE OF THOSE KIDS whose very name made rebbeim sigh. His energy level, personality, and character all pointed to his highly visible ADHD, and often he was just too much to deal with. Rebbi after rebbi had struggled to give Heshy what he needed, and many were moderately successful. But time and time again, Heshy's unrestrained behavior and inability to concentrate were serious detriments for him.

It was with great excitement that Rabbi Chinn announced a change in plans. *Minchah*, which was usually held in the school auditorium, would be *davened*, instead, at a nearby office building. A wealthy businessman—a supporter of the yeshivah—had requested that the boys form a *minyan* in his office that day.

An excited group of eighth-graders filed into Mr. Spiegel's plush office, and Heshy's eyes widened as he surveyed his surroundings. Expensive oriental rugs, dazzling artwork, and exotic knick-knacks filled the large room. Before he knew it, Heshy's senses were bombarded by the stimulation

> There's a world of difference between damage control and creative solutions that let the student shine.

they experienced. His ever-active hands reached out to touch an ornate crystal vase, to finger a mosaic paperweight. His energetic feet led him over to a far wall to examine a small lemon tree.

In the midst of Heshy's exuberant tour, his rebbi suddenly noticed his absence from the group. With warning bells clanging in his head, Rabbi Chinn searched frantically for Heshy, and found him testing out a delicate, velvet-covered ottoman.

"Heshy!" he whispered frantically. "Get over here!"

All the yeshivah needed was for one of their students to break an expensive piece in this luxurious office!

Heshy complied and tried to restrain his hands, but very soon he was picking up an ivory-handled letter opener. Rabbi Chinn motioned frantically to him, but it was quickly becoming clear that Heshy was a danger—the classical bull in the china shop.

Suddenly, Heshy felt a strong hand on his shoulder. He spun around to find the *menahel*, Rabbi Hershkowitz, smiling down at him. For a moment, there was silence in the room, as the boys, the rebbi, and Heshy himself, wondered what would transpire.

"Heshy," Rabbi Hershkowitz said warmly. "Come here, please. I'd like you to lead the *davening*."

A dazed Heshy began reciting *Ashrei*. And his hands, clutching a *siddur*, were still and at peace. ⊞

*all names have been changed

The Write Answer

Retold by Riva Pomerantz

RABBI PINCHAS FRIEDMAN* had walked into the *beis midrash* beaming; after ten minutes of learning time, his smile was already faltering.

"David is a lively boy with tons of energy and a real zest for life. You will enjoy him immensely this summer!" his parents had written on his application, with perhaps just a touch of wry humor. Now, Rabbi Friedman mused grimly, he had come to the startling conclusion that their cheery note was an absolute understatement. In the space of ten, long minutes, David had succeeded in upending an entire bookshelf, sending *sefarim* and *siddurim* flying, and tangling himself in knots as he literally bounced off the walls.

The morning learning, usually a delight, dragged on as the boys tried to ignore their fellow camper's antics.

"David, why don't you come sit next to Aron, over there?" Rabbi Friedman gently suggested. The seat change, though well-intended, was an immediate disaster, when David accidentally knocked off Aron's glasses in his frenzied enthusiasm to kill a mosquito on the ceiling while balancing on a rickety chair.

Amid much laughter and shouting, Rabbi Friedman gritted his teeth and did his best to continue. Something had to happen, and it had to happen fast.

"David?"

The boys were nonchalantly filing out of the beis midrash, heading off to their first sports activity. Upon hearing his name, David, deep in animated conversation with Baruch Klein, popped up his head eagerly.

"Yes, Rebbi?"

Rabbi Friedman suppressed a sigh. as he waited for David to come closer to his desk and for the other boy to leave.

"David," he said, forcing himself to keep his voice steady, even kind. "You had a very difficult time today, during learning. We've got to do something about it."

David nodded guiltily as his face fell. This was obviously not the first time he was having this sort of conversation.

"Well," said Rabbi Friedman, "what do you suggest we do about it?"

David blinked rapidly and looked up at the rebbi with wide-open eyes and a smile erased the furrow on his brow. He had been expecting a hail of angry words; instead, he was being asked to come up with a solution.

"Y'know what, Rebbi?" David said with excitement. "I have an idea! Tomorrow, I'll bring a notebook to *shiur* and I'll take really good notes. That will calm me down."

Rabbi Friedman had his misgivings, of course, especially given the behavior he'd witnessed all morning. But the next day, bright and early, there was David, a loose-leaf clutched under his arm. For two hours, he fastidiously took notes on every word the rebbi

uttered. To his shock and amazement, Rabbi Friedman even saw David adding *chiddushim* of his own, based on what was taught during the learning session. He still could not keep the place in the *Gemara*, but he was clearly learning in every sense of the word.

As the boys ran out of the *beis midrash*, ready for swimming, Rabbi Friedman gave a beaming smile.

"Wonderful!" he enthused. "I'm so impressed!"

"Aww, it's nothing," David said, with an enormous grin of his own. "Taking notes is great. I love writing!" He paused and lowered his eyes. "Actually, I've never before had a rebbi ask me to come up with a solution to my wild behavior. They usually just yell at me," he said quietly.

David Silverman left Camp Achdus that year with plenty of memories, an award for Liveliest Camper, and a loose-leaf full of notes and *chiddushei Torah*. Oh—and a lifetime lesson about the impact one rebbi can make on a *talmid*...when he allows the *talmid* to be part of the solution. ▣

Names and identifying details have been changed.

The Keys to Success

Retold by Riva Pomerantz

THE CHEERY CAMP BANNER WAVED in the warm breeze, ushering in a long-awaited summer season of promise. Sima Goldstein* beamed at her grandson.

"Excited, Moish?" she asked the exuberant eleven-year-old who nodded emphatically. Beneath the encouraging smile, though, Sima was worried. When her daughter had suggested that Moishie come to visit for the summer, she knew exactly what she was in for. Moishie was a wonderful child—But! Known as an absolute terror, Moishie Feuer inspired fear in the hearts of rebbeim and counselors in the greater Brooklyn area, a fact which made Sima cringe as a tall gangly counselor approached.

"Hi, Moishie! I'm Yisroel, your counselor. Come with me and I'll introduce you to your bunk."

Moishie winked at his grandmother and followed obediently.

Unfortunately, the obedience wore away much too quickly, and it wasn't long before the phone call came.

"Uh, Mrs. Goldstein?" the camp director was uncomfortable. "It's just really not working out for Moishie at camp this year. We're going to switch him into another bunk, but after that..." His voice trailed off with an implication that needed no verbalization.

Miracles do happen, Sima reflected days later. Nearly a week had gone by and the director had still not called. Even better, Moishie couldn't wait to get to camp each morning, and he raved about his new counselor, Nussie Hirsch.

"Nussie says that I might be Best Camper," he bragged one day. Despite her inherent "*nachas* instinct," Sima couldn't believe her ears! Weeks passed with not a single complaint about her precious "terror." It was astounding—a child who had been labeled "impossible" by teachers, principals, and Pirchei leaders now ate out of the hand of "his" cherished Nussie.

Sima gave careful thought to the end-of-the-summer gift she purchased for the talented counselor.

After a tearful embrace from Moishie, Sima pulled Nussie aside.

"Look," she said, "I know my grandson is difficult. But somehow you managed to control him so well. I've never seen anything like it before. What's your secret?"

Nussie looked thoughtful.

"Y'know," he said slowly, "every *neshamah* has its key that really opens it up. I guess I just tried to find the special key to reach Moishie's *neshamah*. I'm glad that it worked!"

Sima felt tears prick her eyes as she thanked Nussie. At seventeen years of age, he possessed a rare wisdom and insight that had changed their lives that summer.

*All names have been changed

Shaping with Certainty

▸ If you are certain that there is a way to open the door, you will find it.

▸ There is no room for despair if you are sure there is a solution, even if you haven't found one yet.

▸ In *chinuch* there is no one-size-fits-all, but there is a size that fits each one.

▸ The age of a "teacher"—whether young or old—is not nearly as important as his/her focus. ▣

The Sound of the Shofar

Retold by Riva Pomerantz

THERE IS A BOY IN MY YESHIVAH; a boy with special needs. You may have seen him, hobbling slowly yet determinedly with the cane he uses for his cerebral palsy, always smiling. Ari is a fighter, a true *tzaddik*, even at the tender age of fourteen.

Well, this Elul I decided to expand my students' horizons.

"Boys," I told them, "I want each and every one of you to learn to blow *shofar*."

For my special students, I constantly strive to give them a chance to shine in unique ways, and the *shofar*-blowing activity definitely fit the bill. Especially when Ari put the small shofar to his lips.

"Wow!" I enthused, along with the other boys, awed by the powerful sounds that had just emerged. There was no doubt about it: our Ari was a world-class *shofar* blower. He blushed from the lavish praise, and grinned.

A successful moment can last a lifetime.

I take my boys on various trips throughout the year. When we all piled into the car, the excitement mounted. Driving through the night hardly dampened anyone's

spirits. We sang, we schmoozed, we ate and laughed. When we arrived at our destination we quickly headed over to a local shul to daven *Shacharis*.

The *minyan* was crowded, but the boys hardly noticed. Just davening in an unfamiliar, out-of-town shul was exotic enough to inspire their *tefillos* to greater heights. After *davening*, the *gabbai* made what appeared to be his daily, weary circuit.

"*Shofar*?" he asked, proffering a small, well-worn specimen. One after another, the men shook their heads or looked away, clearly unwilling to attempt the enormous feat of making any sound come out of that meager *shofar*, let alone a *tekiah*!

Perhaps it was in jest, or maybe it was an earnest attempt to bring the *minyan* to an earlier close, but the man standing across from our exhausted group motioned in our direction. As it happened, his finger pointed at none other than...

Ari was balancing nonchalantly on his cane when the *gabbai* approached him with the *shofar*. I watched in silence as Ari's face blanched and he shook his head emphatically. This was a vast audience to a fourteen-year-old kid with a disability, and the *shofar* looked as though it would never emit even a croak.

I caught Ari's eye and gave him A Look. Ari knows that look, as do the rest of my boys. It means "Do it!" His eyes darted back and forth—to the *shofar*, to me, to the *gabbai*, whose gaze was pleading.

Ari took the *shofar*. He held it to his lips. Was it my imagination or did the entire congregation join me in holding my breath?

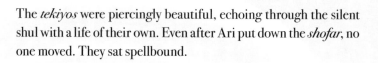

The *tekiyos* were piercingly beautiful, echoing through the silent shul with a life of their own. Even after Ari put down the *shofar*, no one moved. They sat spellbound.

———

End of the year. I took the boys on a camping trip and we sat around the fire, reminiscing.

"What was the highlight of your year?" I asked each one.

It was Ari's turn.

"Remember that time we took a road trip..." he began. "And I blew *shofar* for the whole shul?" He looked at me, and I will never forget the look in those clear, pure eyes. "That was the happiest moment of my life," he said quietly. ▣

———

"Rabbi Nuta Freund once
asked the Chazon Ish
whether one should **treat**
talmidim gently or strictly.
The Chazon Ish answered,
"One must treat them **wisely**."
—*Siach Zekeinim vol. 5*

———

HASHKAFAH, HALACHAH, AND **INSPIRATIO**

A Teacher for Life

Retold by Riva Pomerantz

I SURVEYED THE EMPTY CLASSROOM, overwhelmed with conflicting emotions of excitement and fear. Whoever would have thought that I would undergo the metamorphosis from painfully shy child to classroom teacher? Next week will mark the momentous start of my teaching career. There is a sense of triumph, and of gratitude, as I hang each colorful poster, painstakingly drawn and decorated, on the white-washed walls. In my mind's eye I see visions of the empty desks filled with eager students, imbibing my carefully prepared lessons, and my happiness knows no bounds.

I was about to hang the largest, most prominent poster of all, when Miss Weisselberg entered the room, knocking softly. In a beautiful twist of Providence, Miss Weisselberg, once my elementary school teacher, was now the Principal of the school—the person who I, now a teacher myself, would report to. She, more than anyone, was responsible for my success today, for my euphoric emotions and my fearless undertakings. My mind was suddenly flooded with memories...

Throughout early childhood, my shyness was a real impediment to me. I was so withdrawn that I couldn't even bring myself to enter the classroom each morning. I don't know how I would have ever gotten through the school year if it weren't for Miss Weisselberg, my first-grade teacher. With intuitive compassion, she immediately sized up my situation, and she drew upon all her resources to help me.

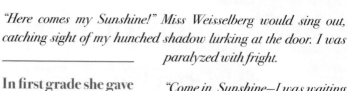

"Here comes my Sunshine!" Miss Weisselberg would sing out, catching sight of my hunched shadow lurking at the door. I was paralyzed with fright.

In first grade she gave me wings to succeed. Years later, as I spread those wings, she lovingly set my flight path straight.

"Come in, Sunshine—I was waiting for you," she would exclaim, in a voice so sweet it lifted my soul. She practically drew me into the classroom physically, each and every morning, until slowly, ever so slowly, I came out of my shell.

How things have come full circle! Here I am, a teacher myself, working for my compassionate mentor, Miss Weisselberg. Here is my chance to offer the same love and warmth to another student, just as she did to me, so many years ago.

Miss Weisselberg's gentle touch on my arm shook me out of my reverie.

"Your classroom is such a pleasure, Chaya. You students will be lucky to have you as their teacher," she said warmly, her voice reverberating with love. She pointed to the large chart I had just hung and asked about it.

It was my pride and joy. I had spent hours designing it, and it hung in the center of the room, where it was sure to be seen.

"It's my 'Honor Roll,' Miss Weisselberg," I explained proudly. "I have a whole system worked out for students who get high marks. When they get a good grade, they'll get a star on their chart, and then prizes—it's to reward the students who are at the top of the class academically."

Miss Weisselberg looked at me.

HASHKAFAH, HALACHAH, AND **INSPIRATION**

"What do you think, Chaya?" she asked softly. "Do we have to 'reward' Hashem for giving a child a good head? When we award stars only for good grades, it's like saying to Hashem, 'With this one You did good, but that one, she could have used some more brains!' Do you see, Chaya? If your chart rewarded effort, or good character, that would be another story. But so often, we get caught up in academics and fail to appreciate what is of real, lasting worth. The girl who struggles with all her might and earns an 80% on a test might be more worthy of an Honor Roll than the girl who daydreams all morning but is blessed with a quick mind and an easy 100.

"You're embarking upon a wonderful opportunity, a sacred task, Chaya. Make sure that you are guided in the right direction. I know you will succeed."

Miss Weisselberg's soft-spoken words pierced my perspective with their clarity and insight. In a blinding flash, I realized what she was teaching me. In *chinuch*, we often get caught up in intellectual stimulation and good grades alone, but in truth, what's of unparalleled importance is how our students use their abilities to work on themselves and grow—and that surely deserves gold stars.

Miss Weisselberg waited patiently until I had taken down the "Honor Roll." I would replace it with another chart, one that rewarded students for what really counted. The wonderful teacher who had brought me out of my cocoon of shyness would now help me spread my own wings as a teacher, committed to the principles of true, effective *chinuch*. ▣

In an illuminating flash of hashgachah pratis, *the week that this article was first published in Impressions several years ago turned out to be Mrs. Weisselberg's yahrtzeit. She was a beloved teacher and principal, and there are thousands of women—now bubbies—whose hearts are still warmed by her love and whose lives are enriched by her guidance.*

Fixing Perfection

T HIS STORY, WHICH OFFERS MUCH FOOD for thought, was originally submitted to IMPRESSIONS by the teacher involved.

Chaya* sat in my ninth-grade Chumash class still as a stone. From the beginning, she wore a permanent frown on her face. After inquiring about her from the principal, I was told that she's just very intense.

Before the first test of the year, I found out that it went much further than that. Her mother called me to discuss the fact that Chaya felt very stressed about studying for the test. Chaya was an extreme perfectionist. Studying took her an inordinate amount of time because she felt had to get 100% on every test. I feared she was slowly working her way toward a nervous breakdown. I told her mother that Chaya should stop studying and I would test her only in small manageable amounts. (I also recommended that she get therapy—which she did.)

This went on before every test.

Chaya was absent for the last test. Her mother called me that night and I realized that even with the therapy, nothing had really changed. I felt it was time for me to speak to Chaya myself.

The next day during break, I sat Chaya down with the blank test paper in hand. I asked her if she was ready to take the test. She said she would like to review the material one more time.

I asked her, "If you would take the test now, what do you think you would get?" Barely audibly, she said, "Perhaps a 90?"

I said, "That's a good grade. Would you be happy with that?"

She stammered, "No... I would rather get a hundred."

"Why?" I asked. She could not answer.

"Chaya," I said gently "A hundred on a test is a perfect score. You can't be perfect all the time in everything. It's an unrealistic goal to expect of yourself. There is only one Being Who is Perfect all the time. Do you know Who I mean?"

"Hashem," she whispered, as the realization hit her.

I continued to impress upon her that if you expect to be perfect all the time, you are bound to be disappointed. And expending all that energy on being perfect in schoolwork leaves you no time for other important things in life, like friends, family, sleep and other hobbies.

I asked her what she thinks she deserves on this test, based on effort alone. She could not answer. I told her that from what I understand, she puts in many, many more hours of study than the average student. She did not deny this.

"I think, based on effort alone, you probably deserve a 300%. Do you agree?"

Slight smile. "Yes," she whispered.

I wrote a big 300% in red on top of the test paper. "But," I frowned, "What a shame, because I really only give 100%. That's the maximum you can get on my test. It's a pity

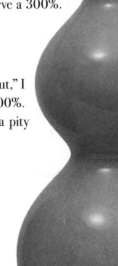

> I had no idea if she would go home and cry herself to sleep, or if she perhaps understood my message.

because you really deserve a 300%!" And I crossed out the 300, and wrote 100%.

I looked up at her. Her face remained blank, but her eyes widened.

I said, "Chaya, what matters to me is not so much the grade, but that my students learned and did the best they can." I explained to her that she was judging herself by the grades she got, while she didn't realize what a great girl she was regardless of whether she got that 100 or not.

I told her that on this test she already received a hundred, yet she could still take the test if she wished. She declined.

As she left the room, I wondered how this girl really felt inside. She was so unreadable. I had no idea if she would go home and cry herself to sleep, or if she perhaps understood my message the way it was meant.

The next day, I received my answer in the form of a bouquet of flowers and a beautiful card. The card was so touching that I know I will treasure it for a long time. (Her mother told me afterwards that Chaya came home that day a changed person.)

I would like to think that from now on, Chaya will no longer drive herself crazy over tests, and that she will lighten up and enjoy life a bit. However, it's too soon to tell. But I feel that Hashem gave me the *siyata d'Shmaya* to reach this girl in a wonderful way, and hopefully, the impact will last. ▣

*Names have been changed.

The Sixth Sense
From a Parent's Diary

Retold by Chany Feldbrand

IT WAS WINTER. The fall jackets had all been put into hibernation and the hats, mittens and scarves came out of storage. The kids learned to leave an extra five minutes for "bundling up" and returned home with reddened cheeks and stiff fingers.

It was winter. Besides for all the extra outdoor gear, I geared myself up for the other side effects of the season; colds, flu, chapped hands and stuffed noses. Of course, like all good mothers I knew that I had to stock up on vitamins, Kleenex tissues and hand cream. I knew everything that was *supposed* to get done and I seemed to manage most of them quite well. Sometimes though, my "To Do" list had the same small errand or two that just didn't get seen to.

Like little Dina's chapped lips. Every morning, she would come to me with a crunched, spotted tissue in her hand to show me "how much it's bleeding." While comforting her, I'd make a mental note to go to the drugstore *today* and get a tube of Chapstick. But then, the day would slip through my fingers, and suddenly, there she was again, home from school, little lips cracked from the cold. Again, I'd resolve to go out and get that moisturizer, but of course half the week passed and the baby's ear infection, the urgent deadline at work, the pile of unpaid bills... found a way of interfering with Mom's best intentions.

Until...

Dina came home that Wednesday with stars in her eyes. Quivering with excitement, she could barely wriggle herself out of her coat. "Mommy," she panted, with flushed cheeks (and cracked lips, I noticed again helplessly), "I'm so excited! My Morah gave me a present!"

"A present?" I wondered aloud.

"Yeah, a present! Just for me!" she gushed. "Nobody else in the class got it! Morah sneaked it into my hand and whispered to me that she bought it just for me, because she knows it will make me happy." My little daughter rummaged through her briefcase as I wondered what could possibly cause all this excitement. I watched as out came crumpled pretzels, yesterday's homework stencil, and a host of broken crayons. Suddenly, Dina straightened gleefully. "Here it is, Mommy!" she called out triumphantly; face shining, as she held up her Morah's gift.

In her upturned hand was a little pink tube of Chapstick.

My "baby" was starting school. This was no ordinary event, please realize. You would think that with child number six I would've gotten used to the experience. But there is something about the youngest child that touches a chord in even the most seasoned mother, and here I was, a worried mother hen. Would the teacher be understanding? Would my sensitive, little sweetheart be okay?

Then there was another small thing. Or maybe not so small. My little nursery girl was still attached to her pacifier. And she had a hard time leaving her "security" when it was time to go to school. So together, we devised a plan to ease her into the separation.

Rivky would take the pacifier with her in the car and when I'd drop her off, she'd carefully place it into the pouch of the seat. Then, when I picked her up for the ride home, she'd have it as soon she'd reenter the car. This arrangement worked admirably, until...

> **I pictured the "catastrophe"; my sensitive, shy daughter entering her classroom.**

It happened. I dropped Rivky off, arrived back home, and horror of horrors, noticed that the pacifier was not in its place! Rivky must've forgotten to leave it behind. I pictured the "catastrophe"; my sensitive, shy daughter entering her classroom, clutching a pacifier... the other children taunting her, calling her a baby... My heart contracted, but there was nothing I could do but brace myself for the torrent of tears that was sure to come.

Lo and behold, Rivky entered the car with a big smile. I could not contain myself. "Rivky," I exclaimed. "Your pacifier! What happened?"

"I came in and realized I was holding it," she said. "I was so scared what would happen, 'cause some kids saw already. And then Morah said, 'Oh, Rivky, you have your little sister's pacifier? Come, I don't want you to lose it. Let's put it into your briefcase.' Mommy, she made me not be embarrassed! And," giggled Rivky, "I don't even have a little sister!"

Thank You Hashem, for the "sixth sense" You've endowed our children's educators with—the gift of understanding and sensitivity! ⊞

"When a child's toy boat
sinks in the bathtub,
he feels the **same**
pain as an adult who
loses his private yacht in
a raging storm."

*Being sensitive to such
feelings is no easy task.*

—*Rabbi Yisroel Salanter*

HASHKAFAH, HALACHAH, AND **INSPIRATIO**

A Lifeline of Love

Retold by Riva Pomerantz

THE YESHIVAH IN ISRAEL WHERE I teach is housed in a small building, nondescript except for the boys it attracts. From long hair to no hair, our clientele can be pretty eclectic, but the very fact that they are attending a yeshivah of any kind bears testament to their strength of character.

Nonetheless, when I saw today's visitor I was more than a little taken aback.

He looked as though he had stepped out from a previous century. A flowing gray beard hid his face, save for piercing blue eyes framed by old-fashioned glasses and a rounded black hat. His garb was clearly Chassidic—a black frock and knickers, ending in black stockings and a pair of sturdy shoes. An elderly man, he must have taken a wrong turn into our inner city-like environment, I thought, and went over to ask where he *really* intended to be.

My approach was interrupted, however, by an excited shout, followed by an exuberant figure bursting in on the scene. It was Moshe, liveliest student of the bunch, a young man whose recent style of dress, body piercings, and shaved head set him apart as a real "star" in the yeshivah.

> While we cannot guarantee that a child will not go astray, the strong bond that we form with a student is the lifeline by which he can always return.

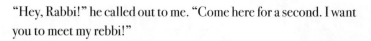

"Hey, Rabbi!" he called out to me. "Come here for a second. I want you to meet my rebbi!"

Rebbi? I came towards him, smiling in confusion. Surely he was not...but indeed he was: beckoning enthusiastically to the elderly figure who was modestly beaming.

"This is my *talmid*," announced the rebbi to the astonished onlookers, in a broken, accented English. "My *talmid*!"

His voice bespoke such depths of pride that it made the breath catch in my throat. The emotion was not lost on Moshe. His smile stretched from ear to ear, as he summoned the rest of the *chevrah* to meet his itinerant rebbi.

"Whenever my rebbi comes to Israel he visits all his *talmidim*," Moshe announced. "So he came to visit me, too."

At this pronouncement, the rebbi embraced Moshe, saying gleefully: "No—it's not '*you*, too'—you are my favorite *talmid*!"

It is difficult to describe the love and warmth which underscored those words. They were genuine, uttered without artifice or expectation. To all present it was clear that the rebbi loved the *talmid*, and that love was unhesitatingly reciprocated. This was a rebbi in the true sense of the word—a rebbi who may have lacked the "polish" and "pizzazz" of a modern, more contemporary educator, but who saw past the rough-and-tough exterior with remarkable clarity.

Later in the day, after the rebbi had departed, Moshe confided in me quietly.

"Without him, I'd be nothing," he said pensively.

"I wish I'd had a teacher like that," remarked another student with envy.

The incident touched me in very strong way, charged as it was with such emotion. But it was the final piece of information, imparted almost off-handedly, that clinched the encounter as breath-taking.

"When did he teach you?" I asked Moshe, noting that the tie between rebbi and *talmid* was obviously quite fresh. "Junior high? High school?"

"Nah," Moshe replied. "He was my third-grade teacher."

———————————

Here was a rebbi who was clearly far from "cool," able to nurture a strong relationship with a student who appeared to hail from a different world. And their connection was still burning bright since third grade! One of the more subtle beauties of the story is that the rebbi did not only reach out to the "off-the-derech" student. In fact, he made an effort to visit all his talmidim when he came to Eretz Yisrael! The unfathomable love and devotion of this rebbi surely continues to make a lasting impression. It is worth noting that after this incident, Moshe began to re-grow his hair and take his mitzvah observance more seriously. The rebbi's unconditional love was a winning impetus. ▣

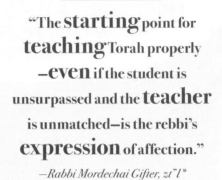

"The **starting** point for **teaching** Torah properly –**even** if the student is unsurpassed and the **teacher** is unmatched–is the rebbi's **expression** of affection."

—*Rabbi Mordechai Gifter, zt"l* *

* *in a private conversation with Mr. Avi Shulman*

A Lasting Impression

Retold by Riva Pomerantz

FOR RABBI ROSEN*, THE END of the school year involved one extra bit of effort beyond collecting the books and tallying the final grades. During the year, he had a photo taken of himself with each individual student. On the final day of school, he gave each boy a sealed envelope containing the photo, and an index card attached to the back inscribed with a personal message specific to the child.

Each year, as the rebbi carefully prepared his envelopes, he smiled inwardly at what he thought just might be his own delusion of importance. "For all I know," he would remind himself, "this will end up in the garbage the minute the boy gets home."

Yet Rabbi Rosen did it anyway, and he did it with his whole heart. He sat studying each picture, looking into each boy's face and trying to discern what words might give that particular boy the *chizuk* he needed.

And so the rebbi came prepared for Ari's last day of fourth grade. The class was wild with excitement. The weather outside screamed "SUMMER!" and the boys were barely able to sit in their seats. Ari and the rest of his class watched with barely suppressed impatience as Rebbi dug into his briefcase and extracted a neat stack of envelopes.

"Remember, each of you has a special message on the back of your picture," he reminded them. "Don't forget to read it."

OR THOSE WHO INSPIRE OTHERS

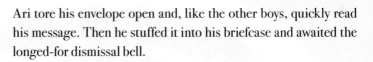

Ari tore his envelope open and, like the other boys, quickly read his message. Then he stuffed it into his briefcase and awaited the longed-for dismissal bell.

As the years progressed, the formerly attentive and conscientious Ari began daydreaming in class. His learning began to suffer, and his classmates began to regard him as "a spaced-out loser," which was the description he applied to himself as well. More and more, he kept to himself, both in school and at home. His parents and teachers worried about the steep decline his young life seemed to be taking.

By the time Ari was 17, he had become a confirmed loner. At home, he only emerged from his room to eat. At school, he occupied space and did as little as possible. His parents searched for answers, but none could be found. Then, seemingly by magic, Ari began emerging from his long spiritual coma. He needed a place to make a fresh start, and his parents found a yeshivah out of town that fit the bill.

The day came for Ari to leave for yeshivah. He packed what he needed and departed, full of hope that life could finally be different. The room in which he had dwelled in solitary self-confinement for the past four years was finally vacated.

Soon after Ari left, his married sister ventured into his room. What she saw there was graphic testimony to a mind in turmoil. The bed was piled high with papers, books, CDS, used plastic cups and plates, discarded packaging—everything but bedding. On the floor lay a rumpled quilt and flattened pillow. That's where Ari had been sleeping, perhaps for the past four years.

Then she scanned the rest of the room. Amid the chaos, there was

one island of order. In a small clearing on Ari's desk was a photo—a little-boy Ari and his fourth-grade rebbi, standing together smiling. She picked up the photo and read the inscription on the back, upon an index card that had been smudged and softened by years of handling: "Ari, you asked such great questions this year. Keep it up! You CAN do it. Love, Rebbi."

Tears welled in the sister's eyes. These few simple words, set apart like a holy shrine in this boy's room, had sustained him. They had been his lifeline to his better self, to his potential. They were there for him to grab when he felt that he was sinking, and there to guide him back to where he wanted, deep in his heart, to go. ▣

> **She read the inscription upon an index card that had been smudged and softened by years of handling.**

> What **you** think of me
> **I** think of me
> And what I **think** of me
> I'll **be**.

All names have been changed.

And the Lessons Never Fade

By Libby Engel

MY SIXTH-GRADE CLASS THAT YEAR was a dream. Never before had I been privileged to teach such a class—girls who genuinely cared about each other and modeled beautiful *middos*. They drank in the lessons, and I eagerly put all my efforts into teaching them as much as possible. Aside from the stories I related and the lessons I taught, I constantly emphasized the *pasuk* "*Lo hamidrash hu ha'ikkar, ela hama'aseh*, the action is more critical than the learning." This became my "quotable quote" to the point where the girls would chorus it on their own, before I even had a chance to say it.

At the end of the year, we emotionally parted ways as I wished my wonderful class much *hatzlachah*. I went on to the next class, but out of the corner of my eye I kept watch over my special sixth-graders as they went on to seventh and then eighth grade. Each year brought change to the class—new girls came in, some girls moved out—and slowly the class dynamic began to shift.

I received the phone call late Wednesday evening.

> The action is
> more critical than
> the learning.

"Mrs. Stern*?"

"Yes."

"This is Breina Davidovitz*,"
said my mysterious caller.

"Oh—aren't you the substitute for the eighth-grade class?" I asked, with a sinking feeling in my heart. To my sorrow, it had become known that the eighth-graders had been giving their newly inaugurated substitute teacher a terrible time and that their chutzpah had gotten out of control.

"Yes," she confirmed. "I have a story to tell you. Do you have a few minutes?"

I'm always game for a good story, especially one that I can pass on to my students.

"Sure," I replied.

"I think you remember my class whom you taught in sixth grade," she began.

"How could I forget them?" I broke in fondly. "They were the apple of my eye!"

There was a pause.

"When I began teaching the eighth-grade class, we ran into a few obstacles," she said tactfully. As a teacher, I knew the volumes hidden beneath these mild words. "There was a certain point not so long ago that I decided it just wasn't the job for me and I was ready to speak to the principal about switching me to a different class.

"I gave it one more day. Resolutely, I walked into the classroom, bracing myself for a difficult time. To my amazement, a group of thirty angels sat there, smiling at me with perfect innocence. I hesitatingly began my lesson and the sterling behavior continued. Not a single word of chutzpah or defiance was uttered; the girls cooperated beautifully!

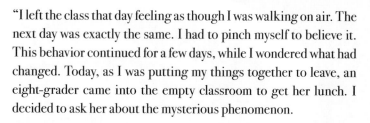

"I left the class that day feeling as though I was walking on air. The next day was exactly the same. I had to pinch myself to believe it. This behavior continued for a few days, while I wondered what had changed. Today, as I was putting my things together to leave, an eight-grader came into the empty classroom to get her lunch. I decided to ask her about the mysterious phenomenon.

"'I've noticed a terrific change in this class,' I told her. 'Can you tell me what caused it?' At first she looked embarrassed. Then she said: 'In a different class we learned about doing *teshuvah* for saying or doing things that are hurtful to another Yid. One of the *teshuvah* suggestions was a *taanis dibbur*, literally a "fast from speaking," [as a form of repentance, whereby one undertakes to refrain from speaking for a set period of time (except when absolutely necessary)]. As Morah was teaching this lesson, we all looked at each other guiltily. We realized that we were causing our substitute a lot of pain through our misbehavior. We all decided to accept upon ourselves a kind of *ta'anis dibbur* and start behaving properly in class.'

"The girl paused for a moment and then she smiled. 'We had a teacher in sixth grade,' she explained, 'who taught us a very important lesson which helped us decide to make a real change. She always said '*Lo hamidrash hu ha'ikkar ela hama'aseh*'—The action is more critical than the learning! So we took action!'"

Mrs. Davidovitz finished her story triumphantly.

And I?

I wiped away the tears in my eyes and thanked Hashem for giving me the privilege of making a difference in the lives of so many. ▣

Names and identifying details have been changed.

Planting a Seed, Savoring the Fruit

By Libby Engel

IT WAS LATE ON A THURSDAY AFTERNOON, and I had yet to do my Shabbos shopping. Having just finished teaching, I had decided to stop at the grocery store near school—a store in which I had never before shopped. Standing in line, I noticed the cashier's kind, friendly manner with the customers before me. He was an older *bachur*, or perhaps a young married man, and he had a knack for putting everyone at ease as they went through the paces of waiting, unloading their groceries, paying and carting it all away.

My turn came, and it was time to pay. I handed the young man my credit card, and he glanced at it once, then examined it more closely for a moment. *Oh, no,* I thought. *Maybe it's expired.* But then he looked up at me with an even broader smile and exclaimed, "Mrs. Kramer!* Is it you?"

"Well, that's what my credit card says, so yes, I guess that's me," I joked in response.

"Do you remember me? I'm Benjy Goodman. Remember you taught my brother and me?"

It had been many years ago, near the beginning of my teaching career, when I had been working in a *kiruv* school near Los Angeles. I did remember Benjy and his brother, Josh. Now that I

looked more closely, I could see that it was the same face, just matured and bearded. The boys' family hadn't been religious in those days, so I wondered how this new persona had evolved.

"I'm going to walk you out to the car and tell you a story if you don't mind, Mrs. Kramer," Benjy said.

He got someone to cover the cash register, and helped me out with my bundles. And here is the story he told me:

"When my brother was in your fourth-grade class, he asked you a question that was quite deep. You didn't have an answer, but you smiled at him and told him, 'I need to go home and ask my husband. He may be able to find the answer to such a fabulous question.' And the next day, you came in with the answer.

> "I don't know the answer Josh but I'll ask my husband."

"Many years later, when Josh and I were in public high school, our family had just come back from a Saturday afternoon baseball game when we got into a discussion about what kind of families we boys would raise. My father made it known that he expected us to marry Jewish women.

"'But why?' Josh asked. 'What difference does it make? What do we do that's so different from non-Jews? If you marry a Jewish woman and you have a Jewish family, you have to be able to be the leader of the family. You have to know about being Jewish and be able to answer your wife's questions and your kids' questions. And you have to have a rabbi to answer your questions. Mrs. Kramer always said she would ask her husband if there was something she didn't know. What kind of husband or father will I be to a Jewish

family, if I don't even do anything that's too Jewish?'

"That was the start of a revolution in our family. We enrolled in a *frum* yeshivah and the family began learning and keeping the mitzvos in earnest."

The story stunned me. One little comment, more than a decade earlier, had planted a seed that had sprouted into this. No one remembered the question, and no one remembered the answer, but I was so grateful that I had taken time to respond. I was more grateful still that I had admitted my lack of an answer, and that my husband was the one to whom I turned for Torah wisdom. Something in those words made Josh want to be that kind of husband too, and today, both he and his brother are fulfilling that role beautifully.

*All names have been changed.

Shaping with Responses

▶ Every teacher is torn between covering ground and giving his/her students time to ask questions. Imagine what an opportunity would have been missed had the teacher ignored the question.

▶ A teacher may feel that letting a student know that s/he doesn't know the answer will cause the student to lose respect for the teacher. This story shows the fallacy of that approach.

▶ The greatest show of respect and concern by a teacher to a student is giving credence to his/her thoughts and queries.

▶ No one remembers the question or the answer—but their lives were forever changed by how they were spoken to. ▢

Please Leave a Message

Retold by Ben Shalom

"**I** WONDER HOW YOSSI IS DOING."

The school year had ended five weeks before, and Rabbi Silver was reflecting on the whereabouts of each of his "children." Mentally he reviewed the class list, recalling each student's precious face with pride in his growth over the year. As Yossi's troubled countenance came to mind, Rabbi Silver's forehead creased with concern, and he wondered if he should give him a call.

Yossi was not your average child. He had trouble making the transition from one setting to another, and his mornings were often beset with unruly behavior. Rabbi Silver had learned to respond to Yossi with soft words and a soothing tone of voice. Yossi's bus arrived early, and there were many mornings that Rabbi Silver would take a few moments to talk or play with him, helping him unwind. With patience and tender care he had developed a very special relationship with this overanxious boy who blossomed under his care.

"Perhaps I should have called him," he thought worriedly. Rabbi Silver knew how much his presence had impacted Yossi, and he hoped that his *talmid* had not lost the ground he had covered. With firm resolve to do something immediate, Rabbi Silver reached for the phone and dialed Yossi's summer number.

"Hello," came the answer machine's greeting. "You have reached 111-2222. Please leave a message after the tone."

Rabbi Silver hesitated momentarily, debating whether to leave a message or call back later. The thought ran through his mind—"I'd better not take the chance of forgetting to call again later." His decision was made, and Rabbi Silver spoke into the machine.

"Yossi, this is Rebbi speaking. I was thinking about you, and wondering how your summer is going. I miss seeing you, and think of you all the time. Hope you're having a great time in your bungalow colony. I just wanted to remind you that Rebbi thinks you're a great boy! You can do it!"

The rest of the summer rolled by, and Yossi's family returned to the city. One morning Rabbi Silver stopped in the neighborhood bake shop for a cup of coffee. Yossi's father entered as Rabbi Silver sat down with his drink. His eyes met Rabbi Silver's and his face lit up. "Rebbi," he cried. "I am so happy to see you. I owe you a tremendous *yasher koach*. You have no idea what your phone call did for my son."

Rabbi Silver looked up in surprise. He had been so disappointed that day, not to have reached Yossi in person, and he hadn't even known for sure if Yossi had ever heard his words on the machine.

Yossi's father joined Rabbi Silver at the table and continued to relate what had happened.

Yossi had been extremely disruptive in camp, often acting out aggressively toward his peers. On the day his rebbi had called, the head counselor had also phoned Yossi's parents informing them that Yossi was getting one last chance to make it in camp. One more incident and they would have to kick him out!

When Yossi walked in the door that afternoon, his mother greeted him with a warm smile, and brought him gently over to the answering machine. "Listen, Yossi," she said, "your rebbi called and left you a message."

His mother pressed "Play," and Yossi heard the sound of his beloved rebbi's voice filling the room, telling him how much he missed him, and reminding him that he was a great kid. The scowl slowly slipped from his face and the corners of his mouth lifted into a smile. If Rebbi thought so, maybe it was true. His eyes shone with pride. Yossi felt like a million dollars.

Every morning before Yossi went off to camp his mother would play the message on the answering machine for Yossi to hear. His eyes would light up anew, and he'd go off to camp with a smile on his face.

The head counselor could not believe the change in Yossi's behavior. He asked his father how he had managed to perform such a miracle, turning Yossi's behavior around overnight.

Yossi's father looked at Rabbi Silver, and finished his story with these words.

"I invited the head counselor into my bungalow to listen to your message. As your words filled the room once again, I looked at the counselor, and I saw tears in his eyes. He was so amazed that a rebbi could show such compassion and concern. My wife and I are so touched by your care for Yossi, and so grateful for turning his summer around. Thank you... thank you... thank you."

Shaping from Afar

There are two overriding lessons in this story:

► A rebbi whose concern did not stop when no one answered.
► Parents who understood the motivational power of a rebbi's message. ▣

"Can't Is Not in My Dictionary!"

As told to Riva Pomeratz

MY STORY BEGINS THE DAY I WAS BORN, the day my parents were told that their brand-new baby daughter had spina bifida and hydrocephalus and would be physically impaired for life. Although they knew I would be physically challenged, my parents made a firm decision: Leg braces and all, I would attend a regular Bais Yaakov school and I would be treated like a regular child. Little did they know then just how crucial this decision turned out to be.

For six years I managed a normal workload, played at recess, and did chores at home. My life was reasonably stable and quite normal, my gait notwithstanding.

And then, my whole world caved in. I walked away from being hit by a car, unscathed, with just a few stitches on my forehead. But several months later, when I started complaining that I couldn't see the blackboard, tests confirmed our worst fears. The tube that had been installed to shunt spinal fluid away from my brain was broken and the spinal fluid had built up in my brain, putting pressure on my optic nerve. I went into the hospital to repair the tube, but I never regained my sight.

Now I was a sixth-grader with two handicaps, and I was terrified. My parents, friends, and teachers reassured me that I could go on

with my life, that I could triumph over my disabilities, but I was despondent. "I can't do it!" I told my teacher endlessly. She countered with a very firm, very wise slogan. "Can't is not a word in my dictionary," Morah A told me over and over again. Until this day, I repeat her uplifting motto like a mantra. It enabled me to do things I never imagined I could do. Things like participate in class, take tests, learn Braille, and even attend summer camp, where I white-water-rafted down the Delaware River with the rest of my bunk and was accepted as just another camper.

> **Morah never wavered in her belief that I could do whatever was demanded of me.**

Morah A, my sixth-grade teacher, never wavered in her belief that I could do whatever was demanded of me, and she went out of her way to treat me exactly the same as any other student. This was an immense comfort to me; being singled out for preferential treatment would not have done me an ounce of good, whereas this candid, firm approach was just the right medicine. To this day, I am still close to this kind and caring teacher. When people ask me who inspired me to become what I am, I readily point to Morah A, who went above and beyond to support me and guide me every step of the way.

In eighth grade, Morah C's dedication went far beyond the call of duty. At the beginning of the year, when we were assigned an important term paper, I created mine in the only way I could— typing it out on my Braille typewriter. My devoted teacher taught herself to read Braille in order to mark my paper. It was the most loving thing she could have done for me. When we learned about the Beis Hamikdash, using diagrams that I could not see, Morah C

asked a friend to trace the diagrams with glue. When they dried, I could feel them and learn their structure and appearance. She found out about a technique called "sighted guide" whereby a blind person holds onto the wrist of a guide and can feel, by virtue of wrist movements, when the guide is ascending or descending. Realizing this would be a valuable tool to help me navigate in school, Morah urged me to teach it to the class. I reluctantly agreed, and from then on, sighted guide became a natural part of our school routine as girls slipped their wrist into my hand so I could navigate the hallways.

Today, I work as a lecturer, speaking publicly about people with disabilities. I also run a support group for young women with physical disabilities. I am, *baruch Hashem*, the grateful mother of a precious son. I cook, clean, and keep house, albeit

> **My devoted teacher taught herself to read Braille in order to mark my paper.**

with help, and I even run a small company, manufacturing tactile books for children. I may need a support cane and a walking stick, but there's no question that today I'm an independent, joyous person, thanks in large part to my teachers and family who never allowed me to give up or give in. The gift they have given me is priceless. ▣

The **greatest** gift
you can **give** a child is to
see him **not** only as he is
but as he could be,
and **help** him get there.

The Peace Initiative

MUCH HAS BEEN WRITTEN ABOUT *the value of teaching by example. We were therefore delighted to receive this letter from a yeshivah student who wanted to share with others his rebbi's remarkable reaction to a problem. The story speaks for itself.*

Dear Impressions*,

I am an in-towner who learns with an out-of-town chavrusa in a Brooklyn yeshivah. A few weeks ago I had reason to be in my chavrusa's city for Shabbos. Even though he wasn't going to be home, I was privileged to stay at his house. Before I went, he asked me to bring back a few things for him. After spending a spectacular Shabbos with my chavrusa's parents, I gathered my things along with the items he had requested and headed back to Brooklyn.

When I returned to yeshivah, I went to my chavrusa's dorm room and told him that I had his things and left them there for him. He thanked me and I left the room. But I made a mistake. I inadvertently took out my personal bag of cake and left it there.

The next morning, I went to the refrigerator to take some of my cake. When I could not find it, I suddenly remembered what had happened. I quickly made my way

This letter was originally sent to Impressions, the newsletter for teachers produced by Chofetz Chaim Heritage Foundation which forms the basis for this book.

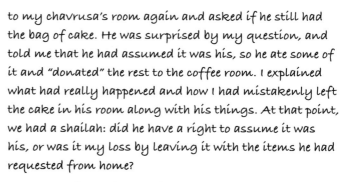

to my chavrusa's room again and asked if he still had the bag of cake. He was surprised by my question, and told me that he had assumed it was his, so he ate some of it and "donated" the rest to the coffee room. I explained what had really happened and how I had mistakenly left the cake in his room along with his things. At that point, we had a shailah: did he have a right to assume it was his, or was it my loss by leaving it with the items he had requested from home?

We began discussing the issue and found ourselves late for seder. When we came rushing in to learn our rebbi asked us what happened, and we told him our story. Our rebbi is not a posek, but his reaction was remarkable. He claimed that, regardless of whoever is right from a halachic perspective, I nevertheless deserved the cake. He asked me how much the cake was worth. We determined that it was around $10, whereupon he promptly removed an envelope from his jacket and handed me $10. He explained that most arguments among friends are concerning money. Therefore, that envelope is the "Shalom account" which he uses to settle small monetary debates and arguments.

The story continues:

The next day, I asked the yeshivah's posek about my situation. He answered that my chavrusa is not liable to pay for all the cake, only that which he benefited from—the amount he saved by not buying a snack or small meal—which is $2. I went back to my rebbi and told him the psak. I suggested that in view of the psak, perhaps I

should give him back $8. He declined, saying that the money was intended for peace, and it should be kept peacefully.

My rebbi is a true example of a rodef shalom—one who pursues peace!

Sincerely,
Aaron Shalom

Shaping by Example

Here are some points we drew from this story. We're sure you can find more.

▸ **Do as I Do**
The rebbi's actions taught more than his words ever could.

▸ **Sensitivity**
The rebbi's reaction showed he understood that although it may have seemed trivial, the cake was important to his student.

▸ **Being prepared**
The rebbi already had a "Shalom" envelope.

▸ **Impact**
The rebbi's actions made a tremendous impression—enough for the student to take the trouble to write to us about it. ▣

To **effectively** transmit
spiritual values, a teacher must be
a **salesman**, not a policeman.
—*Rabbi Daniel Mechanic*

A Lifetime of Inspiration

As told to Riva Pomeratz

WHEN RABBI TEICHTEL WALKED INTO THE classroom, all the natural boredom, fidgetiness, and irritability that teenagers are known for flew right out the window. It wasn't only his lessons—rich with knowledge and down-to-earth wisdom. No, much more than that, it was his *simchah*. Rabbi Teichtel was simply bursting with *simchas hachayim*, and it was eminently contagious. So much so, that its effects stayed with us long after the bell rang.

I will never forget Rabbi Teichtel's *simchah*, the way his face lit up with joy. He walked around like a man without a care in the world, deeply devoted to Torah and *avodas* Hashem, but with an unparalleled joy. I remember thinking, hoping, yearning to achieve the same level as Rabbi Teichtel, at the same time wondering whether it was even attainable by me.

> Imagine our horror when we discovered that Rabbi Teichtel's daughter had been sick all year!

And then, out of nowhere, the bombshell. A young girl had passed away. The *levayah* was tomorrow. The family was sitting *shivah*. The father...was none other than our beloved teacher, Rabbi Teichtel. To say we were

shocked was an understatement. Imagine how our horror and disbelief was confounded when we discovered that Rabbi Teichtel's daughter had been sick all year! Every day, when he walked into our classroom with his signature smile and jovial, warm greeting, he had been dealing with a dangerously ill child, and we had never once known it!

I found myself, together with my classmates, sitting at the *shivah* house, and the experience was surreal. Even as he sat before us, on a low chair, Rabbi Teichtel taught us. He taught us about the concept that each *neshamah* has a role to play in this world and about *Olam Haba*. His soft-spoken words engraved themselves in my heart forever, but at the time they were theoretical; I never imagined that they would ever have any bearing on my own life. True to form, Rabbi Teichtel was back to teaching after *shivah* was over. With the same smile, the same demeanor. His attitude and outlook spoke volumes. My friends and I were in awe.

Fast forward a dozen years, and Rabbi Teichtel's smiling face never left my mind, even as, *baruch Hashem*, my own children were born and the vicissitudes of life sometimes made my weary smile fade. While the school I had attended had been quite modern, I had done a lot of learning and growing and my husband and I were raising our children in a beautiful Torah path.

> **Rabbi Teichtel's smiling face never left my mind, even as, the vicissitudes of life sometimes made my weary smile fade.**

When our fifth child was born, however, life as we knew it ground to a halt. A serious congenital disease left his heart,

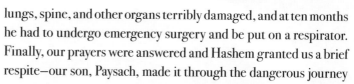

lungs, spine, and other organs terribly damaged, and at ten months he had to undergo emergency surgery and be put on a respirator. Finally, our prayers were answered and Hashem granted us a brief respite—our son, Paysach, made it through the dangerous journey and came out alive, *baruch Hashem*. He would need minute-to-minute care, countless surgical procedures, and our home took on the qualities of an intensive-care unit, but we were endlessly grateful that he had pulled through.

> **A hush settled over the room as everyone instinctively realized that this was someone special.**

Shortly after Paysach's third birthday, the doctors were adamant that he was in desperate need of a complex and difficult surgery. His chances of surviving the surgery were very slim. Again, a barrage of *tefillos*. Again, a deeply wrenching emotional journey as we contemplated the fate of our precious son. And this time, Hashem claimed this special *neshamah* for on High. Paysach was *niftar* and we were bereft.

We sat *shivah*, mourning the loss of our beloved child. The house was crowded with visitors, when a distinguished-looking gentleman made his way over from the men's side to where I sat in mourning. His bearing and the sense of purpose that seemed to permeate his very being were electric; it seemed that a hush settled over the room as everyone instinctively realized that this was someone special, not a run-of-the-mill *shivah* call. I looked up from my low stool and...standing there was...Rabbi Teichtel! How had he heard? We weren't quite sure. But his caring eyes and his nurturing smile were exactly the balm we needed. Rabbi Teichtel's indomitable *simchas hachayim*, taught through his unfaltering example, imbues me with strength to this very day, more than twenty years since I left his classroom.

L'ilui nishmas Paysach Aharon a"h ben Naftoli Lavrinoff, y"lcht

---

Shaping with Simchah

Can a person teach himself to have *simchas hachayim*?
By Mr. Avi Shulman

The answer is a resounding yes. Hashem gave every person the ability to teach himself anything if he is determined and committed to put in the time and effort.

There are many ways to achieve *simchas hachayim*. Here are some basics.

► Surround yourself with people who are positive, inspirational and who exude *simchas hachayim*.

► Read material, books and articles that are upbeat and present a positive view.

► Listen to CD's by people who radiate *simchas hachayim*.

► Collect and share stories of people who exemplify this trait.

► Fill your mind with reasons to be *b'simchah*.

A friend made a list of reasons why he should always be happy. He read the list each morning and it changed his entire demeanor as he became a person who embodied *simchas hachayim*.

Projecting Simchas Hachayim

► Practice your smile—so many people look up to you each day.

► Share happy thoughts and ideas.

► Use upbeat language.

► Accentuate the positive when speaking, and tone down the negative. ▣

Letters*:
Dear Teacher

Dear Impressions,

I wanted to take the opportunity to express my hakoras hatov to a very special teacher by sharing my story with you.

My daughter was a poor student, with below-average intelligence, and a diagnosis of ADD. It was hard to send her off to school each day, knowing how difficult her day would be. In some classes she would feel like a failure, because she could not comprehend anything the teacher said. During recess and lunch break she would face the rejection of her classmates. I wished that somebody would take note of her and ease her distress, that someone would acknowledge her and her individual needs.

There was one high school teacher who did just that. Rebbetzin L. always greeted my daughter with a warm smile, took the time to converse with her, and even called her at home. One memorable day my daughter came home glowing with pride. Rebbetzin L. had given her a beautiful siddur as a gift. This amazing woman did everything within her power to make my daughter feel loved.

Now, years later, she is B"H married, a very successful housewife, running a happy, immaculate home, baking for a chesed organization, and holding a job. She says openly, "Rebbetzin L. always said, 'You can do it.'" It's true, she couldn't when it came to scholastics, but, when she sends her children off to school in the morning with smiles on their faces, when she cooks and cleans and bakes, when she serves her children supper and puts them to bed with tender loving care, she hears her teacher's words ringing in her ears "You can do it," and she does it well.

HASHKAFAH, HALACHAH, AND **INSPIRATION**

One can search the world for chesed projects to undertake. Rebbetzin L. understood that a teacher has invaluable chesed opportunities built right into her job.

Sincerely,

Mrs. B.

"The greatest act of chesed a person can do is to give a Jewish child a Torah education."

—Rabbi Avrohom Pam zt"l

Dear Impressions,

Things are finally quieting down after the beautiful simchah of marrying off our oldest daughter and I feel I must take the time to share with you an incredibly touching story that I'm sure all the teachers who receive your newsletter will appreciate.

As the flurry of activity before the wedding reached a peak, and we sat down to send out invitations, we decided to allow each of our children to invite two of their friends. While our daughters took a bit of time to decide, our son immediately told us who he had chosen. You can imagine our surprise when he said "I want Rabbi Tov •and his wife to be my guests at the wedding." When we asked about his choice, he simply explained, "I want Rabbi Tov to come because he loves me and understands me. He treats me with respect." Now it was our turn to begin thinking. Rabbi Tov had been Yosef's first—grade rebbi and Yosef was in eighth grade! The details finally came tumbling out. Sixth grade had been a very difficult year for Yosef. (We thought we were on top of the situation, were in contact with the rebbi and the principal regularly and encouraged our son as best we could. Somehow Yosef made it through the year.) He did not get along with his rebbi, but we did not know until now that he had been sent out of class on an almost daily basis. Our son knew that he could always go to Rabbi Tov's class and he would receive a warm welcome and a lot of encouragement.

There was no question, Rabbi and Mrs. Tov would receive an invitation. I called to give them the heads-up about the invitation and they graciously agreed to attend. At the wedding as I watched Yosef dance with his beloved rebbi, I knew what it meant to make a lasting impression on a talmid.

May Rabbi Tov and all those like him continue to see success as they reach out to their students in the spirit of true chinuch.

Sincerely,

Mrs. Kohen

*All names have been changed.

*These letters were originally sent to Impressions, the newsletter for teachers produced by Chofetz Chaim Heritage Foundation which forms the basis for this book.

Dear Rebbi, shlita,

It's been so long, but I still remember your third-grade class. I loved it and it was very enjoyable. I never really thanked you for being so accommodating for my siyumei Mishnayos. Although your schedule was packed, whenever I finished learning a mesechta at home you allowed me to make a small siyum in class and give out cupcakes. That year was the first year that I was getting into Mishnayos, and your encouragement served as a springboard. Mishnayos is the reason I've gotten as far as I did. I began reviewing Shishah Sidrei Mishnah in high school and later began teaching it. That knowledge helped a lot in my finishing some mesechtos in Gemara. That all started when I was encouraged by your going out of your way in helping me make some siyumim.

For that I owe a hakaras hatov that I thoughtlessly never gave you, and I ask mechilah for that. When I finally realized the hakaras hatov that I owed you, I had no way of contacting you, but B"H, I was told about a package going to you, and was able to send this with it. Only after teaching someone else can I begin to understand the time, patience, effort and love that was put into me. Belatedly, I now say thank you.

Thank you,

Your grateful talmid
Yerushalayim 5770

"A yeshivah is **not** measured by
how **many** good or bad students
are in it, **but** by what the
students **consider** good or bad."

—Rabbi Yosef Yoizel Horowitz,
The Alter of Novardok

We hope you have enjoyed this book which was culled from 8 years of "Impressions"

For more inspiration and insight subscribe today!

Bring This Publication to Your School!

IMPRESSI NS, a dynamic newsletter made specifically for teachers, is a one-page publication, designed with busy teachers in mind and distributed through schools to thousands of Jewish educators across the United States and Canada. Teachers have been lavish in their praise of Impressions, commenting how the short, powerful thoughts and stories have raised awareness about the power they wield while inspiring them about the greatness of the work they do.

Now in its tenth year, Impressions has gained recognition throughout the chinuch world.

Your subscription entitles you to as many copies as you need for your school.

Call today to order (718) 438-6869

Chofetz Chaim Heritage Foundation • 361 Spook Rock Rd. • Suffern, NY 10901 • (845) 352-3505 Lakewood office (732) 905-9909

> **"Impressions is a perfect title for the newsletter that leaves a lasting impression on the moral fibers of our *mechanchim* and *mechanchos*."**
> —Rabbi Binyomin Ginsburg, Dean
> Torah Academy of Minneapolis
> Chinuch columnist, The Yated Ne'eman

▶ "Teaching is something for which one needs constant chizuk and encouragement. This type of continuous reminder of teachers' valuable impact is invaluable."

—Veteran *mechaneches*, West Coast

▶ "The articles are practical and they touch on real issues that teachers face."

—Mrs. Altschuler, Principal
Bais Yaakov D'Gur in Brooklyn

▶ "Impressions articles require us to sit down, think, and reconsider our responsibilities in dealing with our students."

—Rabbi Charner
Torah School of Greater Washington

▶ "Even if one story or one quote affects one interaction with a student it will have accomplished a world!"

—10th grade teacher, Midwest

▶ "The issues presented by Rabbi Lowy in Impressions have raised my awareness about the lasting impact of a rebbi's actions. Some of the questions address issues I never realized could be problematic from a halachic viewpoint. I'm so grateful someone brought it up."

—Junior high school rebbi

A Shining Example

Several years ago, Rabbi Lowy received a phone call from a woman who had been offered a position as principal of a school. "Rabbi Lowy," she said, "I am very hesitant about accepting this responsibility. It is inevitable that this job will lead me to speak or listen to *loshon hora*, and that is a serious concern for me. What should I do?"

Rabbi Lowy did not share her hesitation. "Please," he responded, "please take the job. It is precisely the individual who is so mindful of the serious consequences of *loshon hora* that is the right person for this position."

This noble woman accepted his reassurance, and took the job. She continues to call him regularly with halachic questions pertaining to *loshon hora* that come up in her daily work.

It is worthwhile for us to contemplate the ways of this principal, and resolve to make it an example that we will follow.

EVERY PERSON WORKING IN *CHINUCH* NEEDS:

A. A GOOD UNDERSTANDING OF THE *HALACHOS* OF *LOSHON HORA*.

B. A *HALACHIC* AUTHORITY WHOM HE/SHE FEELS COMFORTABLE CONSULTING ABOUT *SHMIRAS HALOSHON* QUESTIONS.

CREATING A CULTURE OF CARING...

In elementary school...

NEW!

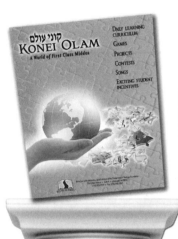

קוני עולם
KONEI OLAM
A World of First Class Middos

- *Middos Curriculum*
- *Grades 3-4*
- *Also available in Yiddish*

שומרי הלשון
Shomrei Haloshon

- *Shmiras Haloshon Curriculum*
- *Grades 4-6*
- *Sep. boys and girls versions*
- *Also available in Yiddish*

מושלי הלשון
Mastering Sensitive Speech

- *Ona'as Devarim Curriculum*
- *Grades 6-7*
- *Sep. boys and girls versions*
- *Available soon in Yiddish*

To Bring These Fantastic Programs to YOUR School:

Morning Machsom L'Fi

For one hour, from 9 until 10, the immeasurable merit of Shmiras Haloshon will intensify and draw its unique brachah down to the hundreds of thousands of people joining together in the Chofetz Chaim Heritage Foundation's global initiative, the Morning Machsom L'Fi. Jews within each community unite with each other, and with other communities throughout the world, creating one hour of increased harmony, sensitivity and achdus. To join call: 212.444.9898 or email join@morningmachsomlfi.org

Bringing Brachah into Your Life

The Chofetz Chaim Heritage Foundation

Wonder Words Children's Story Line

WonderWords, a free children's story line, puts the power of a good story to work, conveying lessons of Shmiras Haloshon in an entertaining and engaging way, presented by master storytellers including Rabbi Yitzy Erps and Rabbi Fishel Schachter. WonderWords currently receives over 12,000 calls weekly. Call: 212.444.1119

Since 1989, the Chofetz Chaim Heritage Foundation has successfully launched innovative methods of promoting the Torah's wisdom on human relations and personal development. The foundation utilizes a vast array of effective communication tools including books, tapes, video seminars, telephone classes and newsletters, designed to heighten one's awareness of such essential values as judging others favorably, speaking with restraint and integrity, and acting with sensitivity and respect. The Chofetz Chaim Heritage Foundation's programs reassert the Torah's timeless recipe for building a world of compassion and harmony.

An Answer at Your Fingertips...

CD & Tape Binders

A wide array of audio CD's on a variety of timely topics by renowned speakers to inspire and guide you on your own journey of growth. Call to order: 845.352.3505 x 116

The Shmiras Haloshon Shaila Hotline

This telephone hotline puts callers (anonymously) in contact with expert rabbanim who can answer halachic questions concerning proper speech. This free service is available at 718.951.3696 from 9 to 10:30PM Monday through Thursday and Motzei Shabbos.

To purchase or sponsor a book or CD or for more information on our programs please contact:

The Chofetz Chaim Heritage Foundation
The Zichron Yaakov Zvi Center for the Teachings of the Chofetz Chaim
361 Spook Rock Road, Suffern, NY 10901
845-352-3505 ext. 116 or email: catalog@chofetzchaimusa.org

CHAZAK INSPIRATION LINE

A free inspirational telephone hotline is available 24 hours a day. Chazak offers chizuk and inspiration by some of the world's best speakers, including: Rabbi Yitzchok Kirzner, z"tl, and yb"l, Rabbi Yissocher Frand, Rabbi Paysach Krohn, and Rabbi Abraham J. Twerski, and includes an array of topics for personal growth, better relationships, Torah thoughts and insights, facing life challenges, meaningful prayer and timely topics for every season. Chazak currently receives over 50,000 calls weekly. Call: 718.258.2008 or 845.356.6665

SPREADING THE LANGUAGE OF AHAVAS YISRAEL

EMAIL

Thousands participate in Shmiras Haloshon Yomi through one of our daily learning emails, which include three choices of text to study from and our new mp3 daily, 5-minute SHY audio. Additionally, more and more people are receiving our daily email reminders for the Morning Machsom L'fi as well as daily learning of Lessons in Truth, Loving Kindness and our popular biweekly newsletter, Chosen Words. Email: editorial@chofetzchaimusa.org

BOOKS

With over 350,000 volumes in print, our best-selling books for daily learning, for both adults and children, have created a worldwide revolution of speech and deed. Building on that success, POSITIVE WORD POWER shows us how to harness the incredible power of words to nurture and uplift the people in our lives. Call to order: 845.352.3505 x 116

Has something a teacher said or done made a difference to a student you know?

Why not share the story and inspire others?

Please send your story to us.

Not a writer? Tell us your story and we'll write it up.

....

Do you have a halachic question about *shmiras haloshon* as it applies to your job as a teacher?

Send it to us for Rabbi Lowy to answer.

CCHF/IMPRESSIONS
204 Clifton Ave.
Suite B
Lakewood, NJ 08701
Fax: 718.701.5994
Email: Impressions@chofetzchaimusa.org